Heather Merrill has done it again. While her previous book broke new ground by studying the challenges of multi-racial feminist activism in Italy, this new contribution enlarges the picture. Here she takes aim at Italian common sense concerning race, while passionately foregrounding the lives of African migrants and Afro-Italians who daily navigate the deadly politics of exclusion. For all those who read with horror the headlines emanating from an increasingly anti-immigrant and antiBlack Europe, this book is for you. And for those who hold out hope that spaces of oppression may generate life-affirming possibilities, this book is also for you.

Jacqueline Nassy Brown, Author of Dropping Anchor, Setting Sail: Geographies of Race in Black Liverpool

A vital investigation of African migrant experiences in contemporary Italy, *Black Spaces* blends ethnographic methods and Black Pessimist theories to explore the material and symbolic meanings of social life and social death. This nuanced account of national and racial formations highlights mundane, and sometimes extraordinary, actions and utterances that bear witness to individual and collective examples of resistance to the erasure of African subjects from European civic life. *Black Spaces* is a formidable account of the workings of race and nation, power and relation in the modern era.

Daphne Lamothe, Author of Inventing the New Negro: Narrative, Culture, and Ethnography

BLACK SPACES

Black Spaces examines how space and place are racialized, and the impacts on everyday experiences among African Italians, immigrants, and refugees. It explores the deeply intertwined histories of Africa and Europe, and how people of African descent negotiate, contest, and live with anti-blackness in Italy. The vast majority of people crossing the Mediterranean into Europe are from West Africa and the Horn of Africa. Their passage is part of the legacy of Italian and broader European engagement in colonial projects. This largely forgotten history corresponds with an ongoing effort to erase them from the Italian social landscape on arrival. *Black Spaces* examines these racialized spaces by blending a critical geographical approach to place and space with Afro-Pessimist and critical race perspectives on the lived experiences of Blackness and anti-blackness in Italy.

Heather Merrill is Professor of Africana Studies at Hamilton College. She is the co-editor of *Spaces of Danger: Culture and Power in the Everyday* and the author of *An Alliance of Women: Immigration and the Politics of Race.*

TWENTY-FIRST CENTURY INTERVENTIONS

Series Editor:

France Winddance Twine, University of California, Santa Barbara

This is the first in a series of research monographs that intervenes in critical national and transnational debates around race, migration, citizenship, new technologies. The Interventions series provides innovative theoretical, historical and cultural analyses concerned with poverty, inequality and social justice.

Titles in this Series:

Black Spaces: African Diaspora in Italy
Heather Merrill

For more information about this series, please visit: https://www.routledge.com/ Twenty-First-Century-INTERVENTIONS/book-series/SOCINT

BLACK SPACES

African Diaspora in Italy

Heather Merrill

Routledge
Taylor & Francis Group

NEW YORK AND LONDON

First published 2018
by Routledge
711 Third Avenue, New York, NY 10017

and by Routledge
2 Park Square, Milton Park, Abingdon, Oxon OX14 4RN

Routledge is an imprint of the Taylor & Francis Group, an informa business

Library of Congress Cataloging in Publication Data
A catalog record for this book has been requested

ISBN: 978-1-138-04325-1 (hbk)
ISBN: 978-1-138-54937-1 (pbk)
ISBN: 978-1-351-00075-8 (ebk)

Typeset in Bembo
by Taylor & Francis Books

For Donald

CONTENTS

FIGURES

ACKNOWLEDGMENTS

The refugees, immigrants, and Black Italians who shared their stories of struggle, creativity, and resilience with me inspired this book. My greatest aspiration for this work is that it will inform people who will have an impact on the social transformations necessary to improve their lives, and by extension the lives of other Europeans. Scholars, students, activists, journalists, and policy makers who read this work will, I hope, understand, act to wipe out racism, and disseminate awareness of transcultural people and places. In our everyday practices, critical studies, collective short and long-term strategies, we can re-construct a world where everyone has an equal chance at life. We all belong to the same social and cultural sphere, with or without hyphenated and multiple identities. To make our world more stable and unified around democratic values, we must first face our history and its legacies.

We descend from societies that contributed to revolutions centered on ideals of social justice, social equality, and freedom. We carry these histories within us, in spite of systematic measures that are being taken by people in whose interests it is to neutralize and destroy them by promoting fear, ignorance, and social distance. To be in a world where we are taught not to look upon one another as human beings is to live as morally diseased.

As Aimee Cesaire wrote,

> Colonization works to *decivilize* the colonizer, to *brutalize* him in the true sense of the word, to degrade him, to awaken him to buried instincts, to covetousness, violence, racial hatred, and moral relativism ... All these patriots who have been tortured, at the end of all the racial pride that has been encouraged, all the boastfulness that has been displayed, a poison has

been distilled into the veins of Europe, and slowly but surely, the continent proceeds toward *savagery*.

(Cesaire 2000, 35–36)

A Europe that has not faced its colonial history and present of racism and violence will be unable to save itself from itself. Changing this requires self-sacrifice, as well as the willingness to face one's own seduction by racial, material, and hierarchies of prestige and status.

I cannot thank my friends and research participants in Italy enough. They have been generous with their time and insights. Maria Viarengo has been a source of brilliant discernment and direction for almost three decades. She, and the equally brilliant Giovanna Zaldini, have contributed to this work in innumerable intellectual and emotional ways. They have been in my mind through the research and writing process. I thank them deeply, along with their wonderful families who have shown me only kindness, generosity, and joy while in Italy. Thanks also to Francesco Ciafaloni, who is one of the most incisive and informed scholars I have ever had the honor of knowing. Francesco's suggestions influence this work. I wish to thank the women of Turin's Alma Mater, for always opening their doors and inviting me into their interiors. A special acknowledgement to Maryann Akinyi for her insight, vision, and relentless determination. Thanks to Babacar, Mam Fatu, and their families for sharing their lives with us, over wonderful Senegalese meals. And to the luminous late Jean-Marie Tshotsha, your impact on me is unceasing.

I also owe a great debt to El Marouakhi Adil and Mahta Woldezghi of the intercultural center *Mondinsieme* of Reggio Emilio. As director and co-director of Mondinsieme, Adil and Mahta provided us with space to work, invited us to events, gave us access to their rich resources, and helped us connect with people from all over the African Diaspora living in Reggio Emilia. They brought us into their social world in 2014, and provided us with a sense of belonging and inclusion. I am deeply grateful to Adil, Mahta, and the many people in Reggio Emilia who spoke openly with us about their lives. Special thanks to Seni Bandaogo for showing us the Burkinabe community garden, and for sharing with us his Association's plans to build an agricultural system to feed people in Burkina Faso.

Along the way I have presented drafts of parts of this work to a number of different audiences and individuals. I would like to thank the scholars and students who listened and encouraged an early version of Chapter Five at the *Nordic Geographer's* conference in Iceland in 2013. My special thanks to Heidi Nast for organizing our session and for her excellent 2011 collection in *Antipode* that inspired it. I thank Heidi for her generosity, creativity, and wonderful intellect. Thanks also to James Tyner for his valuable insights and encouragement.

In 2016, I was invited to present several draft chapters of this work to Jacqueline Nassy Brown's graduate seminar at the CUNY Graduate Center in Manhattan. I wish to thank Jackie's bright and dedicated anthropology and geography students for their questions and insights. A special thank you to the always inspiring scholar Jackie Brown for honoring me with the invitation, and for her invaluable insights into these chapters over an all-too-rapid lunch. Thanks as well to Ruth Wilson Gilmore and to the Anthropology department at CUNY for supporting my stay in the Big Apple.

In 2015 and 2017, I was fortunate to have attended scholarly writing workshops organized by the amazing Tanya Golash-Boza. I cannot thank Tanya enough for guiding even a seasoned scholar to learn how to produce creative work consistently and with great fulfillment. I also thank Tanya and the wonderful Ana Aparicio for their valuable comments on an early draft of Chapter Five. At the first scholarly writing conference I attended in 2015, I met a spiritual sister, scholar Ayu Saraswati who led the mediations and has since that moment acted as a force of inspiration and joy. I am grateful to Ayu for her guidance in introducing me to meditation and helping me learn its value, a practice that has made my work profoundly meaningful. I would also like to thank Leslie Bartlett and Sarah Ovink for their insightful and encouraging comments on my introduction while we attended another life-affirming writing retreat organized by Tanya Golash-Boza and Ayu Saraswati in 2017. I will never forget you, or the other women, with whom I made truly creative connections at that retreat in Bali, Indonesia.

I also owe an enormous debt to people who have invigorated me as I developed a critical interest in understanding Euro-American, African cultures, and myself, in our complex racialized social world. Individuals who have given generously of their knowledge and insight, and have encouraged me to make these contributions, date back to my years in Cameroon in the early 1980s. I wish to thank in particular poet and teacher Berthe Virginie Tuedjo, a soul sister from Western Cameroon with whom I established a profound and lasting connection. She and her family have remained in my heart and mind, informing my ongoing intellectual travels and commitment to understanding how best to contribute to social transformation.

Along this path, my Black American and Black/Native American friends have been pivotal. France Winddance Twine is more than the editor of this series. She is an unusually brilliant and dedicated scholar, and a friend. I am deeply grateful to Winddance for supporting my work, including her encouragement that I go with Routledge, for her invaluable editorial insights and comments on the first draft of Chapter One, and on the full draft of the manuscript. Beyond this, Winddance has given me a rare and precious friendship that I cherish. I would also like to thank my students in Africana Studies at Hamilton College, especially the wonderful Kayla Cody, Kiana Sosa, and Lucia Kello. You have all brought joy to my teaching, and hope in dark moments.

To my life and intellectual partner, Donald Martin Carter, I cannot express my love and gratitude in writing. Donald has been a source of insight for over thirty years since we first met in graduate school at the University of Chicago in the late 1980s. I wish to thank Donald for his incredible unyielding belief in me, for his patience, for sharing his amazing brilliance with me, and for his valuable comments and insights on drafts of this manuscript. I'd also like to thank our two beautiful children, Nico and Eliana, for being such kind and creative spirits, making me laugh, and bringing me endless love.

I am grateful to my editor Dean Birkenkamp, for taking on this project with enthusiasm and for his generous encouragement. I am also extremely grateful to Dean's assistant, Tyler Bay, who shepherded me through the production process with insight and kindness. I wish to thank Daphne Lamothe for her enormously thoughtful and valuable reading and comments on my book proposal, along with Chapters Two and Three. Thanks also to the two anonymous reviewers for their constructive comments. I am grateful to Hamilton College for supporting my research and the indexing of this volume. A special thanks to Margie D'Aprix in the Hamilton library for her help delivering and renewing many needed materials through inter-library loan. Thanks to photographer Alberto Alpozzi for his kindness in locating two of the colonial photographs in Chapter One that were taken in Somalia by Carlo Pedrini, and for scanning a postcard. And thanks to Massimo Ghirelli, for his kind permission and help in printing images from a private collection, printed in his 2005 anti-racist calendar, *Agenda Razzismo Nonsolonero*.

I would like to acknowledge the spirit of Allan Pred whose work inspired my recent co-edited volume, and whose unbounded creative intellect has confirmed and fostered my work as a geographer and transdisciplinary scholar for decades.

COLONIZATION AND IMMIGRATION TIMELINE

1861	Italian Nation State is formed.
1869	Italy takes strip of land at Aseb (Assab) on the Red Sea.
1882	France seizes Tunis from the Ottoman Empire.
1885	Italy occupies Massawa (Massaua) on the Red Sea and begins to establish its first colony, Eritrea in 1990.
1890	Italy begins to acquire land in what later became Somalia.
1890	Italian military forces invade lands under the Ethiopian emperor's control.
1896	Italian military forces suffer humiliating defeat at Adwa (Adua).
1911	Italy attacks Ottoman rule in Tripoli in the world's first aerial bombardment. This begins a protracted war on the Sanusi fraternity and Bedouin of Cyrenaica.
1912	Italy seizes the Sublime Porte in the Dodecanese Islands from the Ottoman Empire.
1934	Italy consolidates the two coastal provinces of the Fezzan interior, naming the aggregated area Libya.
1935	Italy attacks Ethiopia (Abyssinia) under Generals Rodolfo Graziani and Pietro Badoglio. Ethiopia is an independent country and member of the League of Nations, to 'avenge' its loss in Adwa and complete its effort to take the area in the 1890s.
1935	The League of Nations condemns the Italian invasion of Ethiopia, yet it does not impose effective sanctions because other major powers are not interested in opposing Mussolini.
1936	Italian dictator Benito Mussolini proclaims 'Italian East Africa' (Africa Orientale Italiana (AOI)) through a merger of Italian

	Somaliland, Italian Eritrea, and the newly inaugurated Italian Ethiopia.
1939 (May)	Mussolini enters a formal military alliance with Adolph Hitler, the 'pact of steel.' However, Mussolini remains neutral when Hitler invades Poland in September.
1939	Italy annexes Albania.
1941 forward	Italy loses all its colonial territories, beginning in East Africa in 1941, Libya in 1943 with the fall of Fascism and surrender.
1947	Italy's new government formalizes new treaties in East Africa.
1986	Italy passes law 943 to regulate immigrants' access to the labor market.
1991	Following trade union led protests the government passes its first comprehensive immigration legislation, the 'Martelli Law' no. 39, recognizing the rights and obligations of immigrants. The law failed to define a procedure for legal entry, in spite of demand for a greater number of workers by Italian firms and families. Law 39 regulates Citizenship, a by descent or jus sanguinis law that is hotly contested and a new bill has not been fully endorsed by the Italian parliament. Second generation immigrants are de facto and not de jure citizens, unless they claim and are granted citizenship during a short window of time at the age of 18 years.
1998	The Single Act, 'Turco–Napolitano law' no. 286, further restricts illegal immigration in order to meet requirements of the Schengen Agreement. The law was designed to better manage the flow of immigrant labor and expand measures for integration of legal foreigners. The measure leads to increasing deportations, but some features included the recognition of immigrants' social rights such as access to health care and family reunification, and for the first time separates humanitarian and refugee issues from immigrant policy matters.
2002	Harsh law no. 177, 'Bossi-Fini' introduces criminal sanctions on migrants without legal residence documents. Introduces mandatory employment contracts, strict deportation practices, and the legalization of some migrant domestic workers or dependents of firms. The law tightens the connection between the work contract and residence permit, and requires immigrants to have job contracts before entering Italy. It also doubles the length of time immigrants can be held in detention and imprisoned those caught reentering the country.
2008	Italian Prime Minister Silvio Berlusconi and Muammar al Gaddafi sign an accord under which Italy agrees to pay Libya 5 billion dollars over 25 years in compensation and investments. This is called the Friendship Treaty.

2009	Muammar al Gaddafi visits Rome to celebrate the ratification of the Italy–Libya Friendship Treaty that produces joint naval patrols of refugees and migrants. Human Rights Watch condemns the agreement. Berlusconi promises to provide 200 million in U.S. dollars annually for investments in infrastructure in Libya. Italy provides patrol boats, and helps build a radar system to monitor desert borders via the Italian security firm, Finmeccanica.
2013	Operation Mare Nostrum is launched, following a massive shipwreck off the coast of the Italian island, Lampedusa. The Italian government launches a naval and air operation in the South Central Mediterranean to safeguard life at sea. The Italian mission carries out rescue over an area of 27,000 square miles. It saves thousands of lives in its year of operation.
2014	Operation Triton (FRONTEX) is launched in response to demands from Rome that the European Union step up its help with rescue operations in the Mediterranean. The EU border agency Frontex begins its Triton program, replacing Operation Mare Nostrum. Widely viewed as inadequate, Triton focuses on border surveillance only within 30 miles of the Italian coast and its budget is less than 1/3rd of Mare Nostrum.
2015	Italy establishes four "hot spots," ports where new arrivals are contained, identified, and fingerprinted. In 2016 Amnesty International reports cases where physical and psychological abuse are used to record fingerprints.

GLOSSARY

Afro-pessimism A theory advanced in literary and historical studies. Afro-pessimism considers how Black people live in the context of pervasive and profound anti-blackness. Within the tradition of Radical Black politics, it suggests that the Western world is so wholly infused with anti-black racism that cannot be reformed; it must be re-imagined and replaced with a different system.

Anti-black racism Rooted in White Supremacy and the justification of slavery by dehumanizing and defining some people as property. Derived from the social construction of Africa and blackness as fundamentally inferior to Europe and whiteness. Systematically denied as a system, and part of the routine dismissal of black perspectives and lived experiences.

Black lived experience From Frantz Fanon's conceptualization of how Blackness is experienced phenomenologically and subjectively in *Black Skin, White Masks*. It is part of an argument Fanon makes with Merleau-Ponty, Jean Paul Sartre, and other scholars who ignore the "historical racial schema" and "epidermal racial schema" in which black lives are embedded in the West under a fixing, essentializing white racial gaze. Black geographies of lived experience that have been erased from hegemonic systems of knowledge.

Blackness Assigned value as extrinsic to Western society, yet is central to modern Western binarist identity. Manifest in historical processes such as enslavement and colonialism, blackness has been assigned largely negative value as underbelly, symbol of pathology and crime. Widely assumed (inaccurately) to be acted upon instead of acting and affecting the social world. Blackness is also embraced and revered in Black social life, a source of pride, joy, creativity, resistance, agency, originality, and counterculture.

Black spaces   Describes the sites and expressions of Black lived experiences and social life from the vantage point of people who self-identify as Black or who are produced as such because they are socially perceived as Black in ways that, as Frantz Fanon asserted, "overdetermine" them "from without." Black spaces is an approach to the study of Western societies that captures the social lives of Black people as they cope with anti-blackness, and collectively give meaning to their lives. Can include implicit and explicit affirmations of lived geographies of Blackness and Black-Italianness. Black spaces are often unthought because rendered separate from White spaces, yet they are relational places and are integral to modern Western symbolic and material geographies.

black spaces   Like the CIA's secret or classified 'black sites' that the public is not expected to see, black spaces are sites that exist materially and symbolically, yet are so taken-for-granted as 'natural' and normal that they are rendered socially invisible and easy to dismiss as non-existent. Like Black spaces, black spaces are integral to the modern West, but are systematically unthought in our systems of knowledge. They are sites of anti-black violence, racism, microaggression, and systemic social erasure.

Dublin Agreement   A series of agreements among member states in the European Union that establish responsibility for examining asylum claims. Dublin III began to be applied in July 2013. The member state through which the asylum seeker first entered the EU is usually responsible for reviewing the application, and the applicant must remain in that country of application unless and until they are given full refugee status. The Dublin agreement has created a European-wide fingerprinting database for entrants to the EU.

Ethiopianism   An idea that emerged in the 19th century, linking African history to the ancient classical era and contesting prevailing notions that the continent did not have a history prior to European colonization. Ethiopia is one of the oldest nations in the world. After repelling the Italians in 1896 at the battle of Adwa, it was one of the few Africa nations not under European control. Many embraced Ethiopia as evidence of the Black capacity for self-rule. A tradition of Ethiopianism was expressed in slave narratives, and deployed by anti-colonial activists. It played a role in the South African Zulu rebellion of 1906, and in other parts of Africa was used as a call for the restoration of tribal life, politics, and cultural autonomy.

Fugitivity   Signals potentially transformative action where one practices daily acts of insurgency in an anti-black environment. A concept derived from slave narratives as practices of speaking out against and escaping from repression. The flight among enslaved people in the Atlantic world who stole back the lives taken from them, for instance maroons who created fugitive sites, and the many who resisted social erasure through acts of daily struggle, love, and resilience. Fugitivity suggests places and forms of being where state-sanctioned

violence can be critiqued and social justice nourished in ways the beneficiaries of white supremacy do not easily understand. I employ Harney and
Moten's notion of fugitive social life as part of a generative 'undercommons'
created among people who are rendered disposable because they are Black,
poor, or otherwise nonconforming.

Inter-ethnic divisions   Relationships between diverse ethnic groups whose
identities were often created and fueled under European colonization. In
Somalia, for instance, there are divisions between people from different clans
who fought for or against governing groups. There are also divisions
between countries and ethnic groups whose borders were drawn under
European colonization. Eritrea, for example, waged a thirty-year war with
Ethiopia and gained independence in 1991. Somalia and Ethiopia have been
in conflict for decades over land and borders. In Italy there are movements
toward at least temporary alliance across many national and ethnic divisions.

Interculturalism   A term used in Italy especially in relation to "Cultural
Mediation" (Merrill 2006) to describe intercultural communication,
exchange of knowledge, understanding, and solidarity.

Italian Fascism   An authoritarian political movement in Italy from 1922–1943,
under the leadership of Benito Mussolini. Italian Fascism inspired Adolf
Hitler and German Nazism, and it has been a model for other forms of
Fascism. An ideology of the state as holding supreme power, it combines
elements of Nazism, militarism, anti-liberalism, anti-communism, and
corporatism. Italian Fascism is strongly identified with the Cult of Mussolini.

Modernity   The temporal and spatial period beginning with merchant capitalist
expansion in the 15th century and continuing to the present. Marked by
radical transformations in European economy, culture, and politics, including
the end of feudalism and the global diffusion of European knowledge systems
through the transatlantic slave trade, colonization, advent of industrial capitalism and its attendant domination by capital and propertied social classes.
Baudelaire described modernity as the transient, fleeting, and contingent.
David Harvey in the *Condition of Postmodernity* discusses the continuities
between modernity and postmodernity.

Mussolini   Benito Amilcare Andrea Mussolini ('Il Duce'/The leader), born in
Forlì (Emilia Romagna), Italy in 1883. An ardent socialist in his youth. He
created the newspaper, 'Avanti' ('Forward') to promote his socialist agenda,
and used it to expand his influence. Joined the Italian army in 1915 and
fought on the front lines in World War I. In 1919 he created the Italian
Fascist party, a nationalist party that aimed to raise Italy's prestige to levels of
its Roman past. Organized the 'Black Shirts,' a paramilitary organization that
terrorized political opponents. By 1925 he had made himself dictator and
dismantled all democratic organizations. Mussolini and his partner, Claretta
Petacci were executed by the Italian partisans (anti-fascists) in 1945, their
bodies hung on display in a piazza in Milan.

Ottoman Empire An empire that emerged around 1300 under the leadership of Osman in Anatolia, a small principality in Asia Minor. It was one of the most powerful states in the world in the 15th and 16th centuries. Its rule lasted over 600 years, ending in 1922. At its height it encompassed present-day Greece, Hungary, the Balkan region, parts of Ukraine, parts of Syria, Iraq, Egypt, Israel, Libya, Tunisia, Algeria, and the Arabian Peninsula.

Relational place A term I use to describe the historical and present economic, political, and cultural ties between Africa and Europe. In Italy, these ties are deeply significant in the lives of African immigrants, refugees, African Italians, and Italians in spite of a prevailing absence of knowledge, and colonial amnesia. As cultural and geopolitical entities, Africa and Europe are relational and fluid wholes instead of discreet and fixed. The term suggests transcultural geographies and subjectivities.

Sociogenic Fanon's concept of sociogeny refers to a cultural-symbolic register that emerged with the violence of European colonization. It consists of culture, language, and discourse through which we understand our being in the world. Colonization was grounded in racial distinctions and a form of domination distinct from the non-racialized slave-master relationship. It created the conditions for the colonized to be forced to define themselves as non-beings (Fanon 2008).

Stranieri/e The Italian word for 'foreigners,' with negative connotations that resonate with a translation closer to 'strangers.' The term is frequently applied to "extracommunitari" or people who are not from member states in the European Union.

Transdisciplinarity The intermingling of diverse disciplinary theories and methodological approaches into a single synthetic approach. Different from interdisciplinarity in that instead of intersecting diverse scholarly fields, transdisciplinarity combines them into a singular approach to the study of social life and meaning past and present. Africana Studies at Hamilton College and elsewhere embraces the transdisciplinarity of this unique and theoretically compelling field of scholarly inquiry and activism.

Whiteness Normalized humanness. A social construction of white people as the standard human being. People who are inscribed as part of a transparent 'I' that act in the world or have the human agency to affect and create the social world. Can be understood as a form of cultural capital in which 'white people' (including those who pass as white or who are honorary whites) have access to material and symbolic privileges such as the ability to travel across national borders freely, easily gain residency permits, acquire credit from banks, rent or purchase homes, expect to be treated with dignity, expect to be considered intelligent and responsible. Whiteness tends to be invisible; it works at one and the same time to provide norms against which all groups are measured and to prevent itself from being seen as part of the system and structure of modern societies.

White supremacy/White Privilege From W.E.B. Du Bois who observed that in the United States people were taught to see themselves as white as opposed to developing working class solidarity with enslaved and recently freed slaves. White workers received a psychological 'wage of whiteness' that aligned them with the dominant group and blinded them to their common interests and social conditions with black people. White supremacy involves the ideologies, social policies, and mindset associated with white domination over nonwhite people based principally on physical characteristics and ancestry. European immigrants in the United States (especially Irish and Italian) did not in the early 20th century think of themselves as white, yet were taught to use their whiteness for social gain by for instance forming trade unions that excluded blacks. White supremacy creates racial segregation, and restricts meaningful citizenship rights to a privileged group of 'whites' (see James Baldwin (1984) "On Being White and Other Lies" (1984); and George M. Frederickson (1982), White Supremacy).

INTRODUCTION

Witness to the Unthought Position

In the summer of 2010 I was in Turin beginning a new research project on African diasporic politics in Italy when local residents and dear friends informed me that several hundred African refugees had recently collectively organized to protest their treatment. People from Somalia, Eritrea, and Ethiopia, countries with histories of conflict and tension as well as inter–ethnic divisions, had together occupied abandoned buildings in the urban center. A seasoned researcher of race and power and among Italians of African descent for twenty years, I had encountered few African refugees.

Fearful perceptions of 'non-European' immigrants and scarcity of resources had gripped Italy in a state of national hysteria and denial since the late 1980s when Italians first began to realize the country had become a site of in-migration instead of emigration from Italy to other parts of the world. In order to arrive in Europe, most African refugees in Turin and other Italian cities had survived perilous journeys, but their struggles for survival continued on Italian soil. I learned that their lived experiences in Italy converged in some dangerous ways with those of African immigrants, African Italians, and to an extent second generation Italian Africans who were all impacted by entrenched racial systems of classification that placed them (erroneously) squarely outside of European history and culture. From a critical analytical and experiential vantage point, the relationship between Europe and Africa is long and profoundly intertwined, with both continents acting as fundamental participants in the making of the Modern West. Yet in what Van Houtum describes as Europe's "global apartheid geopolitics" African refugees and immigrants who are classified as not 'belonging to' Europe, are generally forced to travel there illegally at great risk to their lives, as a consequence of a fate of birth (Van Houtum 2013).

On a Sunday shortly after our arrival I noticed a small group of women clothed from head to toe in black abayas[1] and flimsy flip flops along Turin's pale grey concrete streets and sitting under a tree near the main entrance to the verdant Valentino Park that follows the River Po. I'd later learn they were Somali refugees, and when on weekends I'd see them under the trees I would greet and chat with them as best I could in Italian (they did not speak Italian) and with gestures. At the women's intercultural center, Alma Mater, which was the first major intercultural center in Italy and that I was involved with creating in 1990,[2] my participants told me that Somali women who had been awarded refugee or humanitarian protection status were desperate for assistance that was not forthcoming from the Italian government. Women frequented Alma Mater on weekdays and Saturday mornings where they ate modest meals, attended teaching sessions in craftwork, had Italian language lessons, and found shelter and human compassion. When I first met them in 2010, the Somali refugees had been living for months or even years in homeless shelters that only opened their doors at 8pm and pushed them out at 8am. When not at Alma Mater or a municipal training site, I was told, they walked the urban pavement under the scorching summer sun, or in the frigid winter held onto each other to generate warmth. Alma Mater had established a program to help a few refugee women preserve what was described as a "sense of dignity." The city provided them with a modest stipend of 400 Euro coupons per month while they studied Italian. They told me that the coupons (equivalent to cash) a few received from the Italian government (as part of their status as refugees) were grossly inadequate. They used the money to purchase toiletries and medication. As I stood stunned by the conditions the refugees described to me, they received a phone call from the *comune* or urban administration,[3] letting them know that the 400 Euro stipend was going to be cut in half. An Alma Mater administrator asked with frustration, "Now what will happen to these people?" The support had been helping a few worry less about their families, whom they'd left in Mogadishu or other parts of Somalia.

In 1954 Italy ratified the UN Convention in Geneva relating to the status of refugees that obliged governments to provide safe asylum for refugees and accord them the same rights as other legal residents.[4] Participating states agreed to process all asylum applications and give those awarded refugee status the same rights as Italian citizens regardless of 'racial' or national origin. However, while Italy proclaims a right to asylum in their constitution, it also lacks a humane and transparent system for guaranteeing basic human rights (Albahari 2015; Mezzadro and Neilson 2016).[5]

There are no specific obligations for signatories of the International Convention on Refugees to provide conditions that enable one to live with dignity.[6] When released from one of several types of detention or processing centers (and whether or not they have been issued or denied legal recognition as refugees), many survive by occupying or squatting in abandoned buildings, makeshift encampments, or moving in and out of homeless shelters.

This book was initially inspired by the suffering of the Somali women and other African refugees. As an anti-racist, critical race studies scholar and critical theorist who is identified as white,[7] I am invested in illuminating their spatial-ontological experiences. One goal is to provide an analysis that does not elide exploring the lived experiences of Blackness, European colonialism, colonial histories, place, and belonging. I offer a new theoretical approach I call Black spaces. My theoretical approach synthesizes critical, North American critical race studies, African Diaspora Studies, and Afro-pessimism. This strongly theoretical and synthetic exploration is deeply grounded in a humanistic and empathetic ethnography.

I employ Afro-pessimist ideas that have been applied primarily to literary and historical analyses. *Black Spaces* examines how anti-blackness and blackness are produced, lived, and opposed by Italians in their daily lives. My concept of Black spaces is situated in the critical transdisciplinarity of Africana Studies.[8] I argue that we urgently need an analysis of the routinized racial ontology of social life and death in Italy. This is necessary for scholars who are devoted to social justice that encompasses state and international protections.

This work has broad European and global implications. Black spaces signal profoundly racialized symbolic and material sites, how these are embodied, and fundamentally how they are negated from plain sight because they are located in what Saidya V. Hartman refers to as the "position of the unthought" (Hartman and Wilderson 2003). The unthought position is peopled especially by formerly enslaved and colonized Black people who are in Western geographical imaginaries located on the color line in a way that produces their persistent social erasure. Black spaces are also sites of what Stefano Harney and Frank Moten refer to as 'black fugitivity,' a metaphor for Black social life. African Italians, refugees or asylum seekers, and many others from a first generation of Africans in Italy deftly create their own sense of being, and social connection. I explore the 'unthought' aspects of black/Black spaces in everyday social contacts, emerging cultural consciousness and forms of trans-ethnic solidarity, the relational place of Italy-Africa as a product of Italian colonialism in Africa, the Mediterranean crossing, detention camps, occupied spaces, and the rise of Black Italy in expressions of fugitivity and counter-transculture.

I bring an unusual depth and breadth of knowledge and experience to this work. I believe this enables me to develop an original approach that captures some of the complexity and multiplicity of the social, spatial, and ethno-graphically lived realities of Black life. In the 1980s I became a Peace Corps volunteer. I studied West African history and culture, preparing to return to Yaounde, Cameroon to conduct research and see my dear friends in that country. Instead, in 1990 I began conducting research on African Diaspora in Turin where I have since maintained and further built friendships with volunteers in Alma Mater and the many people who inform my research. I more recently conducted research in Reggio Emilia. My friends and research participants are from diverse national and ethnic backgrounds in Africa, and different class and regional backgrounds in Italy, including Ethiopia, Eritrea, Somalia, Kenya, Senegal, Rwanda, the Ivory Coast, Cameroon, Morocco, and the Italian regions of Piedmont, Puglia, and Emilia Romagna. Many of these individuals and their families in Turin and Reggio Emilia are now my most beloved friends. They are always, and profoundly in my heart.

Black Spaces

The concept of Black spaces charts the cultural symbolic and material workings of the lived experiences of African descent in Italy. An elastic concept, it allows me to scrutinize the experiences of African refugees, migrants of African origin, African Italians, Italian Africans, *and also* Italian society. Black space demarcates the discursive and systemic production of blackness as social erasure and even social death, while attending to the social life of black people from Africa or with African ancestry. Local and national Italian governments build metaphorical and grounded black spaces to advance notions of a unified Italian national identity. These spaces are racialized in order to render whiteness or near whiteness legitimately Italian just at an historical moment when there is growing visibility of black African and other formerly colonized immigrants in the public sphere, and broad public awareness of a shifting, increasingly multiply cultured demography. Black spaces also refer to such material depositories of anti-black racism as immigrant detention centers and homeless shelters, places that are there but that nobody seems to see. These are spaces of social control rooted in European histories of racial classification, through which the state seeks to delineate and erase the presence of Black people in the public sphere, and render blackness as nonbeing.

Black spaces are what historian of subalternity Gyan Pandey (2013) suggests are 'unarchived' spaces. They are the taken-for-granted parts of life at scales both of the state and everyday interactions, the spaces where one is taught not to wander in thought or body because dangerous even when directly within a field of vision. The insinuation of power in all that passes for knowledge can lead one to overlook all sorts of things as we filter out what we believe is worth knowing or not knowing. Like the CIA's clandestine "black sites," people know black/Black spaces are here yet nobody knows where.[9] They are racialized epistemological spaces that one doesn't necessarily see, perceives without awareness, or that in some cases one sees, knows, and lives in with considerable unease, stress, and profound suffering. In deploying the concept of black/Black spaces, I am advancing an approach to a radically racialized analysis of space and position, of what geographer Ruth Wilson Gilmore has referred to as the "fatal coupling of race and space" (2002). This is a profound ontological, epistemological, and structural combination that persists because it is so constitutive of Western culture, society, and political economy. This does not mean it cannot be or is not in the process of being transformed, but rather that doing so necessitates beginning with the kind of multifaceted understanding of Western culture and society that can be gained only by integrating multiple disciplinary theories and angles.

My approach is supported and enriched by particular viewpoints that have been advanced by theorists of Black studies as part of the abiding tradition of scholarship that Afro-pessimism follows. Thinkers like Frantz Fanon, Charles W. Mills, Achille Mbembe, Lewis R. Gordon, bell hooks, Stuart Hall, and Sylvia Wynter have sought to characterize African subjectivities in the making of the Western world from various social and philosophical perspectives. My work brings critical geography and the centrality of space and place into a dialogue with these philosophical and social perspectives.[10] I also prioritize lived experience and the ethnographic, building my work on the basis of what I observe, from what people say about their experiences, and from how their experiences are represented and or ignored by others.

This book places black subjectivity and experience at the center of analysis. The generation of creative and often affective and unarticulated social and cultural meanings in an anti-black world deserves more attention. My ethnographic analysis considers the question central to Afro-pessimism: How do black people live within the context of anti-blackness? The African and African Italian subjects of my study do not merely respond to anti-black racism. To be certain, they have to be able to live with and negotiate the realities of this world, our world. There are many different ways of doing this. One's social and symbolic capital among other people of African descent, legal status, freedom of movement, access to resources outside one's own ethnic or religious community all play a role in the negotiation of anti-blackness. However, most people of African ancestry in Italy embrace others with whom they share the experience of anti-black racism and anti-othering, and/or with people who feel and relate to them as human beings with a sense that their lives and social life in general is their own. Black spaces are not merely the property of Whites or Near Whites, but are spaces lived by black people that are habitually ignored.

African refugees, immigrants, and second generation African Italians express complex subjectivities and social lives. Writing about African Diasporic identity and belonging, Stuart Hall suggested there are multiple "presences" among people of the African diaspora colonized by Europe (Hall 2003). They tend to have transcultural subjectivities that, whether intentionally or unintentionally, embrace Africanness, Blackness, Italianness, and Europeanness in a variety of complex and intersecting ways. It follows that in this study, black spaces have several significations. I adopt upper and lower case distinctions, black or Black, guided by a desire to distinguish between what are in practice inter-twined social meanings of blackness, one the presumed property of whites who have benefited from White supremacy and the other of Black subjects. Black spaces with a capital 'B' suggests a conscious or semi-conscious social and political identity, and the production of Black social life in often affective, not necessarily conscious or articulated expressions of Blackness. Social life may be designed to appear to be the exclusive property of Whites or Near Whites; but African refugees, immigrants, and second generation African Italians or Italian Africans express complex subjectivities and social lives.

Afro-pessimism can be employed as a language that supports the impulse to cope with anti-black racism by wholly rejecting whiteness and White allies. However, I find its meta arguments useful in exploring my own ethnographically based material on the *spatial production of anti-blackness and Blackness* and its origins in European history. I do not, as I will explain below, adopt in this study the post-essentialist position that prevails in the United States and also to an extent in other parts of Europe that Blackness must and does refuse assimilation into the mainstream; that Blackness is (along with other nonwhite postcolonial subjectivities), by contrast with Whiteness, immanently autonomous.

A central conceit in Afro-pessimism is that modernity produced an anti-black world that is so utterly broken it cannot be reformed – it must instead be demolished and replaced.[11] Jared Sexton in his discussion of the "tragic-comic existence in black" asks, "What is the nature of a form of being that presents a problem for the thought of being itself?" This phrasing magnifies the pivotal "unasked question," credited to W.E.B. Du Bois over a century ago in *The Souls of Black Folk* regarding how it feels to live a blackness that has been inscribed by Whites/White supremacy into the modern world as by definition a problem. Sexton maintains that because the world imposes on blackness a kind of pathology and decay, the "fact of blackness" is by necessity the position of ontological death, or the social life of social death (Sexton 2011). In other words, it's impossible to escape the conditions of being in a world made through fragile yet also irreducible narratives of anti-blackness, where "the human" is normalized as white, in opposition to a form of black nonbeing. Sexton describes the lived experience of black being as follows,

> Being black means belonging to a state that is organized in part by its ignorance of your perspective – a state that does not, that cannot, know your mind – we might say that blackness indicates a situation where you are anonymous to yourself. Reduced to what would seem its essential trait, blackness is a kind of invisibility.

His sobering claim suggests that transformation is not really possible without a complete overturning and remaking of the world, *as we know it*, a world defined through epistemic, psychological, intellectual, and physically violent anti-blackness (Spillers 2003; Sexton 2011, 2016; Hartman and Wilderson 2003). This argument emerges from within a tradition of Black Radicalism that is committed to the vision of social revolution, as opposed to the social reform of existing institutional structures (Robinson 2000).

Afro-pessimism suggests that it is futile to render anti-blackness legible and visible. Afro-pessimism has no confidence in the capacity to recognize black social life without a comprehensive transformation, rethinking, and reimagining of the world. While I understand this perspective, it tends to over-determine culture and economy. Modernity established racial patterns of social hierarchy that now form part of a taken-for-granted epistemology and ontology. To make sense of this we should begin with awareness that anti-blackness is systematically denied in Europe, the US, and globally. Writing about the black condition in the United States, James Baldwin argues in *The Fire Next Time* that whites are hopelessly trapped in a history that they do not understand and from which they cannot be released,

> Whites (They) have had to believe for many years, and for innumerable reasons, that black men are inferior to white men. Many of them, indeed, know better, but … people find it very difficult to act on what they know. To act is to be committed, and to be committed is to be in danger. In this case, the danger in the minds of most white Americans, is the loss of their identity … the black man has functioned in the white man's world as a fixed star, as an immovable pillar: and as he moves out of his place, heaven and earth are shaken to their foundations.
>
> *(Baldwin 1963, 23)*

Thus, if more people, especially White people, become racially cognizant and committed, transformation *will* follow.

Some may reject the idea that white people will ever give up their privileges and superior position. I respond by asking: Would you be willing to give up your own social and material privileges based on race and or social class? A nuanced understanding of racial, class, gendered, and ethnic hierarchies, and a practiced commitment to anti-materialism is required. Many white people are also unhappy with the alienation and diminishing commitment to social identity, whether or not they enjoy personal privileges from whiteness. I use white people as a strategically essentialized category to portray a pattern of identity that is privileged and taken-for-granted as the reference of the "normal" human being who is therefore unmarked. However, white people are in reality quite heterogeneous, and Italians themselves differentiate each other through a racialized system of classification in which the northerner is depicted as closer to the Anglo-Saxon ideal white than the southerner (also see Dickie 1999).[12] Most white people, too, wish to create and live in a more gratifying, just, and humane world. This must be a world that values the social good above personal material gain and prestige. In addition, my own ethnographic materials suggest that the theoretical agenda of rejecting the existing world *is happening* in some of the ways that Baldwin suggests, i.e., by Africans *moving out of their alleged place*, figuratively and materially. With both conscious intent and subaltern practices, many reject their own rejection and the privileging of superficial performances of race and status in favor of collective responsibility and sharing.

As Jack Halberstam asks in his introduction to Harney and Moten's *The Undercommons*, "If we do not seek to fix what is broken, then what? How do we resolve to live with brokenness, with being broke...?" (Harney and Moten 2013, 5) Black/black spaces is a concept that seeks to address just how this brokenness is lived in experiences, and how one lives with and negotiates it without being able to transform it entirely. Black life is expressed in Italy in manifold ways, including the practice of subterfuge and a rejection of being rejected, the assertion of one's being. It is revolutionary in a system designed to erase blackness that my participants have frequently taken the position of learning and understanding the Italian system and culture while adopting some features as their own, in quite critical and self-conscious ways. They say, metaphorically, "I see you, Italy. And Europe. I am a witness to your systemic cruelty towards me, toward your own people, to your brutality and violence. And I have perspectives that differ from yours and that you cannot erase even though you pretend to be able to do so."

Afro-pessimism, which builds on many of Frantz Fanon's insights into the postcolonial condition, advances a theoretical agenda based largely on textual analyses that I think is quite insightful and useful, yet is a bit over-reaching in its portrayal of a fixed social system that entraps us all without relief.[13] It emerged as a language for addressing the deeply entrenched modern structures of anti-blackness that began with the transatlantic slave trade and have stubbornly held forth, affecting the lives of people in the African Diaspora and Africa in ways that are generally unnoticed by Italians. I am aware that this is a broad statement, and race is an extremely slippery and in fact fluid classification that takes different forms in relation to diverse places and times. However, as Afro-pessimist and many scholars of the African diaspora have argued at least since W.E.B. Du Bois and Anna Julia Cooper in the early 20th century, the color line is built into the fabric of Western culture and society in such a way that it is designed to resist fundamental change, and cognizance of its very existence (also see Mills 1999).

The major value in Afro-pessimism is that it neither sidesteps black suffering and trauma (by focusing solely on resistance) nor does it languish within it; it neither denies nor reifies black suffering and the social violence that informs it. Instead, it looks for the creation of social life in social death, allowing us to bring racial domination and the trivialization of black life to the forefront of analysis, and also to encompass the broad perspective Doreen Massey referred to as a power-geometry of social-spatial relations across space and time (Massey 1994). Fred Moten and Stefano Harney's iteration of Afro-pessimism as radical black fugitivity is focused on the social life produced by people rendered in effect disposable because they are black, poor, and otherwise nonconforming.[14] In a more geographical manner, Katherine Mckittrick refers to "worlds within worlds" that are however interrelated and not entirely distinctive (Mckittrick 2011; also see S. Gregory 1999; Brown 2005).

Race is a set of sociopolitical processes of differentiation and hierarchization that has been manufactured in simultaneously unequal lived spaces throughout the world, positioning Africa and blackness as the "lack of" culture and life, a symbolic void and material space of death and zone of the most absolute alterity, where life is valuable, if at all, only for labor and exotic imaginings of an anachronistic or essentially wild primitivism that contrast with European ideas of what it means to be truly "civilized." Blackness and race are central to the imaginaries of European societies, in parallel with modern knowledge and discourse about "man," and what it means to be human (Mbembe 2017; Trouillot 1997). In Modernity, sub-Saharan Africa came to symbolize the underbelly of the West, where selfhood and personhood were constructed as outside the human (Mills 1998). Frantz Fanon first pointed out that European culture "epidemiologizes" blackness so that people come to symbolize territories heavy with fabricated meanings (Africa) derived from colonial conquest and attendant discourses. In *Black Skins, White Masks* Fanon described the lived experiences of being sealed in a crushing objecthood, one's body abraded into nonbeing; the movement, attitudes, glances of white others fixed, like a chemical solution fixed by a dye (Fanon 2008). It is vital to situate Black Italy, Black Europe,[15] and the global African Diaspora in relation to this modern Western historical-ideological context (see Said 1994).

There is a vast literature on immigration in Italy especially in the 1990s, much but not all of it written by Italian scholars.[16] This important work is primarily focused on ethnic communities and the challenges faced both by immigrants and an Italian host society that was neither institutionally nor culturally prepared to be a country of immigration and port of entry to the European Union, and some of it addresses issues of racial hierarchy and discrimination (Carter 1997; Merrill 2006; Bartoli 2012; Cole 2005; Mangano 2010; Decimo and Sciortini 2006; Dal Lago 1999; Saraceno, Sartor and Sciortino 2013; Hawthorne 2017). Much of this scholarship on immigration focuses on issues of ethnicity, multiculturalism, and postcolonialism (Riccio and Brambilla 2012; Romeo & Lombardi-Diop 2015; Giuliani and Lombardi-Diop 2013; Ponzanesi 2016; Lombardi-Diop and Romeo 2015; Grillo and Pratt. 2002; Grillo et al. 2015; Andall 2000, 2003; Salih 2003; Antonsich 2015). Race is central if not always addressed directly in the burgeoning work on Italian colonialism and postcolonialism (Del Boca 2005; Labanca 2002; Ben-Ghiat and Fuller 2005; Palumbo 2003; Negash 1987; Andall and Duncan 2005; Ponzanesi 2016; Lombardi-Diop and Romeo 2013). However, there is no significant work that offers an ethnographically grounded study of race and racism in Italy from a theoretical and transdisciplinary perspective of black studies and critical geography. Moreover, this book represents the first study of the African diaspora in Europe that incorporates Afro-pessimist and race theory to shed light on black diasporic identity in Italy and anti-black culture. Current research on migration in Europe and its refugee crisis urgently needs a conceptual approach that opens one to a nuanced analysis of the lived experience of Black Europeans and African refugees or, as Lewis R. Gordon (2000) suggests, the existential phenomenological dimensions of racism. For in this world dominated by taken-for-granted racialized practices, a Manichean world that as Frantz Fanon wrote in relation to colonization was and is even today divided into two, blackness functions as an underbelly, a symbol of crime, decay (Guillamin 1995; Hartman and Wilderson 2003; Wilderson 2015; Gordon 2000; Mbembe 2003; hooks 1992; Muhammad 2010) and pollution that is normalized as separate from the presumed purity and life force of Whiteness. I approach and subject to rigorous and transformative criticism the system of anti-black racism that functions as if natural, with attention to black suffering and the experience of social erasure as well as resourcefulness, social life, and transcultural, diasporic identity. Anti-black racism is part of a racial ontology in the modern West and around the globe that we desperately need to make sense of and transform in order to fulfill promises of social justice, including state and international protections, recognition, and regard for human life. We need a theoretical framework for situating discussions of race and white supremacy with the capacity to challenge presumptions of national identity and belonging, subjectivity, immigration and refugee studies, and the very assumptions of Western knowledge (Mills 1998, 1999; Weheliye 2014; Wynter 2003; Gordon 1995, 2000; Ferreira da Silva 2007; Hartman 2007; Sexton 2010, 2011, 2016; Moten 2003, 2008; Vargas 2010; Trouillot 2003). Our understanding of the manifold ways black life is lived in different places, in spite of and in negotiation with anti-black racism, can generate new forms of knowledge about ourselves, and the world we really live in. It might lead us to learn how to transform instead of merely living with what is broken.

Silences about Black subjectivity and agency in Western historiography are as Rolf Trouillot compellingly argued held in place by profound scholarly narratives that control and repress empirically evident truths about the past. The Haitian Revolution for example has been described as if it were orchestrated by the French, concealing the brutalities that the enslaved revolted against, and their reasoned struggle for freedom. Histories were written as if the Haitian Revolution had never happened, for how can one write a history of the impossible? (Trouillot 1997) The systematic exclusion of Blackness from humanity follows a Western ontology, an implicit organization of the world and its inhabitants, and systematic pattern of thought that has been with us for over five centuries. This practice of filtering out Black thought, social agency, and contributions to world history enable and legitimize racial violence, discrimination, and inhumane treatment of people with African ancestry. I concur with Achille Mbembe who in *On the Postcolony* argues that, today, the former colonized is positioned throughout the West very much like the former slave, in that he or she is "The object to whom anything can be done, whose life can be squandered with impunity" (Mbembe 2001, 235).

Frantz Fanon argued that European colonization created a fundamentally violent geographically and culturally compartmentalized world with "native" towns and "European" towns, "native schools" and "European schools." This social world was divided by what racial "species" one belonged to. In Fanon's penetrating analysis of colonial culture and practice, the border between the European and native world was represented by the police barracks and stations, with police and soldiers as the agents of colonial repression. Police ensured that the colonized remained under constant scrutiny, with a threat of violence and death. In other words, the colonized were taught to live in a state of terror. The pervasive potential for violence by police and also citizens who have been given authority by virtue of their racialized whiteness has sadly remained integral to the world in which we live. It has only accelerated under current political economic conditions. Anti-blackness has remained part of a taken-for-granted belief built on false and distorted knowledge that some people do not deserve to be free, or to live at all, while others are destined to survive and thrive. Following the argument of Fanon and other scholars of Africana Studies, I argue that oppressed people are not easily able to carve autonomous spaces free from terrorizing state control and forms of everyday symbolic and material violence.[17] The violent conditions in which Black people often find themselves make life much messier than this. Most of our scholarly work is unable to explain the paradox of agency for former slaves and colonized people who persistently experience forms of sur-veillance, potential violence from military, police as well as micro-aggression while interacting with civilians.

As Hannah Arendt (1973) suggested, one is not a person in European nation states, i.e., a human being, unless one is recognize as a "citizen." In Italy, even people born in the country yet who do not appear "Italian" are repeatedly told they could never become "Italian." This is a highly alienating, potentially debili-tating message. In practice these assumed non-Italians, who nevertheless may feel culturally very Italian subjectively, are denied human belonging. The idea of blackness in the West is used as a way to rationalize anti-blackness, the rejection of blackness. This work addresses the problem of Africa in Europe, of people of African descent and the modern legacies, the lived experiences of anti-blackness or how one lives with and negotiates the experience of being perceived as a threat to Europe, itself a contested field.

Historical Context

In 2015, there were 83,243 political asylum requests in Italy, representing 7% of the total number of the EU.[18] A few have achieved Italian citizenship. Still others, over one million people, live precariously in Italy for years or decades without legal documents, working in the informal economy (see Lucht 2011). During the past four decades Italy has transformed from a nation of emigration to one of immigration. Today 5 million foreign nationals hold residency permits in a total population of 60.5 million. Others have temporary residency but live as second-class citizens in a state of limbo and anxiety in which they must continually seek to renew their documents. Almost a million Italian children have parents who are not Italian citizens, thus have no access to resources and recognition as legal residents.[19]

Italy has a complex relationship to ideologies of whiteness and othering for a number of reasons. Northern Italy internally colonized the southern regions at unification. Italy has historically held a peripheral geopolitical relationship to the rest of Europe as part of the Southern Mediterranean (see Giuliani and Lombardi Diop 2013; Pugliese 2002). Southern Italians who emigrated to Australia, North America, and later to Western and Northern Europe were perceived as dark-skinned and initially discriminated against in their places of settlement (Gabaccia 2000; Lombardi-Diop and Romeo 2015). Southern regions remain relatively impoverished, their development uneven compared with the Central and Northern zones.

Italians have been internally divided along north-south axes. However, as Lombardi Diop and Romeo have argued, over the past two decades such divisions and privileges have been supplanted by underlying ideologies of Italian cultural superiority to Africa and visions of a homogenously White country (Lombardi-Diop and Romeo 2015). In this historical context where blackness is self-consciously emerging as a spatialized identity and anti-blackness is institutionalized, I detail the production and reproduction of Black spaces as experiences and imaginaries (see Smith 2015). The most dramatic current image of Africans in Italy, repeatedly represented in the press, is of boatloads of migrants and asylum seekers, and stories of capsized ships and lifelessness.[20]

On May 29, 2016 in an interview with the BBC, Southern European spokesperson for the United Nations High Commissioner for Refugees, Carlotta Sami pronounced migrant deaths as the "new normal." Over the preceding week alone, an estimated 700–900 men, women, and children fleeing war, human rights violations, and poverty in Africa and the Middle East suffocated, burned to death when the boats caught fire, drowned after their boats sank, or disappeared. Libyan police and military forced many onto flimsy boats and into the Central Mediterranean sea (Albahari 2015). The vast majority of people who die in the crossing are Sub-Saharan African, notably from Eritrea, Ethiopia, Somalia, Ghana, Gambia, Senegal, Nigeria, and Togo.[21]

Sami's reference to the normalization of deaths in shipwrecks suggests that these atrocities have become acceptable among the majority European social and political will. The Italian news has made it clear for over a decade that most of the victims are African, regularly broadcasting images of sinking boats and corpses. They tend to be represented abstractly as hordes of people, or as individuals prostrate on cement or dirt. This image of Africans has become the dominant trope for what has since the early 1990s been represented as an "immigration emergency" in Italy, supplanting the 1990s images of the African "Vu Cumpra"/ Senegalese street seller or Nigerian prostitute (Carter 1997; Merrill 2006). Any quick glance at images in the Italian press since 2000, including the mainstream national newspapers such as *La Stampa, La Repubblica*, or *Il Corriera della Sera* will

FIGURE I.1 Italian regions and provinces

lead one to countless "documentary" representations of Africans in situations of extreme poverty, emotional and physical pain, and in groups on ships, boats, wharfs, and detention centers, often behind barbed wire fences.

Former Prime Minister Matteo Renzi in his effort to garner cooperation from European partners whom he felt had abandoned Italy, warned that the current "refugee/migrant crisis" is reminiscent of the racial holocaust of the Third Reich.[22] These deaths are, however, part of a long pattern in the racialized

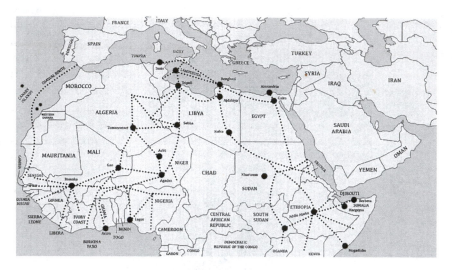

FIGURE I.2 Central Mediterranean Routes
Source: Map made by Mackenzie Doherty.

relationship between Africa and the West. The movements from Africa to Europe represent a new African crossing, a contemporary Middle Passage that tends to be under-reported and or misrepresented by the international press.[23]

The normalization of the death of people of African descent does not end in the crossing space of the Central Mediterranean sea. Racialized spaces are also being produced in the interiors – in camps, detention centers, prisons, and other public spaces. I use the term racialized space to refer to material repositories where people racialized as other are *not considered Italian and are separated from Italian citizens*. Racialized spaces are also symbolic sites where, through affect and gesture as well as social capital and access to resources, people are marked as different and inferior culturally. They are perceived through a racialized system of social hierarchy that Allan Pred, in his study of racism in *Even in Sweden*, described as composed of a "constellation of relations, practices, and discourses that I found myself unavoidably amid" (Pred 1995, xiv). As Pred argued with sensitivity and insight, the hypermodern experiences of capitalism breeds experiences that are reworked politically and culturally into expression that, as he put it, "allow historically sedimented or latent forms of racism to resurface in new guise" (Pred, 1995, 10; also see Brown 2005; Wilson-Gilmore 2007; Mckittrick and Woods 2007; Mckittrick 2006; Wilson 2002).

The prevailing idea that the African Diaspora in Europe is entirely new is inaccurate. However, until the late 20th century Italians had commonly identified people from former European colonies in Africa with a sense of curious paternalism, exoticism, or fear. Neither Italian history textbooks nor popular media substantially discussed Italy's and Europe's long connections to Africa, including the 19th and 20th century relationships forged through colonization. People of African descent have lived in Italy for centuries, evidence in images of black Madonnas and Alessandro de'Medici, Duke of Florence. Until the 1980s, many traveled to Italy to study at the universities. National and international border patrols and surveillance technologies serve to conceal multi-layered and multi-dimensional historical, colonial, economic, political, cultural, and faith-based interconnections between Europe and Africa, a deeply relational Europe-Africa.

There are a number of reasons to include refugees and asylum seekers in analyses of immigrants and citizens of African descent in Europe (see Di Maio 2012).[24] In 2015 alone, asylum seekers from East and West Africa constituted some 100,000 newcomers throughout Europe, with the highest concentration in Italy.[25] In Italy, and in contrast to neighboring Greece in the period from 2015–2016 alone, the vast majority of refugees and migrants who arrived via the Mediterranean Sea were from African countries.

From January to August 2016, the greater part originated from Nigeria, Eritrea, and Somalia; and from Nigeria, Eritrea, Sudan, Gambia, and the Ivory Coast through 2015 (UNHCR report August 2016).[26] Migrants and refugees tend to be conflated into a single category in Italy.[27] The Lega Nord party for instance has long articulated the idea that it's almost impossible to distinguish an asylum seeker with legitimate claims based on international agreements from a clandestine migrant fleeing poverty. This is the expression of a cultural logic fueled by a political culture that has capitalized on and nourished fear and an anti-other structure of feeling (see Chapter Two), along with a contradictory policy of intentional neglect (Merrill 2001; 2004; 2006; 2011; Carter and Merrill 2007; Lombardi-Diop and Romeo 2015).

A foundational principle in international human rights agreements is to protect freedoms against persecution on the basis of racial, ethnic, religious, political differences through the granting of asylum. Race does not otherwise factor into many legal or scholarly discussions of refugees. However, my research on African refugees in Italy reveals that asylum seekers and refugees routinely negotiate anti-black racism, which is part of a shared experience with other African migrants and their Italian-born children (Merrill 2006).

Geographer Derek Gregory described Geographical imaginations as part of a colonial present that marks "other people as irredeemably 'Other' and that license(s) the unleashing of exemplary violence against them" (Gregory 2004, 16). These geographical imaginaries encourage the Italian media to make a spectacle of black people in pain by diffusing now iconic images of Africans in overflowing, sinking, or sunken boats, which is becoming a shared memory, part of a collective Black diasporic identity haunted by ghosts. This resonates with the anti-black experiences of immigrants and Italian citizens of African ancestry. These boats have become iconic images of an immigrant crisis all over Europe, infusing into the contemporary European world view the abstract idea that African migrants are superfluous. How do such images of physical and psychic violence and loss affect refugees, African Italians, and immigrants? There are undoubtedly profound differences in experiences between refugees, people engaged in struggles for citizenship rights, and immigrants struggling to obtain or renew residency permits while trying to survive and contribute to the well being of their families. Nevertheless, in bearing witness to these spectacles of pain and death, African Italians understand their connection to these shared experiences of degradation, whether or not they accept what James Baldwin in a comparable US context referred to as "this dark and dangerous and unloved stranger," that is "part of himself forever" (Baldwin 2012, 32).

"Black" is a complex and incomplete name and identity because it encompasses enormous class, ethnic, gender, and religious differences. Yet one can speak today, using Benedict Anderson's (2016) term, of an "imagined community," of Black Europe, and an incipient, inchoate Black Italy (Carter 2013; Hawthorne 2017). A nomenclature not (yet) widely adopted, the notion of a Black Italy refers not to an essential blackness based in racial and cultural identity, but rather to a multivalent and diasporic identity. This sense of a common black lived experience includes assemblages of people with diverse geographical origins, histories, and relationships to Italy. It encompasses Italian citizens, refugees, and immigrants[28]. Some want recognition and inclusion, others want freedom to move and work, still others want to participate in a changing Italy and Europe that recognizes their ongoing contributions to modernity and their multiple identities. Black Italy describes persons who may have lived in Italy for over a decade or who were born in Italy and in spite of their differences are similarly positioned in the social world. In contrast to the context in the United States and the Caribbean, where Blackness is linked with cultural-political identity and there is an ongoing struggle to (re) define and distinguish it from the mainstream "White" culture, in Italy the first and second generation of African migrants struggle to be included in the national imaginary. They tend to assert human rights and belonging in Europe, and those fluent in Italian tend to be relatively comfortable with multivalent, elastic transcultural identities. There are some first-generation African immigrants who seek to educate the Italian public about particular African cultural practices and beliefs in order to dispel prevailing myths and imaginaries and exchange cultural and artistic achievements (see Merrill 2006).

Africa and Europe

Africa and Europe have long been intermeshed; they made the Modern West together. As Alessandra Di Maio, Cristina Lombardi Diop and Caterina Romeo, and others have suggested recently, the Italian south as part of the Mediterranean and in a subaltern relationship with northern Italy is the site of postcolonial counterdiscourses and countermapping among scholars and artists who are reclaiming it as a highly transcultural, borderless place (Di Maio 2012; Lombardi-Diop and Romeo 2015; Raeymaekers 2017). The reality of Europe's extended, profound, violent, and intimate relationship with Africa that began around the 15th century makes writing about Africans and people with African descent in Europe highly fraught, and challenging. The legacies of transatlantic slavery and colonization produced common experiences in the present, although there are manifold differences and tensions between people with African ancestry living in Italy.

"Is Italy a racist country?" was a frequently asked question in the Italian media in the 1990s. Most Italians responded that when compared to the North Americans they were not really racist. The United States was founded on slave labor and anti-blackness. Today, the prevailing denial of racism remains, or what Ruth Frankenberg called race-evasion, and color-evasion (see Frankenberg 1993). However, outside of the country there is a growing sense that Italy has a problem with racism,[29] instantiated most spectacularly in the treatment of Italy's first Black government minister, Cecile Kyenge, by fellow parliamentarians from the Northern League. Kyenge is of Congolese origin having traveled to Italy to study in 1983. She was a practicing opthamologist in Emilia Romagna before being elected to local government in that region and then becoming the country's only Minister of Integration in the Enrico Letta cabinet from 2013–2014. She was elected to the European parliament in May 2015. As Minister of Integration, Kyenge promoted migrant rights, and urged for inclusion and the granting of citizenship to children born on Italian soil. Yet some Italian members of parliament denied her due respect. A member of the Northern League referred to her as an orangutan and another said she should be raped in order to know how Italians felt when raped by foreigners (Merrill 2015).[30]

Tobias Jones, writing in the *Guardian News,* expressed a growing sense that these are common sentiments in Italy, "The verbal attacks on Cecile Kyenge are shocking, even in a country where racism is part of everyday life."[31] People threw bananas at Ms. Kyenge, as they have been repeatedly thrown at black soccer players throughout Europe. Jones writes,

> Anyone who has listened to Italian political debate, or worse, stood in an Italian football stadium, knows that Italy simply isn't a tolerant place. This is a country where a recent prime minister, Silvio Berlusconi, thought it hilarious to joke that Obama had a decent suntan. This comment is deeply resonant with popular notions of Blacks and others, but also with the racialized divisions and forms of discrimination between the Italian North and South. The racism isn't restricted to right or left, old or young, rural or urban: it is noticeable everywhere.[32]

Following European patterns, Italians are reproducing the racialized divisions produced by colonialism (cf. Mbembe 2009). Italy creates perceptions of African migrants and refugees as "alien," and threatening to national security. By recycling colonial-era policies and practices that divided "natives" from European colonists, they allocate state power to employ extraordinary, extrajudicial measures against non-citizens and people deemed "undesirable."

In the wake of global economic restructuring, a crisis in labor, and a neoliberal phase in history dominated by what David Harvey described as "time-space compression" when all social life it seems is assigned a market value, there is both the reappearance of virulent racism that had been expressed indirectly, and also a sense of social confusion, fear, and growing indifference (Harvey 1991; 2007; Pred 2000). A central characteristic of this social era is creation of disposable categories of people (McIntyre and Nash 2011; Merrill 2011). While the globe becomes ever more intensely interconnected through the market and human movements, a sense of anxiety over unstable labor markets that are generally blamed on newcomers, and the absence of securities that in many industrialized countries had been provided by the welfare state, it is fairly easy to invoke proto-racial, ethnic, and religious differences to nourish a state of fear and anger that divides people who in the absence of these ideologies might find they have common problems. In Italy, where migrants and refugees especially of African and Arab origins have come to signify people of a different "race" and thus spurious or without an authentic place in the established social order, pre-occupations with national cultural purity are common.[33] For example, Marcello Pera, the right wing senate president from 2001–2006 railed against the growing "metissage" and hybridity in Italy (Mezzadra and Neilson 2003). Nevertheless, increasing interculturalism is a social reality, and the relationality of place past to present an ever more apparent part of the social fabric.

Methodology

I published *An Alliance of Women: Immigration and the Politics of Race* (University of Minnesota Press) in 2006. This book analyzed the intersectional struggles and identities among women of African descent and from other parts of the developing world and Italians in Turin, Italy in relation to the so-called "immigration crisis," the challenges of intersectional feminist politics in the face of sedimented racialized hierarchies, and the effects of global economic restructuring on labor and culture. Alma Mater, the first intercultural center in Italy where "Cultural Mediation" was created, was the central focus of this research. I spent seven months in 2014 conducting research in Reggio Emilia and in Turin. Located in the central Italian region of Emilia Romagna, I worked with *Mondinsieme*, an intercultural organization. I conducted formal interviews with forty people in Reggio Emilia and Turin. I informally interviewed or observed another 100 first and second-generation people of African descent. My analysis is based on my research in two cities, Reggio Emilia and Turin. I have been conducting research in Italy for over 25 years. In 2010, I interviewed Somali refugees in Turin, who were receiving support from Alma Mater. They ranged between 18 and 50 years of age and included pregnant women, and women with their children moving in and out of homeless shelters. They recounted horrific stories of their plight in Somalia and Italy. These women grew up under warfare and were denied the right to attend schools. Thus I turned my attention to the several buildings that had been occupied by refugees from the horn of Africa, predominantly Eritrea, Ethiopia, Somalia, and the Sudan.

In Turin and other Italian cities such as Bologna and Rome, people from the Horn of Africa and West Africa have transformed vacant municipal buildings into living quarters. My analysis of their struggles and of other refugees, migrants, and citizens of African descent are the central focus of this book. My ethnographic research on the lived experiences of people of African descent in Italy inspires the theoretical approach, concepts, and analysis I employ. My field research is guided by qualitative anthropological methods of participant observation, based on a theoretically and historically informed yet flexible conceptual framework, research questions, and analytical strategies (Maxwell 2013).

As a veteran seasoned scholar of the African Diaspora in Italy fluent in Italian, my motivation to fill a gap in the literature on European social theory and Africana Studies motivates this book. I am a European-American of Jewish and Hungarian (Catholic) origins whose ancestors immigrated to the United States in the nineteenth and early twentieth centuries. My partner of over thirty years, anthropologist and Africana Studies scholar Donald Martin Carter is a Black American from Oakland, California. We have raised two children together, both of whom have participated in our ethnographic research in Italy that I began to undertake in 1990. I am socially classified as White in Europe and North America. In Italy I am generally perceived as one of the "tribe" of Europeans, and people presume that I am French, Italian, German, or English. This has facilitated my research at times. It has enabled me to be constructed as a type of racial insider without being hypervisible as an observer.

My interest in the African Diaspora in Europe initially grew out of my knowledge of and interest in West African cultural-economic and political practices, in particular anti-colonial struggles and interactions between indigenous cosmologies and capitalist political economy, especially in Cameroon. After learning the anthropological and historical literature on West and Equatorial Africa, I refocused my research on Africans and African descent people in Europe because of my interest in the workings of modern power relations. I deepened my knowledge of North American Black feminist thought, critical race theory, and Black Studies, which developed in the US. This body of literature has been produced primarily by North American and Caribbean Scholars. My life is deeply informed by and structured by my personal and professional relationships with Black natives of North America, Africans, people of African descent in Italy, and my own extended Black family. They have shared knowledge and experiences with me, and I have lived some of this knowledge for over three decades.

In the past few years some North American students and colleagues in the United States have argued that white people are incapable of understanding and bearing witness to experiences of anti-black racism in the context of global white supremacy. I understand the pain and frustration that have lead to these feelings and perceptions, but I believe this argument is both fallacious and counter-productive. Social, cultural knowledge and criticism are gained by hearing, empathizing with, situating the lived experiences of others in historical contexts and making sense of these experiences with rigorous conceptual and critical ana-lytical tools. Without the human capacity to empathize with, to identify with others from different backgrounds, we can learn little about how power operates. It is true that cultural patterns and taken-for-granted beliefs inform our inter-pretations of events, and that our personal, familial, and "tribal" interests tend to exert enormous influence on our renderings of social events and the testimonies we hear or are unable to hear.

This problem of the invisibility and erasure of Black lived experiences as a habitual and central component of modern Western society is my central intel-lectual focus. However, one can – and must – rethink and relearn what one has been taught in the interest of maintaining established power relations, if for no other reason than to be free. Freedom means being able to think for oneself instead of allowing others to do our thinking for us. And many who are inter-ested in gaining or maintaining power are all too happy to take control of our thoughts, if we give them permission to do this.

In her eloquent essay, "'Can you be BLACK and look at this?': Reading the Rodney King Video(s)," Elizabeth Alexander (1994) discusses how crucial it is to understand what black people bring to communally witnessed violence against black people, or what James Baldwin described with the Biblical phrase, the "evidence of things not seen."[34] Alexander compares the representation of black life by documentary photographers and artists. Documentary photographers fre-quently watch and participate, perpetuating state sanctioned violence and brutal-ity toward black people. They follow a pattern of many white spectators, failing to act as witnesses. To be black in America and in the African diaspora more widely is to take images and stories of black suffering and to record them as memories and knowledge needed for survival, for to be black is to be acutely vulnerable to violence. Alexander suggests that black people share a distinctive perspective in which they may experience feeling physically sick when they see or hear violence against black people; they carry these memories in their bodies. By contrast, people classified as "White" because of European colonialism, the transatlantic slave trade and white supremacy accept the brutalization and crim-inalization of Black people. Witnesses feel themselves implicated in the fate, the pain of others. What might it mean to bear witness without carrying cultural memories in the flesh?

In this book, I take the position that white people can and must be witnesses and allies, following the Civil Rights Movement in the 20th century US, where some white people were witnesses. In her memoire, *Incidents in the Life of a Slave Girl* (Jacobs 1861 (2001)), Linda Brent, a light skinned slave, urged the white female reader to identify with the racial and sexual abuse she endured. She asked readers to assume her perspective instead of identifying with the cruel and callous slave-owning White woman.

I have witnessed state-sanctioned violence towards African refugees and migrants in Italy, and the deeply wounding erasure of African Italians from the social order. I feel implicated in their fate, because they are part of my adopted human family. It is my responsibility to tell their stories as long as I can, and to do so from their perspectives along with, crucially, critical scholarly tools and an intellectual analysis that is intrinsically emotional and intuitive.

Chapter Outline

Chapter One examines the intersections between Africa and Italy by tracing Italian colonial history and racialized cultural contacts. I make the case for understanding this as a relational and transcultural place. Chapter Two explains the architecture of my conceptual approach. I explain how Black/black Spaces is a conceptual and methodological tool to explore the hiddenness of anti-black racism, and Black social life. In Chapter Three, I examine how racialization is produced everyday in social contacts and places, and how it is responded to. Chapter Four discusses everyday violence and the emergence of Black diasporic solidarity and subjectivity following death of 14-year-old Sylvester Agyyemang in Reggio Emilia. Chapter Five focuses on refugees from West and the Horn of Africa. I consider shared experiences of crossing the Mediterranean and living in Italy, examine the production of Black spaces in occupied buildings, and the formation of Black fugitivity.

Notes

1 Cloak in Arabic, a loosely fitting robe-like dress covering all but the body's extremities.
2 My first book, a critical geographical, anthropological, and critical race studies-informed exploration of the intersectional power relations of gender, race, class, age, and culture in the interethnic, anti-racist feminist alliance, Alma Mater. It emerged Turin in the early 1990s. See Merrill (2006).
3 The Italian "comune" is the smallest political and administrative unit. We might think of it as the city council, headed by an elected mayor.
4 This Convention does not establish specific state obligations to accept applications, although it does include "nonrefoulement" or the prohibition against expelling or returning refugees to the territories where their lives or freedom might be threatened.
5 The number or asylum seekers entering Italy annually has expanded greatly since I first began this research in 2010. At that time, the so-called "Arab Spring" had taken place and there were a growing number of applications from Tunisia and Libya. The situation has amplified considerably in the wake of opposition movements in Syria, other parts of the Middle East, and Africa. Millions of lives hang in the balance. Italy continues to take in the greatest portion of asylum seekers from West and East African countries. According to AIDA (the Asylum Information Database), in 2016 Italy had

the highest number of requests from Nigerians, followed by Pakistanis, Gambians, Senegalese, Ivorians, Eritreans, Bengalis, Malians, Guineans, Ghanaians, Afghanis, Somalis, Iraqis, and Syrians. Men constituted 84.9% of applicants, women 15.1%, children 9.1%, and unaccompanied children 4.6% (www.asylumineurope.org/reports/ country/italy/statistics, June 16, 3017). This is a challenging situation for Italy, and Europe. The 2007 European Treaty provided for the development of a common policy on asylum, but this has yet to be developed and implemented. The Italian coast guard, maritime police, and organizations in collaboration with the UNHCR, Red Cross, Save The Children, and many other local and international volunteers and human rights monitors such as Doctors Without Borders remain largely responsible for the majority of boatloads of asylum seekers entering Europe via the central Mediterranean, although the European border police, FRONTEX, is also quite active. Italy's 4,720 miles of coastline is difficult to control, and further militarization is not a solution. When the Balkan route to Europe and the Greek borders with Turkey were closed off in 2015, the numbers of people crossing the Central Mediterranean sea to enter Europe further amplified. Not an easy problem to solve, it is effecting Italy's domestic policies and political culture along with its relationship with the rest of Europe. UN international agreements do not obligate states to provide specific protections to refugees, and Italy has long given very little by way of housing, work, and monetary supports to help refugees heal, integrate, and re-establish their lives. Italy provides far less by way of these supports than most other major European countries (see Chapter Five).

6 The international institution UNHCR (United Nations High Commissioner for Refugees) was created to provide protection to refugees by supervising the legal regimes in signatory nations. However, there is a lack of monitoring and supervision: a contradiction between UNHCR responsibilities on the one hand, and the limited accepted obligations of certain nation states on the other. Member states are obligated by Article 35 of the Geneva Convention to cooperate with the UN. But there is a gap between the UNHCR responsibilities and official state obligations. There are UNHCR offices in most states, including Italy. They gather information on domestic laws, decrees, instructions, and practices that they may measure against international refugee instruments. But mechanisms to ensure institutional reporting are inadequate, and Italy has fallen far from the mark.

7 I do not really see myself as White, but the world around me has identified me as such. My family has been Black for over thirty years, and for many reasons I have long identified with people who are not privileged in this world. As James Baldwin said, "As long as you think you're white, I'm going to be forced to think I'm black" (Thorsen 1989). However, I recognize that even though my beginnings were quite rough and I had to remake myself, my struggles were helped by my perceived Whiteness. When I returned from Cameroon in the mid-1980s, I rejected and became even more critical of mainstream Euro-American culture, married a Black American, and raised Black children.

8 I prefer the term transdisciplinarity to interdisciplinarity in Africana Studies, because it captures the synthetic interweaving of multiple disciplinary approaches. This is necessary in the growing field of Africana, where we seek to clarify the centrality of anti-blackness and black lives to the intricate workings of the modern social world, the emergence of the West and its racial capitalism as the dominant social system for the past five hundred plus years.

9 Much of the recent senate review was redacted. Some countries where these sites are held have been indicated.

10 For some excellent work on Black geography and critical geography of race, see the work of Wilson Gilmore (2002, 2007); Mckittrick (2006, 2007, 2011, 2015); Woods (2007); Wilson (2002, 2007); Bressey and Adi (2013); Bressey and Dwyer (2008);

Alderman and Dwyer (2008); Tyner (2005); Inwood and Martin (2008); Inwood (2016); Twine and Gardener (2013); Kobayashi and Peake (2000); Wright and Ellis (2000); Darden and Kamel (2000).

11 Their focus is on the effects and responses to anti-blackness in former slave societies, but they gesture toward a global anti-blackness.

12 For a discussion of "Strategic Essentialism," see Gayatri Chakravorty Spivak (1987). For Whiteness see for example Frankenberg (1993).

13 Fanon's concept of sociogeny refers to a cultural-symbolic register that emerged with the violence of European colonization. It consists of culture, language, and discourse through which we understand our being in the world. Colonization was grounded in racial distinctions that created the condition for the colonized to be forced to define themselves as a nonbeing, because European or Western (hu)manness was defined as white. Fanon wrote that the black man had to be black; and to be black in relation to the white man (Fanon, 2008).

14 See the important work on social abandonment, disposability, and waste by human geographers Cindi Katz, Geraldine Pratt, Heidi Nast, Melissa Wright, and Karen Morin (Harney and Moten 2013).

15 See Blakely (2009).

16 There is also a vast geographical literature on borders, migration, identity, and securitization in Europe. See for example: Gilmartin (2008); Leitner (1997); Ehrkamp (2005); Samers (2003); Mitchell and MacFarlane (2016); Anonsich (2016); Hawthorne (2017); Hawthorne and Piccolo (2016); Giglioli 2016).

17 Angela Davis, Achille Mbembe, Saidya Hartman, Frank B. Wilderson, Jared Sexton, and Frank Moten are among the other scholars whose work may be described as within an Afro-Pessimist arc. They all argue that Europe created a violently anti-black world.

18 International Institute for Statistics, www.istat.it

19 Angela Boccato, "Will Italy Finally Bring its Citizenship Laws into the 21st Century?" 30 May 2016. *Equal Times*. There is a campaign for citizenship among a second-generation of immigrants in Italy called, "L'Italia sono anch'io- Seconde Generazione" or "I'm also Italy – Second Generation." In October 2015 the Lower House in Parliament passed a law that the group proposed, but it has yet to be taken to a vote in the Senate. See the forthcoming dissertation by Camilla Hawthorne, graduate student in geography at the University of California, Berkeley.

20 For evidence one only needs to look through Italian and international newspapers, news magazines, and television news. Even the film industry is taking this up, most recently in the 2016 documentary "Fire at Sea," by Gianfranco Rosi.

21 The International Organization for Migration (IOM)'s Missing Migrants Project estimates that West and East Africans die or disappear more than people from the Middle East while trying to reach a safe country of destination, the majority in the Mediterranean Sea. Estimates of deaths by region of origin over three years are as follows: 2016: Mixed/Unknown: 3694, Africa 2817, Americas 670, Asia 266, Europe 0, Middle East 471; 2015: Mixed/Unknown: 2052, Africa 1935, Americas 505, Europe 0, Middle East 897, 2014: Mixed/Unknown: 1643, Africa 1942, Americas 496, Asia 870, Europe 1, Middle East 333 (https://missingmigrants.iom.int/).

22 Former Italian Prime Minister Matteo Renzi made repeated attempts to persuade the EU to share the burden of refugees with Italy. He urged the EU to introduce joint refugee bonds, but Germany was opposed. Renzi proposed an "Africa Fund" to establish an infrastructure and investments across Africa as a way to help Africans strengthen their economies, but the proposal was rejected.

23 When for example in June 2016 the *New York Times* drew attention to African refugee movements, they characterized participants as "economic migrants" when in fact many are asylum seekers escaping war and human rights abuses (Dionne Searcey,

"Desperation Rising at Home, Africans Increasingly Turn to Risky Seas," June 16). They hail from former European colonies (Ponzanesi 2016). The NYT article portrayed Africans as victims of poverty and culture instead of as people who left their homes because they were politically oppressed, economically marginalized, and courageously sought to make a better life for their families. Some African refugees gradually achieve stability, but many are excluded from protective mechanisms, regardless of their situations (see documentary film, *Other Europe/Altra Europa* (2011) by Rosella Schillaci and Roberto Greco).

24 Other conceptual constructs include "Afropeans" and the "Black Mediterranean."

25 Eurostat-European Commission: ec.europa.eu/eurostat

26 According to the UNHCR's Regional Bureau Europe, "Refugees & Migrants Sea Arrivals in Europe," monthly update August 2016 the number of Syrians, Iraqis, and Afghans arriving to Italy was very low in 2015 and until August 2016. They cite the top countries of origin of people arriving via the Mediterranean in 2015 from a total of 153, 842 as follows: 19.4% Nigeria; 13.1% Eritrea; 7% Sudan; 6.7% Gambia; 6.7% Cote d'Ivoire; 6.5% Guinea (Conakry); 5.2% Somalia; 5.2% Mali; 5.1 % Senegal.

27 The conflation of undocumented immigrants and refugees with Africans is one of many neologisms that have recently appeared in the Italian vocabulary, informing the appellative, "immigrant" ("immigrato") which as I suggested above has been used by the Italian media to refer to every newcomer, independent of his or her juridical status, including asylum seekers and refugees (see Di Maio 2009).

28 I use the term, immigrants, to include both documented and undocumented.

29 In WEB Du Bois' attention to the classification of blackness as a problem, his argument was that the problem was really that White America was racially structured, that White people reproduced racism through daily and institutional practices.

30 See Tobias Jones in The Guardian, "Why is Italy so Racist," July 13, 2013, www.theguardian.com/world/shortcuts/2013/jul/30/italy-racism-cecile-kyenge-esterofilia.

31 Ibid.

32 Ibid.

33 A corollary to the treatment of Africans is the treatment of "Arabs" or people believed to be of the Muslim faith. The notion that Arabs are a threat to Christianity is fundamental to the making of the Modern West. Another group that may be understood as the ultimate outsider is Roma, who are continual targets of discrimination, prejudice, and violence. However, Roma tend not to wish to "fit in" with the rest of society (see Oakley 1996).

34 Alexander adopts and expands on the notion of witnessing that is a theme running through much of James Baldwin's work. As philosopher Todd Franklin describes, Baldwin bears witness to his nation's unfulfilled promise of eliminating racism and white supremacy after Abraham Lincoln declared the emancipation of enslaved people of African descent. Much of Baldwin's writings, especially his essays, grapple with black experiences of being trapped in a racist system that denies their social worth. He is a "somber witness" to what oppresses him. He sounds a note of caution especially in his letter to his nephew, "The Fire Next Time," that new generations would give voice to the subjugated point of view, demand a complete revision of the prevailing US version of history, and the world's perception of "the black person." These youth would first need to come to terms with their past, and with the obliviousness inscribed in whiteness. When blacks no longer believe in their own degradation, whites can no longer maintain their beliefs about who they are and where they come from (Franklin, 2018).

1

AFRICA-ITALY

A Genealogy of Relational Places

At the end of *Adua*, Igiabo Scego's haunting novel about Italian colonialism and its afterlife, the Somali-Italian protagonist and the book's namesake is offered the gift of a video camera by her Somali refugee husband who tells her, "Now you can film what you wish, now you can narrate what you see and like" (Scego 2015).[1] This moment marks a subjective denouement in the novel, signaling that after decades living in Italy, Adua finally has the tools she needs to communicate and record her own story. Her name, which represents Italy's colonizing project and Africa's first fully-fledged anti-imperial victory against a European army at Adua Ethiopia in 1896, suggests that she is courageous and resilient in the face of power. Yet to this point in her life, Adua has been unable to come to terms with and narrate her own reflected being, a life grounded in intersecting memories and experiences from a number of different places and times.

In Scego's story, Adua reflects on her early life in post-colonial Somalia; the intersections between her own experiences and those of her father in his entanglements with Italian Fascism and colonialism in "Italian east Africa," and the current moment when so many refugees from Somalia and other places are lost in the sea while en route to "safe ground" in Europe. When her husband, whom she calls "Titanic" because he survived a sinking ship and who represents the newest generation of Somalis in Europe, hands her a camera, Adua is finally given a chance to record what she knows from her own perspective. Hers is a complex subjectivity informed by the profoundly intertwined histories of Italy and Somalia. Scego's novel elegantly depicts the complexity of lived experiences in the postcolonial African diaspora, underscored by manifold differences and collective affinities (Scego 2015).

As geographer Camilla Hawthorne notes, Scego's story is a meditation on the lived experiences of Italian colonial history and its legacies of violence and intimacy (Hawthorne 2015). In the early years of her life in Magalo, a small city on the Indian Ocean, Adua is inspired and seduced by images of freedom and adventure in Italy. In Magalo she walks along avenues lined with Italian architecture; she frequents Italian groceries and cafes; attends Italian mission schools; and marvels at American films shown in the local theater, while imagining herself as a Somalian Marilyn Monroe or Ginger Rogers. When she receives an invitation from an Italian couple and film production duo to star in Italian films, she is lured away from her unhappy childhood to Rome in the 1970s and into a world where she is degraded by performing the European stereotype of a sexualized and exotic African woman, or what Robin Kelley describes as "the fabrication of the Negro" (Kelley 2000).[2] Scego, one of Italy's foremost contemporary writers, depicts Adua's multifaceted life as she moves between memories of her father's experiences of racial brutality and hostility in Fascist Italy while acting as a translator in Rome and Ethiopia prior to the second Italian occupation in 1935. Adua reflects on her childhood in Somalia in the immediate aftermath of Italian colonialism there; her arrival in Italy in the 1970s and exploitation of her vulnerability as a young woman; and the present moment when many Somalis endure traumatic journeys while crossing North Africa and the Mediterranean in order to find asylum in Europe. Her husband is a much younger man from Somalia, a refugee whom Adua rescues from homelessness and nurtures back to health in body and mind. His strength restored with her support, Adua's husband is able to confront the enormous challenges of rebuilding his life in Europe. Nevertheless for Adua, whose dreams of becoming a film star and ability to claim her life have been suppressed, the marriage enables her to acquire the recognition she needs in order to assert her place in an Italy-Africa. Scego's novel demonstrates quite poignantly, as Hawthorne writes, that "Africans" are not foreign "others" intruding into bounded Italian space (Hawthorne 2015). Instead the interweaved, and as Fernando Coronil suggests contrapuntal histories between Italy and Africa precede Italy's official transformation into a country of immigration beginning in the late 1970s, "Challenging an imperial order requires overturning the Self-Other polarity that has served as one of its foundational premises. This requires that cultures be seen, as Ortiz and Said propose, in contrapuntal relation to each other rather than taken to be autonomous units." (Coronil 1996, 73). Their boundaries should not be assumed.

In this chapter, my primary goal is to examine the profound relationality of Italy and Africa; how the familiarity, violence, and mythologies of Italian colonialism in Africa inform African diasporic identities. Italian colonialism connected Italians and Africans dialectically, producing identities that gain meaning in relation to each other. If national identities were built as multiple and porous, this is not how they have been depicted in Italian popular consciousness dialogues. To understand these spaces of relationality I examine texts and photographs for evidence of the inner lives of humans.

My discussion is brief and exploratory, focused on Italian colonization in Asmarina (Eritrea/Ethiopia), Libya, and Somalia from the end of the 19th century through mid 20th century. Locating Africa-Italy as a relational place is not a simple endeavor. The materials at my disposal are limited, in part because they are generally written from a perspective that seeks neutrality or to critique Italian colonialism while remaining situated in Eurocentric paradigms focused on Italian interests. Still, I ask what might have been experienced and emerged in inter-cultural contacts and encounters. Our frameworks have tended to be unidirec-tional, focused on national interests and the greater diffusion of the capitalist economy including markets, without considering how colonized and colonizers generated irrevocable interdependencies.

Frantz Fanon maintained that colonialism rendered any real recognition and reciprocity between colonizer and colonized impossible. No such recognition was possible in the colonial situation where the master did not perceive the colonized as human.[3] Fanon disputed Hegel's widely accepted dialectical model between master and slave as the universal human mediation of relationships of domination-subordination in which the master *needs* the slave's recognition. Fanon argued instead for a "sociogenic" or cultural perspective on colonization that considered social context and power relations in all social interactions, as opposed to the presumption of an "I" as universally White. Fanon's sociogenic perspective sug-gests a radical relationality of colonialism that is at once a deliberate blindness on the part of the European colonizer to (the unthinkability of) Black spaces, and also a transformation of the worlds and therefore the subjectivities of the colo-nized. Fanon argued that the racially hierarchical system of Western knowledge made unthinkable the colonized as part of the same human family as the coloni-zer. I will explore how the oppression that Europe structured by imagining itself as inclusively White was at once incomplete, resisted, and consented to.

People born in Eritrea, Ethiopia, Somalia, and Libya, which were colonized by Italy in the late 19th and through much of the first half of the 20th centuries, generally became reluctant "subjects" of the Italian empire. They were forced under circumstances peculiar to colonization to submit to cultural domination. They established colonial relationships with an occupying and at least initially foreign people and their institutions. From the moment the process of Italian colonization began to unfold, there was no turning back. Violence is a pivotal but not singular feature of colonialism. Desire, and the intersubjectivity of all human beings in practical contact, leads inevitably albeit unintentionally to transforma-tions of place and persons. Within and surrounding the massive violence, new world views resonate with and contribute to emerging Black European diasporic subjectivities. Here, I consider what Stuart Hall described as multiple coexisting "presences," diasporic cultures created in colonization (Merrill 2013; 2014). Hall argued that cultural change, as a consequence of contact zones, the movement of peoples, and different types of transcultural communication, is *not the exception by the norm.*

The common presumption that Europe made itself in its "Renaissance" and Age of Enlightenment/Age of Reason that initiated the Modern world in its various permutations is grounded in a myth. *Europe was not the only historical agent in the drama of exploration, expansion, and empire.* An imagined self-other, white-nonwhite polarity that predates European modernity (Jordan 2012) has become a controlling racial discourse that conceals and mutes the interactive, and interdependent relationality between individuals and places. Modernity has presumed worlds separated not just by space but also time, imposing a linear concept of time as progressive, and a geographical imagination of Africa as symbolically and materially anachronistic, distant from Europe along a scale of development and its implied value judgment of "civilization."

As a structure, modernity requires an Other and an Elsewhere. Parts of humanity are dropped off the path of progress, silencing not only histories of the colonized but also of the West as it is subsumed in an imaginary construction and narration of itself against which the rest of the world is evaluated. The movement of global commodity flows through the transfer of finance and merchant capital that linked peoples and places across vast international borders and deeply affected practices and beliefs of all, involved all sorts of people – the merchants and ship builders, the Africans purchased as commodities and displaced, and Africans left behind (see Hartman 2007).

Rolf Trouillot argued that the massive global movement of people, capital, and goods exerted immense influence on the practices of daily life. Everyone involved conceived of themselves and the world around them, creating hybrid and diasporic identities and cultures (see Hall 2015). Forms of communication encompassed the exchange of commodities like people, horses, sugar, coffee, corn, and livestock that in their dissemination became part of local cultural economies, long forgotten as having originated elsewhere. There was of course confusion and resistance to the changes and repression, but it is important to realize that from the early years of the movement of trade and people in the Atlantic, identities became much more complexly diasporic than we have been lead to believe (Trouillot 2003).

Africa and Europe are positioned dialectically. I deploy the idea of relational place principally as a modality for exploring the diasporic worlds and subjectivities produced through Italian imperialism. I do this while challenging conventional oppositions, classifications, and boundaries by attending to geographies that are inhabited, embodied, and aesthetic. Employing empire and colonization as primary units of analysis allows for an examination of how local life worlds both escape from and are also profoundly impacted by colonization. This calls into question definitions of nation and ethnicity (Cesaire 2010; Fanon 2008; Trouillot 1997; Wilder 2015).

The Myth of Italian Innocence: Erasing Colonialism

The myth of Italian innocence has licensed avoidance of serious discussion and scrutiny of Italian colonialism in Africa. Crucially, this unofficial policy of evasion denies the profound relationships between Italy and Africa that inform the experiences and complex identities of several generations of de jure or de facto African Italian and Italian African citizens.

The silence on the Italian colonial record was deafening until the mid-1970s, when it began to be critiqued by left-leaning historians (Rochat 1978, 2005; Del Boca 2003). Until the turning point that corresponded with increasing immigration, a crucial part of the Italian story was obscured by a cultural forgetting, deliberate state repression, and the Italian cultural myth of "Italiaetta," referencing the mildness of the Italian character and "Italiani brava gente" or the notion that Italians are good people (Del Boca 1996, 2003, 2005; Andall and Duncan 2005). In spite of opposing evidence by scholars since the 1970s, the belief that Italians were exceptional colonizers, that they were benign and welcomed by colonized in contrast with other colonizing nations, persists into the present.[4] Knowledge of Italian genocides and concentration camps with high rates of mortality in Italian colonial Africa that were constructed prior to and as experimental predecessors to Nazi and Fascist camps of the Second World War has been repressed.[5] The prevailing collective self-representation in histories and memoirs from the early 20th century is that Italians were victims who suffered atrocities especially in the Second World War, not victimizers who carried them out (Walston 1997; Fuller 1996).

Across the Mediterranean basin, Africa and Europe have entertained close ties for centuries if not millennia. While national territories and cultures are enacted, represented, and lived as real, so too are the relational and transnational places forged through the interactions between Africans and Europeans, most intensely during the 19th century colonial encounters. As Alessandra Di Maio maintains, the nation state is not a place of monolithic or homogenous identity, nor is it in a binary relationship with other nations. National spaces are instead comprised of diverse, multiple intersecting spaces, and the Italian nation may be considered as part of a broader "Black Mediterranean" (Di Maio 2012).[6] Yet the formation of this multiplicity and relationality has a violent, coercive, and hierarchical history, fraught with suffering and inequality. In the commerce between Europe and Africa in raw materials, manufactured products, ideas, people, traditions, and human beings, as Aimee Cesaire argued, Europeans did not conduct themselves with respect for human dignity, or with even intellectual rigor. They were interested in domination of a monetary economy and social system, and to this end would eliminate everything that got in the way of their personal and national enrichment. Cesaire asserted that colonizers did not engage in human contact or exchange, but instead *took from* colonized lands and labor in a relationship of dominance and subordination (Cesaire 2010). The institutions of the colonizer were celebrated and those of the colonized denigrated or ignored. The discursive and material structure of this relationship has never been quite transformed, binding Europeans to Africans and Africans to Europeans long after the demise of colonial rule even though the enduring socio-cultural links have been repressed from active memory (Iyob 1997, 2005; Andall and Duncan 2005).

The Italian colonial record is fairly consistent with Cesaire's critique. While Italian colonization began later than other European powers, it was situated in the broad and aggressive imperialist movements that characterized late 19th century Europe. A colonial ideology and cultural consciousness was forged in the mid-19th century through visual and print culture. Interest in East Africa intensified after 1869 during the construction of the Suez Canal that would open the commercial and strategic importance of the Red Sea coast. The first Italian geographical society was founded in Florence in 1867, and transferred to Rome when it became the capital in 1871 (Atkinson 2003; Cerreti 1994). Dominated by diplomatic, military, political interests, and the influence of an intoxicating nationalism, the geographical society lobbied for expansion. They embarked on expeditions in Abyssinia to study African botanical and geological phenomena, but also to monitor Italian settlement there and later in North Africa and Somalia. Neapolitan elite, Milanese industrialists, merchants, and financiers agitated for aggressive expansion in North and East Africa to serve as markets for Italian commerce and homes for Italian emigrants. Post-Unification (1871) Italian school textbooks to promote literacy included many references to Africa as exotic, and images constructed from stereotypical beliefs were widely diffused at the popular scale (De Marco 1943; Novati 2005).

Geographical societies appeared in multiple Italian cities in response to the lobbying efforts of local elites, and they disseminated knowledge, including pictorial and photographic representations of Africa. The societies, founded by leading colonial advocates and geographers, were highly influential, and supported a growing eagerness to expand Italy's geopolitical influence, an enthusiasm that intensified in the early 20th century and during fascism. Geographers collaborated with colonial authorities to identify, isolate, and rank the "races" of the regions, classifying Africans according to racial typologies, while using the self-conscious practice of science to legitimize the Italian presence and render the region more governable (Atkinson 2003).[7]

In 1885, an official Italian presence was established at the Red Sea port of Massawa. They began their effort to move into the Eritrean highlands. Ethiopian leaders sought to stop Italy's advance through armed resistance, and Italians suffered defeats but also played on rivalries among local leaders and conscripted young men for service in the Italian military. In 1889, Emperor Menelik II agreed to allow Italians to expand their territory northward after Italy had secured control over a significant portion of territory to the west and south of Massawa where they announced the creation of "Eritrea" as their first colony, with the capital in Asmara.[8] The Italian treaty severed the north from the south as people living in the territories north of the river Mareb became "Eritreans" while those to the south were integrated into the consolidated empire of Emperor Menelik. Many switched their allegiances from Abyssinian overlords to the Italian crown, and were nourished by the myth of inclusion in modernity through the European "civilizing mission" (Iyob 2005).

Italy's participation in the imperialist projects of the late 19th and early 20th centuries does not seem to have been underpinned by market saturation and a need for overseas investment that Lenin and Hobson argued had motivated other capitalists (Segre 1996). Italy was on the same path as other European powers toward finance capitalism, but had not yet reached this point in market capacity, so it was relatively economically weak. The Italian state supported investors, inducing them with special government contracts, tax, and tariff privileges. Colonization served as a route for interest groups including entrepreneurs, professionals, bureaucrats, military officers, and southern capitalists to guarantee themselves slices of the public revenue.

Italian colonialism was in part a response to the power vacuum left by the decline of the Ottoman Empire and an Italian bid for power (Segre 1996). Beyond commercial advantages, desire for diplomatic prestige garnered through military power and racial supremacy seemed to have motivated the new Italian state (formed in 1861), in partnership with the Italian Crown and nobility, to pursue colonization.[9] Italian capital expanded through colonization, promoting a booming trade for example between Eritrea, India, Austria, and Saudi Arabia. From 1910 onwards, 50% of Eritrean exports went to Italy and more than 50% of Eritrean's imports came from Italy (Negash 1987).

Italian colonialism is frequently characterized as exceptional and relatively insignificant because it was short lived, weak, and because Italians have a mild national character; they are "brava gente" or "good people" (Del Boca 2005; Labanca 2005). But scholars have argued that Italian colonization was authoritarian, brutal, and at times remarkably ruthless (Del Boca 2003, 2005; Negash 1987; Labanca 1999, 2002, 2005). There were certainly nonviolent trade and land tenure agreements between Italians and East African leaders, as well as periods of relative peaceful co-existence in Eritrea and Somalia and extended moments of paternalism. Yet from its beginning, the prevailing policy was domination at any cost, informed by anti-black Euro-American political culture (Labanca 1999; Tabet 1997).

An intensely aggressive approach became especially acute and pressing after the Italian military defeats, most prominently at Adwa in 1896, when Ethiopian Emperor Menelik II successfully challenged European expansion (Jonas 2011). This victory over the better-armed Italian forces resonated powerfully in the African Diaspora in the post-Emancipation United States and Caribbean. However, even after experiencing a humiliating defeat at Adwa, Italians did not abandon their dream of colonizing Ethiopia, and they used Eritrea as a launching pad for their broader designs. Eritrean leaders who did not support the Italian presence were frequently deported with their families to sordid prisons in Italy or Africa, for instance to the Nokra prison on an island off the coast of Eritrea (Labanca 2005).

In Somalia, Italians initially acquired territory in the 1880s through agreements with Sultans, but when Benito Mussolini became prime minister in 1925 he authorized his General De Vecchi to annex more lands by bombarding and razing areas of resistance (Hess 1966). Mussolini invaded Ethiopia in 1935, and employed extraordinarily repressive measures that included the use of chemical bombs and warfare almost entirely by air that were also used in Somalia (Labanca 2005).

Italy created its Office for Colonial Settlement in 1890, directed by Leopoldo Franchetti, a British-trained conservative baron from Tuscany. Franchetti and Prime Minister Francesco Crispi, an architect of Italian unification who came to be authoritarian, envisioned Italian settlement in East Africa as a way to resolve Italian rural problems of landless peasants, especially in the South. Eritrea was Italy's "colonia primogenita" or first born colony where Italians seated a military government and expropriated some 400,000 hectares of land declared available for Italians. However, land was available only to those with some capital, and the colonial settlement policy was a failure.[10] In the early years following the losses in Adwa, *Italian Native Policy* was developed under Fernando Martini to consolidate colonial rule and ostensibly to "civilize the native," but this discourse was not reflected in practice. As Negash argues, the fact that Italian soldiers summarily executed up to one thousand Eritreans believed to be resisting colonial rule says a great deal about the position the colonized would be assigned under Italian admin-istration (Negash 1987). Eritreans had obligations to the colonial administration, but they lacked corresponding rights over their own lives and property.

Racism as a cultural psychological and political phenomenon was intrinsic to colonial imperialism, and it existed in Italy prior to imperial expansion in Africa (Tabet 1997; Gaia and Lombardo-Diop 2013). In Europe, Jews and Africans have long occupied the role of "estraneo" or stranger, an "evil that menaces the tribe" (Goglia 1988; Mosse 1997). Anti-blackness was implicitly present in Italy at the mass scale, even though as Luigi Goglia argues, it took the form of a diffuse sentiment of political and cultural superiority (Goglia 1988).[11] Among the African popula-tions Italians encountered, there does not appear to have been a corresponding predisposition to render Italians inferior or even as competitors. When Italians first entered Eritrea, for example, local rulers such as Bahta Hagos, the governor of Akele Guzai, welcomed and even embraced their Catholic religion. But when between 1893–1895 Italians had claimed over half of Eritrea's arable land, Hagos led a popular uprising in 1894 with some 1,500 well-armed men. However, because the region had experienced famine exacerbated by local conflicts, many reportedly welcomed the peace that Italian occupation advanced.

Italy invaded Cyrenaica and Tripolitana, Libya in 1911. In the Acroma[12] Accords of 1917, they agreed to share power with local tribes in the Cyrenaica region, an area governed by the Bedouin Sanusi fraternity, an Islamic order created in 1843 whose social philosophy promoted an austere, simple observance of Islam. In 1922 when Mussolini rose to power, the rights of Bedouin were rescinded, accords were abandoned, and a campaign was waged to force the nomadic and semi-nomadic people to surrender their authority, triggering a bitter and bloody war that lasted for a decade. The Italian state deployed spatial strategies to produce a controlled and pacified people by cutting off their mobility and communications.[13] Mobile Bedouin were forced to live in fixed designated zones near Italian military bases where they were under continual surveillance and subjected to all sorts of restrictions (Atkinson 2012). Mussolini mandated brutal treatment of the native populations. By 1930, the Italians operated 16 concentration camps in Cyrenaica, and other such camps were established in Somalia, Eritrea, and Ethiopia where the regime interned people suspected of thwarting Italian policies.

In East Africa there were several phases in Italian colonization as part of a process in which Italians tended to use a heavy hand in matters of colonial order, including a campaign to produce racial apartheid as Italian Fascism gradually took root. Before the invasion of Ethiopia in 1935, Italian racial policy was already discriminatory and autocratic. Yet in Eritrea especially where there was a modest settlement of Italians that grew considerably in the 1930s, Italians intermingled, coexisted with, and constructed place with Eritreans (Pankhurst 1969a). Italian settlers included landowners as well as craftsmen, workmen, masons, and many poor whites that mixed with Eritreans as a matter of survival. There was some tension among Italians and Africans who competed for jobs. The military was comprised for the most part of Eritrean soldiers, or "Askari" whom Italians trusted (Barrera 2003b).[14] The racial and class hierarchies didn't always correspond, and this was of concern to the colonial government. The Italian settlement was not large enough to produce businesses serving only whites, and in the early years, members of the colonial elite, for instance attorneys, often worked for Eritreans. Nevertheless, a body of military personnel and other members of the Italian middle class such as entrepreneurs and public employees interacted with Eritreans in a hierarchical manner.[15]

Until 1930 most settlers were male, and Italians held the record among Europeans in creating a score of Italian-Eritrean children (Pankhurst 1998). Their Eritrean mothers were an integral part of Italian colonial life and a central feature of African-Italian encounters. To formalize what were in effect arrangements of cohabitation between Italian men and Eritrean women, the colonists institutionalized the institution of *Madamismo*, a contract to provide "the comforts of home" to male settlers limited to their stay in Africa (Pankhurst 1969a; Carter 1997; Iyob 2005).[16] The Eritrean women rapidly became familiar with the workings of European households, and some of the Italian officers doted on them. But the governor was vehemently critical of the system as incompatible with the maintenance of control and discipline. The colonial government had in

1897 established principles and guidelines to inform colonial legislation and practices, including the strengthening and underscoring of European superiority over the natives. Even so, memoires and other writings by colonial officers like Alberto Pollera, an Italian aristocrat and leading administrator in Eritrea who was married to an Eritrean woman with whom he had a family, argued that Eritreans and Italians were similar in many ways, and that intermixing would be inevitable. I must emphasize however that even Pollera, who is noted as an early ethnographer, did not advocate for regular inter-marriage; he adhered to the British idea of the "White Man's Burden" to civilize, and did not believe Eritreans and Italians were equal (Pankhurst 1969a; Goglia 1985, 1988; Sorgoni 2003). Colonists who sought to curb abuses of power and violence against Eritreans nevertheless adhered to the idea that their role was to preserve white prestige (Barrera 2003a, 2003b), and appropriated the best lands for Italian settlers and corporations.

A distinctive feature of Italian colonialism was that the Italian government's aim was to secure authority and prestige not only over natives, but also over Europeans in the colonies. Ruth Iyob argues that the effort to concurrently Italianize colonizer and Europeanize colonized gave rise to an enduring connection between Italians and Africans (Iyob 2005). In Eritrea the Italian community was until the 1930s small and economically weak, comprised principally of state employees. Therefore, compared with other colonial settler communities where they could press for regulations that would permit them to harshly exploit the colonized, the Italian state sought to secure prestige and authority over their own citizens and the colonized with an iron fist, believing a firm grip even more crucial in Africa than in Europe. This conduct helped mitigate the extent of daily exploitation of the colonized (Barrera 2003a, 2005; Larebo 2005). However, Italians took enormous pride in their domination of the colonized "natives" and their exercise of control over their territory. Formally, racial discrimination was widespread and institutionalized in schooling, employment, and the courts (Pankhurst 1969a). Courts practiced racialized adjudication and Whites always prevailed in disputes. In the 1930s, indigenous people were confined to the "native quarters." They did not have access to clerical positions, and little of the manual labor. Over 50,000 Italian construction workers and mechanics were brought to Eritrea to work on the docks and building roads. Most employment obtained by Eritreans was in the military where they were conscripted as Askari[17] for Italy's colonial wars in Libya, Somalia, and Ethiopia.

Abbay suggests that colonized populations both "reaped the fruits of modernity" and also bore the "hardships of colonialism" (1998). Food and consumer goods were low-priced, and this helped forestall public discontent. Many local agrarian elite collaborated with Italians to further their own interests. Italy imposed a capitalist system on Eritrean pre-capitalist social formations that had been dominated by a patriarchal communal economy and long distance trade. This capitalist mode of production was superimposed on Eritrean societies in a manner that promoted only primitive accumulation.[18] Eritreans were given precarious work and low wages that coerced them to rely on the pre-capitalist economic system. They were positioned to supply labor, principally for seasonal work for Italian capital. As Negash suggests, Eritreans were integrated into the capitalist economy just enough to mitigate the adverse effects of Italian rule. Food, clothing, sugar, and liquor were imported and consumed in proportion to exports. Colonization increased the autonomy and independence of the colony against famine and drought by providing salaried employment to some 10–15% of the population.

After the advent of fascism, Italians in Eritrea and Ethiopia became much more straightforward than the French or even English about not expecting cultural assimilation. The prevailing philosophy was that if the colonized were for instance granted voting rights, they would be able to destroy the social system. The Italians who governed in the colonies seem to have most closely resembled Albert Memmi's (1991) description of the "colonizer who accepts," i.e., they accepted being usurpers and in trying to legitimate their role created and recreated racism on a daily basis while remaining dependent on the colonized. Italians were however in practice less distant from and more intimate with the colonized than the racial colonial ideology prescribed. Albert Memmi, whose point of reference is French in North Africa, describes colonialism as intrinsically racist and likens it to fascism in that both systems delight in racialized police torture, oppression of the many for the benefit of the few, and political machinery that produces human relationships on the basis of contempt and inequality guaranteed by police authoritarianism. He distinguishes class oppression from colonial racism, for in the former there is hope for escape through social mobility, while in the latter there is no hope for social mobility, as one can never move into the privileged class even if one earns more money or wins more titles than others in that class. Racial differences in colonialism are in his view immutable, and there is a taken-for-granted belief that servitude is natural to the colonized. Italian colonialism followed Memmi's conceptual structure in a rather loose and porous manner. Italians sought prestige, yet many colonists, especially from Southern Italy where they had been colonized internally by Northern Italy, did not look upon the colonized with the same contempt Memmi and Frantz Fanon describe in French colonial Africa, in spite of its cultural assimilationist policies.

Africans living with Italian colonialism in East Africa were not passive; they negotiated or resisted racial colonialism in a variety of ways, including full scale armed and guerrilla resistance especially in Libya and Ethiopia, and masked forms of resistance and "hidden transcripts" for instance among "madames," monks, and colonial or "native" soldiers. Silence does not always mean agreement or compliance (Scott 1987; Kelley 1996; Hanchard 2006). As in other European colonizing countries, Italians deployed methods of cooptation and the division of ethnic and religious groups in order to weaken and short-circuit the formation of potential alliances against the state. They engineered complicity by compelling Eritreans to accept a structure of chieftainship, to encourage the creation of new centralized political systems based on ethnic identity, and create local divisions that pitted them against each other and a colonial state that defined itself as European and nonnative.

The impacts of this system designed to weaken local symmetries and advance colonial domination had to have affected profoundly not only the newly named Eritreans, but also to have placed heavy burdens on the perpetrators whose moral development was compromised. As Memmi suggests, all colonized and oppressed share and are bound together by common experience, "Oppression is the greatest calamity of humanity. It diverts and pollutes the best energies of man – of oppressed and oppressor alike. For, if colonization destroys the colonized, it also rots the colonizer" (Memmi 1991: xvii). Italian colonizers were likely usurpers not only in the eyes of the colonized, but also in their own implicit self-visions if and when they realized the arbitrariness and illegitimacy of their privileges.

Spatial Technologies of Violence: Genocide and Concentration Camps

There's a prevailing Eurocentric vision produced in historiographies informed by cultural stereotypes that Italian Fascism was less cruel than others. This perspective has predominated even among the most trenchant critics who have located the origins of Italy's 1930s racial laws in Germany's Nuremberg Laws (1935) while turning a blind eye to the genocides and concentration camps in Africa that preceded Germany's death camps. The camps in Africa set the precedents for Germany's policies of racial genocide (Ahmida 2006).[19] Ali Abdullatif Ahmida argues that Italian atrocities committed in Libya have been trivialized, even though this dehumanization profoundly impacted generations of Libyans. Soon after Italy invaded Libya in 1911 and Ethiopia in 1936, violent repression of resistance, terrorism, and destruction of local ways of life reached heights that were perhaps only paralleled by the German genocide of South West African Herero and Namaqua in the early 20th century. Italian soldiers systematically destroyed nomadic and semi-nomadic Bedouin of Eastern Libya, and they used chemical weapons to destroy resistance in Eritrea, Ethiopia, and Somalia. The colonies were racialized "spaces of exception" for European law, where strategies of warfare outlawed in Europe were implemented and developed.

Libyans challenged Italy's invasion of Libya in 1911, and while Italians had repressed the resistance in the western and southern regions by the early 1920s, the anti-colonial nomadic and seminomadic groups mobilized by the Sanusi social and religious movement in the eastern desert region of Cyrenaica continued to present a daunting challenge. They waged a guerilla resistance movement that involved networks of spies, facilitated by their familiarity with the geography of Green mountain valleys, trails, and caves. When the Fascist Party assumed power in Rome in 1922, they advocated military force to "pacify" natives in Africa. Their policy was based on an ideology of racial supremacy in which daily life was marked by violence more vehement in the colonial territories than on the mainland. Between 1929 and 1933, Italians deployed spatial strategies as they committed ethnic genocide against Libyans (Atkinson 2000; Ahmida 2006). Mussolini ordered his Generals Pietro Badoglio and Rudolfo Graziani to crush the resistance by any means necessary. For his actions in Libya, General Graziani earned the appellation "the Butcher of Fezzan or the Hyena of Libya." He and Badoglio directed a scorched earth policy that cut off supplies by building a 300-kilometer fence from the Mediterranean coast southwards toward the Libyan Egyptian border, and seized livestock.

The Italian colonial administration shut down Sanusi lodges and poisoned their wells. With their aircraft and an Italian-Eritrean military on camels, they encountered fierce local guerilla resistance. They responded by rounding up two-thirds of the population, including over 100,000 predominantly pastoralists, and deporting them by sea and foot to concentration camps; in one recorded instance some 657 miles. In February 1931 the Italian military had succeeded in occupying the town of Kufra deep in the desert that would later become the site of a detention center (see Chapter Five). They captured and hung the leaders, arrested and killed their aids.

Atkinson argues that Italians built concentration camps as a spatial measure to restrict nomadic populations (Atkinson 2000). The camps represented the *export and expansion of institutions of mass incarceration from Europe to Africa* where they tested and perfected such technologies and practices of state violence and the suppression of opposition (Muhlhahn 2010). Labanca argues that Italians were motivated to colonize Africa not only by national expansion and prestige, by the chance to create penal colonies (Labanca 2005). The imposition of 16 camps to control mobile, and anti-colonial populations was also part of an effort to impose European concepts of spatial boundaries (Atkinson 2012). Imprisoned were certain ethnic groups and other categories of people classified as socially dangerous and extraneous.

Double barbed wire fences surrounded the camps. Food was rationed. No one was permitted outside, except by permit. Labor was forced. There was no medical aid. The conditions were devastating for independent, semi-nomadic populations. The herds died and people slowly starved. The camps decimated the population; at least 60,000 people died (Ahmida 2006). Ahmida, whose analysis included interviews with survivors, suggests that this was an act of ethnic cleansing: not merely states of the exception as part of the modern West in general, but exercised on the basis of white supremacy (Ahmida 2006; see also Gregory 2015). His interviews with survivors such as Salim al-Shilwa reveal experiences of racialized humiliation and suffering at the Agaila camp when in one instance a man was whipped one hundred times for failing to salute the commander. When he then refused to recite, "Long live the king of Italy" he was lashed another seven hundred times. This scene is resonant with the experiences of African Americans in the Jim Crow Southern United States who were frequently beaten or killed for not saying "Yes sir" to a White man.

In his poem included in Ahmida's study, Al–Minifi, another survivor expresses the impact of living in the camp:

I have no illness except this endless aging,
loss of sense and dignity,
and the loss of good people, who were my treasure.

(Ahmida 2006, 187)

About the Italians he writes,

They bring nothing except rule by torture
and the long....
And the tongue rived and sharpened with pounding abuse.

(Ahmida 2006, 188)

In Italian East Africa, the situation was not very different. Del Boca describes the concentration camps there as "lagers" (Del Boca 1987). The Danane, a "hell hole," was built in 1935 in an isolated area some 40 kilometers from Mogadiscio, Somalia. In less than a year it had been filled with some 1,800 Ethiopians and Somalis whom General Graziani as Viceroy defined as "people of little importance, but in any case dangerous" (Del Boca 1987, 298) They were African notables and functionaries of middle and lower rank, for instance ex-officials of the Ethiopian anti-colonial leaders, ras Immiru and ras Desta; Coptic monks[20] who had escaped genocide at Debre Libanos, Assabot, and Zuquala monasteries in Ethiopia; partisans of some Ethiopian brotherhoods; fortunetellers, bards; and Somalis who had exhibited their opposition to Italian colonialism. Like the Nocra camp in Eritrea, Danane had a sinister reputation from its beginnings. Del Boca describes the director, Mazzucchetti, as having made every effort to humanize the site, although it remained a well of disease and death where some 6500 persons were imprisoned from 1936–1941 and some 3175 died from disease and poor sanitation (Del Boca 1987, 299).

Italy was the first European nation to deploy airplanes in war during the 1911–1912 conquest of Libya, and they were used extensively in subsequent campaigns in the Libyan interior. When Italy invaded Ethiopia in 1935 they employed aircraft more intensively there and throughout East Africa than in Libya to bomb populations and destroy life sources (Rochat 2005). Italians built airbases in Somalia and Ethiopia where hundreds of bombs, gases, and other weapons were shipped. Ignoring the international protocol against the use of chemicals in war it had ratified in 1928, Fascist Italy used noxious substances against civilians. When they invaded Ethiopia and also when then waged campaigns to "pacify" Somalia, Italians practiced arial bombardment and forms of surveillance that attacked any forms of life with mustard gas bombs and machine guns (Rochat 2005). In addition to mustard gas, they also used arsine shells that can produce suffocation, and explosive bullets (Sbacci 1977). Corrosive drops rained down on Somali and Ethiopian citizens, penetrating their clothing and producing fatal internal lesions. When Ethiopian leaders and rebel groups did not submit to Italian occupation, Graziani imposed a "reign of terror," decreeing total destruction.[21] The Ethiopian resistance or the Patriots had no airforce with which to retaliate, and few gas masks (Novati 2005).[22] Nevertheless and quite significantly, Haile Selassie fled to Europe, and his power was undiminished by the Italian occupation (Novati 2005).

Mussolini was interested in generating a new racial consciousness among Italians, making them a conquering race, and calling on a renewal of the "greatness of Italy" evocative of the Roman empire (Goglia 1988). He began a campaign against the "plague of miscegenation," or inter-racial mixing. Before this time, the government had permitted Italian men to recognize their children who had been given Italian citizenship and encouraged to assimilate into the Italian community – even though individuals of "mixed race" were classified as inferior and the pre-Fascist colonial governments had sought to prohibit Italian cohabitation with Eritreans (Barrera 2005). Fascist racial policies were diffused throughout East Africa, affecting the lives of all who had been touched by Italian colonialism. Until fascism escalated, there were no specific provisions for children of Africans and Italians, and their status had depended on a June 1912 Italian citizenship law that linked citizenship with parentage by an Italian father and on occasion mother. In July 1933 (n. 999), an ordinance for Eritrea and Somalia allowed children born in Eritrea or Somalia of a parent of the "white race" to assume citizenship only at the age of eighteen. From this point forward, the notion of "race" that had referred to ethnicities was incorporated into law as a representation of the status of a people who were either members or outsiders in a nation state. In 1940, Italians were prohibited from acknowledging and supporting the children they had with Africans, and the children were assigned the status of colonial subjects. Italians on the mainland were bombarded with fascist racist propaganda inspired by state legislation, and in a short time such discourses and imagery had colonized the minds of the youth.

After the Italian occupation of Ethiopia in 1935 the colonial possessions were reorganized. Eritrea-Somalia-Ethiopia was merged and the entire region named, "Italian East Africa" as part of the Italian empire (Novati 2005). Fascist propaganda depicted "mixed race" people in the most degrading light, and sought to delegitimize their identity as Italian (Barrera 2005). However, many individuals defined themselves as Italian and were so perceived by Eritreans. Mussolini was a man of violence who had eliminated his political opposition in Italy by murdering his opponents, so his colonial policy was one of ruthless repression of any hint of Ethiopian resistance. Worried about the threat of racial mixing to Italian racial domination, he legally distinguished Italians from Africans, enacting a decree (no. 880 of 1937) that prohibited conjugal relationships and the practice of Madamismo and marriages between Italian citizens and colonial subjects on penalty of imprisonment. Another decree proscribed that nationals and other white Europeans live in quarters populated by indigenous so that they could not interact with natives. Codes were established to prevent social contact and equal treatment in public places. Natives were barred from walking on the sidewalks of the main streets, or from frequenting cafes and other public places alongside Italians. A sort of white supremacist apartheid or Jim Crow was attempted by the fascist state, with separate seats on buses, separate taxis, separate dishware in restaurants. This must have created extreme emotional stress for Eritreans and Somalians especially in the urban areas. It is important to remember however that there were always Italian scholars and functionaries who did not accept this racial turn, and who publicly expressed their opposition (Goglia 1988).

In Somalia, society was fragmented into conflicting groups who were often nomadic and sometimes feuding, and this along with environmental conditions prevented Italy from practicing its policy of demographic colonization there. Italian military, including Askari, met with armed anti-colonial pastoral resistance that transcended clan feuds. Until the end of the Second World War Somali territories were under Italian jurisdiction. In the 1920s the Fascist government appointed the first governor-general of Somalia, and from that time forward Somalis were subjected to a divisive rule by the colonial administration. Italians operated a trust administration in Somalia after the war, and continued to exert substantive influence there, expending considerable energy in the country as the main recipient of Italian external aid in the 1960s and 1970s (Hess 1966; Lewis 1980; Novati 2005).

Forgotten Voices: The Debre Libanos Massacre

Generations of Africans' lives are deeply, irretrievably transcultural in relation to Italian economy, politics, and culture. Italy influenced Eritrea, Ethiopia, and Somalia through culture and trade. Its violent effort to repress opposition in the making of its own national identity impacted generations of East Africans. The successful Ethiopian defeat and repulsion of a European power and its wide resonance in the African diaspora is a symbol of resolute independence, thriving communities of resilience, and creativity. But another and generally unknown part of this story is that thousands of innocents were killed. The stories of lives lost in a European imperial quest for domination remain, hidden yet impactful on the generations that have followed.

The massacre at the Debre Libanos monastery in Ethiopia was until recently an untold story, concealed by the Italian and Ethiopian state because it tarnishes the Italian narrative of the country's relative innocence in colonization and absence of responsibility to the surviving African people with whom its own history became embroiled in violence. In general, neither Italians, nor Ethiopians, nor people of the African Diaspora wish to revisit such incidents. Michel Rolf Trouillot argues that silences about the horrors of the past can keep us from writing counter-histories against the dominant, and therefore from preventing repeated patterns of violence. Silences about grim histories may also contribute to the concealment of resistance and triumph, for the Debre Libanos massacres were allegedly planned as retaliation for an attempted assassination of Viceroy Graziani. And in the aftermath of the Debre Libanos massacre, there was a broadening of popular support for the anti-colonial Ethiopian Patriots. It is also worth mentioning that birth and death are twins, so the Italian and Eritrean military who took part in the massacres were irreversibly reborn by killing. The traces of their acts, of the lives they took, endure. Far from bounded spaces, Ethiopia and Italy made themselves and each other in ways that we must re-cognize as relational. Yet, instead of being seen in Italy as a war criminal, in 2012 taxpayers funded a mausoleum and memorial park in honor of Graziani the Butcher of Fezzan that was built in the Italian village of Affile south of Rome: a memorial to "the fascist hero" under whose command thousands of Africans were murdered.

Ian Campbell uncovered the story of the Debre Libanos massacre over a period of some ten years by interviewing survivors and witnesses whom nobody had ever asked about their experience (Campbell and Gabre-Tsadik 1997; Campbell 2014). His singularly detailed account of this history provides an invaluable window into a much forgotten yet pivotal moment in African-Italian history when over three days an estimated 1,800–2,000 Ethiopian monks and others connected with the Debra Libanos monastery were killed with clubs, bars, and cudgels; burned alive, and shot on orders of the Viceroy and his military commanders. Thousands more were imprisoned and died in concentration camps like Danane, in Somalia. Campbell writes,

> In the entire history of world colonialism one will not find another episode in which a religious community has been illegally attacked and destroyed with such brutality. It is without doubt an awful distinction, for which Italy must carry the blame.
>
> *(Campbell 2014, xliiii–xlv)*

The octagonal stone monastery of Debre Libanos was founded in 1275 and rebuilt at the end of the 19th century under the personal supervision of Emperor Menelik II. A sacred site and seat of learning, it had long been Ethiopia's most cherished burial ground where according to a vision by its founder, Tekle Hymanot, God promised that all buried there would go straight to heaven. It was a Christian pilgrimage site that had continued to play a vital role in the affairs of church and state at the time of the massacre in 1937. There was a long association between the Ethiopian nobility and the monastery. Holy water was said to fall from the roof of the site. Yet in his autobiography, Graziani boasted about the massacres and wrote that nobody cried for the deacons and other victims who were killed, "because Africans are different" (Campbell 2014, xIvii).

Ethiopian popular opposition and resistance to the nominal Italian occupation remained poorly armed, but tenacious. On March 31, 1936 the resistance fell at Tigray when Italian Fascists asphyxiated the Emperor and his army with toxic gases. The initial Viceroy was General Badoglio with Graziani as Marshall, but Mussolini rejected Badoglio's plans to manage the country by indirect rule through local leadership and replaced him with Graziani who was the incarnation of a superhero in Italy in an era when the military and war were glorified. Mussolini gave Graziani, who saw himself as a modern Caesar, unlimited powers. He decreed a strategy of direct, totalitarian rule. The Italian military advanced extraordinary brutality to suppress civilian resistance and shoot in cold blood anyone suspected of being a "rebel," even after they had surrendered. The government routinely terrorized the civilian population as a way of blackmailing Ethiopian Patriots into surrendering. They bombed and sprayed men, women, children, animals, crops, and drinking water with toxic chemicals, destroying entire villages on the slightest of pretexts with the most sadistic of spectacles.[23] The Ethiopian Patriots held on throughout the five years, launching many successful attacks against Italian military commanders (Pankhurst 1969b; see Ghermandi 2007). The Patriots contributed greatly to the ultimate overthrow of the Italians and dissolution of Italian power in East Africa. They were encouraged from abroad by the Emperor Haile Selassie I, who was in exile in Bath, England.[24] Many Ethiopians who witnessed the brutality joined the Patriot movement. They held on, but the Italian strategies of control were ultimately dominant especially in Addis Ababa and the surrounding area.

After an attempt on the Viceroy's life and his revenge in the massacre of thousands of Ethiopians in Addis Ababa, Graziani focused on liquidating the heart of the Ethiopian Orthodox church, Debre Libanos, which he believed was a sanctuary for rebels and a center for Ethiopian nationalism. Graziani sought to liquidate everyone connected with the monastery, and a whole generation of Ethiopian intellectuals. The massacre was planned in the holy days of the saints as recognized by the Ethiopian Orthodox Church (12 Ginbot) when the faithful make a pilgrimage to the monastery for a special feast that was in this instance supported by the viceroy's government. A hidden gorge on the plain of Laga Welde was chosen as a site for the massacre; soldiers dug for five days. The monks and followers were to be brought to this place and executed, out of the sight of witnesses. Most of the Eritrean, Libyan, and Somali soldiers deployed on this mission were Muslims.

Convoys of truckloads of soldiers arrived to surround the church and its surroundings including the adjacent nunnery. Hundreds of pilgrims arrived in their finery with friends and family prepared to perform the rites of their faith as part of the joint festival of St. Tekle Haymanot and Archangel Mikael with their healing powers for the sick. Craftsmen, workers, gardeners; servants young, elderly, and disabled as well as monks, priests, and deacons were greeted by gun wielding black shirt, jack booted Fascist soldiers who herded them around the sacred sites, imprisoned them in the monastery, rounded them into lorries, and took them to the site where they were executed on May 20, 1937. According to witness testimony from a then fifteen-year-old boy who with his father had a view from a nearby bridge, people who were tied together were lined up and shot with machine guns, their bodies falling into a riverbank. No mercy was shown toward the approximately 1,200–1,600 people slaughtered. The soldiers then shoveled a bit of soil on the bodies, without performing proper burials. The final toll, including people butchered in other sites or left to die from starvation imprisoned in one of the Debre Libanos buildings, was over 2,000. Following the carnage, Italian soldiers plundered the monastery searching for gold, taking the most prized and sacred objects to General Maletti and Viceroy Graziani, including for example gold crowns and a gold bible from the 16th century. The church had been among the wealthiest in Ethiopia.[25]

This story was suppressed for decades, and even at the end of the 20th century was being recounted to Campbell in hushed tones. Fearing Fascist reprisals, people did not recover the bodies of their loved ones. For several months after the massacre Graziani continued his campaign of terror, dragging people on the slightest of pretexts of suspicion of sympathizing with the resistance from their houses to be executed or imprisoned in the Danane or the Akaki camp outside Addis Ababa where many also died. The bodies of loved ones were left to be devoured by hyenas and vultures and swept off by the rains.

What was the afterlife of this massacre? How must those left behind and the survivors have experienced the aftermath of this act of deception and virulent barbarism by Europeans and the institution of the Askari soldiers? Some Askari refused to participate, and those who did had been compelled or bribed into a system designed to build and sow divisions and to destroy inter-ethnic and inter-religious unity. Askari were given the only jobs available in a repressive monetary system that had promised to reward conformity with security, but also rendered them mute-men.[26] For some time if not longer, those who lost loved ones must have been in a state of mourning, and fear (cf Rankine 2015). They must have known that the Italian determination to erase the lives of Ethiopians who objected to Italian colonial forces was more than an act of political terrorism. It was an act of racial genocide, engineered by a heroic figure of Italian racist colonialist fascism that did not emerge out of a void in Italian and European history. Survivors and loved ones left behind must have realized that the European lexicon of racial hierarchy, the idea filled language of blackness as ontologically different from European humanness, was a taken-for-granted that had been drilled into the Italian colonist mentality. At a time when the lynched bodies of black Americans across the Atlantic were a reminder and warning to black Americans that they should not dare to even question the prevailing racial order, the bodies of those massacred in Ethiopia were desecrated by being left hidden in public, unburied.

Everyone knew the massacre had happened, but they were threatened with death if they presented themselves openly as sympathetic witnesses. This did not forestall their mourning.

Memories of loved ones had to have remained; their lives passed on from one generation of direct and indirect witness to the next. Kinship ties were the institutional adhesive binding the person to the community and society, so if one person vanished he or she left an absence that foreshadowed consequences for all those left behind. If the deceased had been an eldest brother for example, they did not cease being a "mother's brother" or "head of the house." They could not have been forgotten. The wake of these losses will have profoundly impacted the living.[27] Their disappearance into the world of the deceased deprived their families of sources of support and sustenance. What must it have been like to be kept away from the bodies of one's son, daughter, mother, father, sister, or brother; to have been unable to bury and mourn them through burial ceremonies? And to have been unable to expose the crimes committed against them, and all that they represented?

Ways of Looking

Thousands of photographs were taken during Italian colonialism in Africa, diffused widely in school textbooks, exhibitions, and museums, through private collections, and the popular press. Many of the images represented stereotypical beliefs that remain potent today (Andall and Duncan 2005). Exhibits of these photographs taken from state archives and private collections have appeared especially since the 1980s. They provide excellent materials for scholarly discussion and analysis (Goglia 1989; Labanca 1992; Triulzi 1995; Pennacini 1999; Del Boca and Labanca 2002).[28] These invaluable discussions explore the sedimentation and contradictions of Italian anti-blackness in the wake of the intensified presence of people of African ancestry in Italy.

In the 19th and early 20th centuries they were referred to as "moretti," meaning dark haired, dark skinned boys. Prompted by the growing visibility of people of African ancestry living in Italy, the *Piedmont Center of African Studies* in Turin launched an exhibit, "L'Africa in Piemonte tra '800e '900" in 1999 ("Africa in Piedmont between the 18th and 19th centuries") that explored the common histories between Italy and Africa in contrast with the idea that the presence of Africans in Italy was novel. The organizers wished to promote mutual acceptance, to advance knowledge and understanding of the colonial past, and of the suffocating prison of stereotypes. In their publication about the exhibit, Cecilia Pennacini, an anthropologist at the University of Turin, describes Italy's expansion through commerce, funded in part by the King of Sardinia who was very interested in the Horn of Africa. Italian commercialists, "explorers," journalists, and scientists produced an abundance of visual images of Africa and Africans including goods, objects or "specimens," and "fetishes" that were displayed in travel writing, novels, postcards, circuses, and public exhibits that "invented" scenes of African people and their daily lives (Carter 2010). An area of inquiry first carved by W.E.B. Du Bois, Frantz Fanon, Edward Said, and others, this important work on the production of a European geographical imaginary of Africa has contributed a great deal to our understanding of how Europeans constructed themselves spatially and temporally in contrast with and as superior to non-Europeans cast as permanent Others. Africa became for Europe the archetype of anachronistic time and space.[29] These images can tell us more about European culture, economy, and politics than about Africa and Africans. Yet when we examine further, colonial images of Africans can also tell about the subjects in these photographs, their interior worlds, identities, relationships to the colonial world, and what Kevin Quashie describes as their inner "quiet" (Quashie 2012).

From photographic images we can interpret the history of apparently reified cultures of difference the photographers might have hoped to capture, but more importantly we can glean a sense of what the people photographed understood and felt when the photograph was taken, and what was being expressed about their social position (cf Campt 2012, 2017). Persons on the receiving end of colonization did not have much opportunity to commemorate their experiences, yet the photos narrated by Italians suggest African versions of colonial encounters communicated implicitly, and accessible to viewers with cultural and political knowledge and attentiveness.[30] The colonial gaze is powerful, but it is not the only history. Documentary-style and artistic photographs narrate stories that have not yet been told. In the colonial context we can read coexisting exploitation, pleasure, affection, independence, resistance, and intimacy. The interior lives of the photographed Africans are not apparent to us, as we have been trained to see images in specific ways informed by dominant cultural codes and systems of classification. Yet it's important to try to do so, for inner thoughts and feelings are vital parts of what makes us human. As Kevin Quashie poignantly captures in the language of quiet, the interior being of black people is "a stay against the dominance of the social world" (Quashie 2012, 6). The richness of the inner life is frequently missed when images are read through the colonial gaze, which "overdetermines" Africans "from without" as formerly colonized, "primitive," and or rebellious (read criminal) subjects without complex thoughts and relationships to the world. The photographs taken even at the height of European colonization present counter-stories and counter-geographies about the bonds between Africa and Italy.

In an image on the back cover of an agenda by *Nonsolonero* from 2005, *BELL'ABISSINA: L'Italia coloniale nelle foto private* (Figure 1.1),[31] an Askari soldier holds the novel, *Il Fuoco*, written by Italian General D'Annunzio who was also Prince of Montenevoso and Duke of Gallese (Ghirelli and Valenti 2005)

The soldier sits with his legs crossed displaying the book on his chest while looking straight into the camera. His facial expression is one of gravitas with a hint of irritation, and his tender holding of the book suggests his knowledge of

FIGURE 1.1 Photograph of an "Askari" soldier holding the book, *Il Fuoco* (The Flame), a novel published in 1900 by Gabriele D'Annunzio. The back cover of the 2005 Agenda, *Bell'Abissina: L'Italia coloniale nelle foto private. Agenda Nonsolnero.*

Source: from Agenda Nonsolonero 2005, Ghirelli family collection, Rome.

and participation in Italian culture and society. His pose suggests a man not only literate in Italian language but also well read and with an intimate understanding of what is most dear in Italian and European culture. *Il Fuoco* is a story set in late 19th century Venice about a young poet, Stelio Effrena, and his mistress who is a famous actress. In Latin, the protagonist's surname is "Ex Frenis" or "senza freni" meaning, without brakes. The novel is evocative of the Italian classics, especially of Dante Alighieri and his relationship with Beatrice, and includes D'Annuzio's theories of drama inspired by Friedrich Nietzsche and Richard Wagner. The Agenda's text that accompanies other images for the month of April describes this and others taken with the caption, "Il mio ascari" or "My ascari" as a signal of the special relationship that existed between Italians and Africans who acted as personal attendants, servants, and battle companions. The back cover photograph of the soldier suggests an entirely self-possessed man who is conscious of the complexity of his hybrid and multifaceted identity, a man with insight into Italian culture, and with a great deal to say about the world, and his own place in it.

Pervasive in the iconography of colonialism were portraits of African women, many of them nude or semi-nude. The *Nonsolonero* Agenda text describes images of nude African women as trophies of war, but also as "mia moglie e mia cognata" (my wife and my sister-in-law) in poses that express violence, innocence, and cultural domestication of African women by the piccolo Borghese (Petit Bourgeousie) in Italy. Some of these photographs were intended to reproduce or innovate on classical European images of nude women.

A studio photograph from 1930 in the collection, *Colonialismo e Fotografia: Il caso italiano* for example presents a young Somali woman smiling widely into the camera. She lays nude front forward on her elbows on a wooden bed, in a pose more suggestive of Manet's assertive subjectivity of Olympia than of the more erotic or arguably objectified images of women by for instance by Titian and Boticelli (p. 134 in Goglia 1989).[32] What is exceptional in this image is the woman's appearance as relaxed and at ease with the photographer and with herself being photographed in a studio. She is seen to partake in European aesthetic and gender traditions as a member or insider instead of an outsider. And even though she is nude in the photo, her demeanor is one of self-possession and confidence, not the vulnerability and or disgust expressed in the facial and bodily gestures of other nude photos of African women from the 19th and early 20th centuries.

A comparable image is in a postcard also taken in Mogadiscio around 1930 of two Somali men stand beside each other smiling, wearing traditional style white cloth, that fits loosely around them and resemble Togas from Ancient Rome (Figure 1.2; Goglia 1989, 108)

They, too, appear quite comfortable with the professional photographer, and integrated into a cherished Italian history that at the time the photo was taken was being invoked by Mussolini and Italian Fascists in their bid to reproduce the Roman Empire in East Africa. The facial expression of the young man in the left

Somalia Italiana   *Tipi di Bimal*

FIGURE 1.2 A postcard of Somali men taken by A. Parodi in 1930

of the photo is active, as if he is were the middle of a sentence that expressed joking or light-hearted questioning, and the second man is gently smiling while holding a regal staff.

In what appears to be a close and intimate family style photo of two African girls who appear to have been sisters in the Agenda by *Nonsolonero* for November, the older and taller girl holds her arm around her sister with a slight smile on her face while her younger sister is wide eyed and gently questioning (Figure 1.3).

Both girls look straight into the camera, and express a sense of participation in the complexly interconnected African–European world in which they are living. Another photograph in the *Colonialismo e fotografia* collection presents three Somali men described in the caption as "Operai Somali alla torchiatura" (Somali workers at the oil press; Figure 1.4).

A man stands facing the camera with his hands resting on the machinery for what appears to be an impromptu photograph. This man's facial expression is one of self-containment, dignity, and perhaps a bit of annoyance, while the man behind also seems to look at the viewer as he is being viewed. The third man's back is to the photographer because he is in the process of pressing the oil. This image, like the others, demonstrates Africans and Italians enmeshed in an intrinsically transcultural world.

These photographic stories, along with the histories of exchange through economy and trade, and of unspeakable Italian violence and repression in its long historical relationship with Africa that began just after it became a nation state, can tell different versions of history. European capitalist expansion, which as Marshall Berman argued involves the continual melting into air of all that is solid, needed the labor and resources of the colonies in order to build the industrial revolution. Yet as Fernando Coronil argued, our knowledge has been molded by Western representations of "otherness" guaranteed by implicit creations of self-hood in which observers are distinctive from observed, insiders from outsiders, and the world is mapped into discrete bounded units of asymmetrical histories and peoples. This method of understanding prevents us from recognizing the mutuality and intimate connectedness between the peoples and societies of the colonies and metropoles that produce/d the world as we have been living it for at least a hundred years (Coronil 1996). The self-other duality that continues to be taken-for-granted in much of social science and the humanities renders nonwhite others as dependent subjects without agency, instead of coauthors in the ongoing making and remaking of Europe.

In this intervention, I contribute to Italian colonial history by building upon an approach that attends to the formation of subjectivities (Ahmida 2006; Ghermandi 2007; Scego 2015). The brutality and imperialist racism of Italian colonization was informed by perspectives on self and other, along with the daily interactions at moments when Italians and Africans were not inhibited by prescribed racial codes and systems of differentiation. By exploring the hidden spaces of violence along with resistance, negotiation, and familiarity we begin to

FIGURE 1.3 Photograph of young girls. From the 2005 Agenda, *Bell'Abissina: L'Italia coloniale nelle foto private. Agenda Nonsolnero*
Source: Agenda Nonsolonero 2005, Ghirelli family collection, Rome

FIGURE 1.4 Three Somali workers at an oil press
From *Colonialismo e Fotografia: Il caso italiano* (1996) based on an exhibit of private photographs, October–November 1989

contradict the taken-for-granted oppositional understanding of the relationship between Africa and Italy. Hierarchies of power and race generate divergent yet intersecting perspectives on the world, and all of these matter for a full understanding of history, and the historical present. Igiabo Scego's novels and the autobiographical, fictional writing, and films of other Italian and immigrant authors and artists of African ancestry call into question official versions of autonomous, bounded spaces and cultures by presenting polyphonic narratives of the postcolonial African diaspora in contemporary Italy (see Di Maio 2012; Chambers 2008). The enduring cultural linkages have generally not been celebrated. Instead Africans have continued to be marginalized while the cultural institutions of the colonizers are celebrated. In this conceptual configuration and cartography, the non-west is external to the west, so there's little mutuality or relational imaginary. Nevertheless, relational identity of place and people is a reality.

Re-cognizing the realities of how foundationally and fluidly relational African and European lives are will compel us to think more broadly about what it means to be human, to be an individual and a collective self, and how to redeem humanity.[33] We can begin to rewrite humanness by re-cognizing national and bodily spaces as peopled by human actors with profoundly interconnected transcultural and enduring histories.

Recently arrived Africans in Europe were often already on the move before they settled in Italy, having lived in other parts of their own country of birth or migrated outside to other African countries and European countries. As Stuart Hall (2003) eloquently argued, Diaspora is good to think with, because in Europe and the colonized world that includes the entire globe, identity is not just being, but also becoming, always emergent in response to different historical conditions. The human subject is a subject of culture that is continually positioned by and in the process of re-positioning itself. This understanding entails understanding non-essentialist conception of post-colonial diasporic subjectivities, culture, and ethnicity in order to, as Frantz Fanon suggested, free ourselves from the deforming burden of racialized categories; to unsettle the idea that we have and need a root identity in tradition. And to perhaps free colonizers and colonized from the nightmare of their violent histories.

Notes

1 The translations are my own.
2 Like the protagonist in Ken Bugul's poignant *The Abandoned Baobab* (2008) about a Senegalese woman's performance of European imaginaries of African women as intrinsically exotic and erotic, *Adua* was "overdetermined from without" as Frantz Fanon put it. She was imprisoned in a "racial epidermal schema" made by Europeans (Fanon 2008), and compelled to perform the role of the "naturally" and unreservedly sexualized African woman in direct contrast with the more reserved Italian-white women.
3 What Sylvia Wynter has termed, the "Coloniality of Being/Power/Truth/Freedom," can only be challenged by calling into question the very being of being human as it is

personified in a globally hegemonic Western and middle class system of classification (Wynter 2003).

4 This includes the rebirth and normalization of Italian neo-Fascist politics in the 1990s through Mussolini's granddaughter's far-right party, the MSI (Movimento Sociale Italiano) that she later broke from to form another group, AN (Alleanza Nazionale) that became a member of Silvio Berlusconi's coalition government. As Abdullatif Ahmida has pointed out, fascism has become respectable again, and is even romanticized in popular films about Mussolini (Ahmida 2006).

5 For more on pre-war camps, see Iain R. Smith and Andreas Stucki (2011); James Walston (1997).

6 See also Timothy Raemakers' blog, "Liminal Geographies."

7 The Italian Colonial Institute presented public lectures, films, exhibits, newspapers, magazines, and pamphlets on colonization as heroic. The Italian Touring Club was a patriotic organization that celebrated travel to "exotic Africa."

8 Negash writes that Italians actually first entered Eritrea through a shipping company purchased at the Port of Assab in 1869 (Negash 1987).

9 Italy established penal colonies in Africa for Italian dissenters and peasant uprisings. This also factored as an incentive for colonial expansion (Labanca 2005). Labanca suggests that in the early years, Eritrea was treated as a territory where dissidents and criminals were interned.

10 Gramsci and others believed Italian colonial expansion was motivated by colonial settlement of peasants. But Negash argues that this was only a secondary motivation and moreover a myth produced by the Italian ruling classes to divert attention from Southern agitating Italian peasants (Negash 1987).

11 Filippo Manetta, an Italian exile and editor of *Il Proscritto* who spent time in the U.S. working in the cotton industry at the end of the 19th century and supported the Confederacy, wrote about his shared White Supremacist idea that the West needed to conquer Africans in order to change their religions, customs, and institutions. In other words, he was virulently anti-black, and believed Africans and people of African descent in the Americas were "people without history." Benedicte Deschamps argues that Italian editors like Manetta became propagandists for the Confederates when they returned to Italy. They served as conveyors of cultural representations between the United States and Europe, shaping Italian images of the United States (Deschamps 2011).

12 A settlement signed by Italy and the Senussi leader, Idris-al-Senussi that exchanged recognition of the Islamic Brotherhood as the governing body of the Cyrenaica region of Libya or Italy's right to preserve direct rule over a slice of territory in the north.

13 This can be compared to U.S. strategies to contain Native Americans.

14 The "Askari" (Soldiers in Arabic) were voluntarily recruited until the early 1930s. Once recruited, soldiers were obliged to go overseas. There were some 60,000 Eritrean soldiers stationed in Ethiopia to consolidate the new empire in 1935 (Negash 1987).

15 In Eritrea, education was initially viewed as a method of elevating natives to intellectual parity with Italians, but the concern to dominate soon became the centerpiece in Italian racial colonialism. Especially after 1934, native education in Eritrea was regarded as a means to consolidate colonial rule by teaching Eritreans of Italian "glories and her ancient history in order to become a conscious militant behind the shadow of our flag" (Negash 2005, 111). A two tiered education program for Natives and Italians was put in place. The colonial government was supported by scholars such as anthropologist Lidio Cipriani who argued that Africans were destined to be ruled by Europe, justifying colonial use of force and the separation of the "races" at all levels, especially the schools. The need to produce and maintain Italian prestige justified instruction for Africans as manual laborers instead of classical education. However, the Catholic

Mission, which played a principal role in colonial education especially in Somalia, helped spread Italian culture. Negash suggests that the church and state were not separated in the colonies (1987). The Italian colonial cinema was also used to teach imperial and racial consciousness, grounded in an ethos of display and possession. Italians did not subtitle their films, and yet as Ben-Ghiat notes, transcultural differences mediated the reception of intended meanings as for instance in distinctive ideas about comedy and drama in Africa (Ben-Ghiat 2005).

16 Sandra Ponzanesi argues that the conquest of Africa by Italians was intended to offer both ideological and personal rewards via the unlimited access to African women awarded to Italian men. She discusses portrayals of Eritrean women with the trope of the "Black Venus," a highly sexualized and exoticized woman, close to nature who presented an alternative to European middle class sexual mores and social codes. Postcards and other iconography of a sexualized Eritrean woman were widely circulated and used to entice Italian men to the colonies where they could enjoy sexual freedoms not licensed in an Italy saturated by the sexual mores endorsed by the Catholic Church. Italian men who could afford it would cohabit with a "Madame," while the lower ranking soldiers would frequent prostitutes. But instead of being mere objects and passive victims of the European gaze, Ponzanesi argues that African women were also agents in a complex racial regime of domination and subordination. Becoming a Madame offered these women the chance to improve their social position and become influential in local society as intermediaries between the colonizers and colonized (Ponzanesi 2012; see also Barrera 2003a; Carter 1997; Iyob 2005; and Pickering-Iazzi 2003).

17 The Arabic word for "Soldier, Pawn, or Guard."

18 Primitive Accumulation refers to pre-capitalist modes of production.

19 Ahmida (2006) criticizes the otherwise excellent work of Victoria de Grazia and Hannah Arendt for their Eurocentric omissions. He also applauds the writings of pioneers who long ago criticized Italian policies, including Antonio Gramsci and Evans-Pritchard.

20 Coptics are members of an Orthodox Christian church based in East Africa and the Middle East.

21 Sbacci estimates that between May 1936 and June 1940, Italians used approximately 459 bombs against the Ethiopian Patriots and 1,972 C500 T bombs in the war of occupation in the northern front and roughly 2,000 poison gas bombs in Ethiopia (Sbacci, 1977, 48–9). Ethiopians reported these war crimes to the League of Nations, but they were left to protect and defend themselves. The League did not oppose the Italian occupation of Ethiopia.

22 Japan also used poison gases in China in 1937, and the French employed it in Morocco. All major state powers used poison gases between the two world wars (Sbacci 1977).

23 Campbell describes methods such as skinning alive, burning families alive in their homes, beheadings and public displays of severed heads, hangings by the wrists and slow death, and throwing out of airplanes alive.

24 When Mussolini entered the Second World War as an ally of Germany, he set off a series of alliances between the English, French, and Ethiopian Patriots in East Africa. The English and other European powers had not offered external support to the Patriots until Mussolini's declaration of war, and once he had done this they funneled arms and other resources to the Patriots and merged the five-year struggle between the Patriots and the occupying forces with the wider global war between the allies and axis powers. Without the knowledge and participation of the Ethiopian Patriots the British may not have defeated the Italians in East Africa. In June 1940, Haile Selassie established himself in Khartoum, Sudan where he signed leaflets distributed to the Ethiopian people urging them to "harass the enemy" in any way they could. He called on

the Askaris to leave the Italian military and join the Patriot forces, and many did (Pankhurst 1969a, 1969b).

25 There's a film on YouTube that recounts the story of the massacre, by Antonello Carvigiani. https://www.youtube.com/watch?v=NKSBN_0fMmI.

26 For more of this type of discussion, see Achille Mbembe (2001) *On the Postcolony*, and Frantz Fanon (2008) *Black Skin, White Masks*.

27 See Christina Sharpe (2016) *In the Wake: On Blackness and Being*, for a thoughtful application of Afro-pessimist arguments about blackness as death and mourning in the wake of the transatlantic slave trade, and the many creative ways this is coped with and transformed.

28 Also see Roberta Di Carmine (2011) on Italian films about Africa.

29 For a discussion of Italian racial science, see Donald Carter (1996). Also see Jan Nederveen Pieterse (1995).

30 See Tamar Garb (2013); Deborah Willis and Carla Williams (2002).

31 Archivio dell'Immigrazione in collaborazione con l'Associazione Baobab, L'Archivio delle Communità straniere e L'Isliao. I thank Giovanna Zaldini for this gift.

32 See John Berger (1990).

33 My ideas about relationality and relational place in this chapter and elsewhere were buoyed and inspired by Andrea Smith's argument about "radical relationality" against the notion of a transparent and universal I to which all seem to aspire, people at the top of social hierarchies and at the bottom. Smith suggests that real freedom cannot be acquired without disrupting the present structures and social order by understanding the self as wholly constituted through other beings. Selves are part of interrelated collectives instead of bounded by land ownership. Instead of the notion of ourselves as transparent and self-defining subjects in opposition to who we are not, we must build on the parts of ourselves and our living, situated geographies constituted in and through our relations with other human beings with whom we are always interconnected. The outside ceases to exist as such, and we build on the incompleteness of hierarchies and forms of oppression that have been made to appear universal, towards understanding our selves as interrelated and mutual, in relational places and spaces (Smith 2013).

2

BLACK/BLACK SPACES

Lived Experiences and Geographic Logics

Who is the stranger in Italy? In 2015, Italy had 5,0124,437 immigrants (8.2% of the total population), and at the end of 2016, 247,992 refugees or asylum seekers.[1] Straniero/a is the Italian term for foreigner and also for enemy, and her prototype is African.[2] A subject who in modern European thought has long held the position of subordination, mysterious allure, anachronistic space-time, and danger. In the present day, African descent people who are claiming their right to live and thrive in the territories of the merchants and colonists who built Europe with the help of African labor, land, and natural resources are encountering time worn, naturalized imaginaries of an Africa outside European and world space and history (space-time). Enduring ideas about place, belonging, and personhood are reasserted in state policies, media, popular representations, and daily social interactions. As a consequence, people who appear to be of African descent are as Frantz Fanon suggested in plain sight and hyper-visible yet routinely reduced by the white gaze to a sort of nonbeing, perceived and classified as people who do-not-belong-here,[3] must be scorned, feared, exoticized, rendered silent and hidden.

Black subjects represent and inhabit Black and black spaces, absent present spaces of taboo that are forbidden and prohibited both materially and symbolically.[4] Black spaces are symbolic sites where anything can happen and everything is permissible. This is part of a dualistic social cartography.[5] In their daily practices, some people have reported that they frequently take alternative routes. For many African Italians and Italian Africans, immigrants, refugees, and asylum seekers from Africa who inhabit them, Black spaces have distinctive meanings.[6] For first and second generation African Italian subjects, they are Black spaces with a capital "B," where they exercise some degree of control over their individual lives and those of their families, knowledge of self and one's social position, and where they build communities that crisscross established ethnic, racial, and sometimes class divisions. Black spaces are where one practices daily acts of insurgency, "fugitivity," and subterfuge in an anti-black environment. As Fred Moten argues,

> What is required … is not only *to reside* in an unlivability, an exhaustion that is always already given as foreshadowing afterlife, as a life in some absolutely proximate and unbridgeable distance from the living death of subjection, but also *to discover and to enter* it.
>
> *(Moten 2013, 746)*

For many African descent people in Italy, Black spaces are the fulcrum of a Black radicalism dedicated to social survival, justice, and transformation.

The hyper-visible, yet invisible presence of black Africans and other formerly colonial subjects in Italy highlights the transition from a nation-state divided by cultural localisms to one that produces a unified sense of national identity in opposition to those ossified at even further distances from local and regional identities, i.e., people socially and juridically classified as 'non-Italian.' Italy was unified as a nation rather late, in 1861. The historical Italy of an uneasy nationalism moored in immense regional inequalities and countless and distinctive local customs has since the late 20th century begun to reimagine itself with difficulty as 'multicultural,' in tension or even a tug of war with collective sentiments that hold dear to an imagined yesterplace where social hierarchies and cultural distinctions were articulated in a vernacular of small Italian towns, villages, and regions.

Many blame '*stranieri/e*'[7] and any municipal administration that supports them for the social and economic hardships working and middle-class Italians face today. There is a longing and nostalgia for a time before immigrants arrived or as a shopkeeper in Reggio Emilia remarked, when "'those people' were not here." Blaming the newcomers for crime and shop closures, she added that before the "bad elements" arrived, "I could walk at night safely," and "I could tell people where they could eat a meal that was characteristically Reggio Emiliano. Now, these restaurants have all closed and there is nothing left of our local culture."

An Italian teacher in her sixties described how in the little town of Correggio on the outskirts of Reggio nell'Emilia, the hometown of one of Italy's most beloved popular rock artists, Luciano Ligabue, the daily market is simply startling. Flipping through clothing and sundry items or awaiting services at fresh vegetable stalls are countless people who do not appear to be Italian, who have darker skin tones, and who may wear turbans and head scarves. They are typically Pakistani and Bangladeshi men drawn to Correggio because they possess the pastoral skills needed for work on dairy farms. The famous parmigiano-reggiano and ricotta cheeses are produced here. In the larger adjacent city of Reggio Emilia itself, African women and men, many with young children in tow, frequent the Tuesday and Friday morning markets. Often in small groups and speaking African languages, they are seen haggling with vendors and quietly conversing with friends or family members in African languages while sifting through mounds of apparel.

Portraits of Everyday Life

In the small city of Reggio Emiliano a small city that prides itself on its local customs and ways of life, African, South Asian, and Chinese people are among the vendors with stalls in the outdoor market. In one of the three market piazzas, a group of West African women sit comfortably with their children and shopping bags every Tuesday and Friday chatting for hours while their children play or are rocked in carriages. They look forward to these mornings when they leave their homes and relative isolation on the urban peripheries for the center of town to chat with friends and purchase household goods. African women sit comfortably for hours in an Italian market surrounded by crowds of customers holding the hands of small children or pushing them in carriages, shoulder to shoulder with friends and spouses while slowly walking or combing through stalls filled with mixed goods 'on sale,' speaking Italian or Italian dialects and numerous other languages to each other and to the vendors with whom they may be involved in bartering exchanges. And even in the moments when the markets are closing and the crowds have dispersed, the women sit, perhaps with less ease than before, but still chatting and quietly joking in the middle of an Italian piazza that by their actions they are claiming as their own.

Chinese-Italian baristas own and serve in the café-pasticceria-bars, fixtures of Italian culture. African, Eastern European, and other newcomers frequent the streets of Reggio with their young children, some in strollers, baby carriages or with infants and toddlers astride their backs. While Italian birth rates have continued their long decline,[8] African and other newcomers are having children[9] who frequent the local schools and are socialized in Italian culture. The country has one of the oldest populations in Europe and lowest birth rates in the world among citizens, and yet many children of "non-Italians" are neither legal nor cultural citizens. Nevertheless, and as a factory worker in his 50s from Burkina Faso eloquently remarked in Italian, *his* children and the children of others from *Africa and diverse places outside of Europe*'s real and imagined borders represent, "the future of Italy."

To many Italians, the presence of visible African, Asian, or other nonwhite people signifies the negative economic transformations and cultural challenges facing Italian families and communities. What I call an *anti-other structure of feeling* and cultural logic tends to preclude inquiry, while "stranieri/e" increasingly "Africani/e" are blamed for disrupting the social order and triggering social degradation and economic strife. This is a profoundly rooted cultural logic. Anti-other and anti-black imaginary are circulated in national and local media images that have blanketed the papers and television news since the 1990s. This began with representations of African street sellers or the so-called 'Vu Cumprà' competing with Italian shop-owners and market sellers, and West African prostitutes.

Black Social Death

In the early 21st century these degrading portraitures have been replaced by images of boats filled with Africans in Lampedusa, an Italian Mediterranean island off the coast of Sicily that is proximate to Tunisia and Libya, and more recently Sicily.[10] The archetypical image of the migrant is African, frequently referred to as "poveri disgraziati" (poor wretches) or "poveri disperati" (desperate poor). The reference point of the anti-other structure of feeling that has come to pervade Italian culture since the early 1990s is now the iconic boatloads of people arriving almost daily from Libyan ports, the majority seeking political asylum. In 2014, many of these people were Sub-Saharan African, or Syrian. Images of black pain or death overshadow attention on these human lives. As much as possible, African and other refugees and migrants are scurried out of sight to the spatial peripheries of towns and cities, or what are euphemistically called 'immigrant processing centers' that many former residents and Italian activists describe as contemporary Lagers or concentration camps that represent spaces of the exception where state laws are suspended. These are black spaces of social control, and moreover, black spaces of social death.

Anti-Blackness is part of common sense European ontology. People presumed to be of African origin are typically classified as "essentially different" from Europeans. Scholars have argued that Italians are xenophobic but not racist, in contrast with Americans, French, and other Europeans. In my research, I found that Italians discriminated against people on the basis of their national origins and skin color. In Sicily and other parts of the Italian South racism appears to be less marked.[11] Southern Italians have also experienced considerable internal prejudice from northern Italians. However, in the Southern regions where hierarchies of rank based on social-political power tend to be palpable, people of African origin are at the very bottom.

Asylum seekers are obliged to wait in Italy until awarded full refugee status. The European Dublin Treaty (1997) mandates that one must be fingerprinted and request protection in the country of first arrival. Somali, Ghanaian, Senegalese, and people from other parts of West and East Africa with *permesso di soggiorno* residency documents or citizenship who had lived in Italy for decades have departed for better lives in other European countries, the United States, or returned to their countries of origin. They describe routine discrimination in the job and housing market. Daily micro-aggressions and other expressions of contempt and or social invisibility accompany general absence of compassion among Italians. Many who feel socially erased are striving to transform the social terrain.

Shop owners and other residents of Reggio frequently remark, "There are too many of them. And the Africans are too different from us." They are perceived as intruders in a mythologically white place that defines community in relation to 'pure' Italian blood ties.[12] Like slaves in the Caribbean and the Americas, they are socially classified as strangers in a land where they have no citizenship claims and genealogical ties. Their place in the family tree remains outside the territorial borders of Europe (Patterson 1985).

As Toni Morrison argued in *Playing in the Dark,* for European Americans, blackness is an "absent presence." Morrison suggests that this absence is a foundation of Western (read: white) identity. The Western subject is spatially located in the West in relation to imagined 'third world' and 'different' others symbolically classified as separate from and outside of modernity (see Carter 2010). Although blackness is assigned a largely negating value, racism is taken-for-granted and thus invisible. It doesn't register. If Black lives and worlds are symbolically designated as out-of-bounds and taboo, racism (if admitted to exist at all) is both popularly and academically assumed to be a 'natural' phenomenon, its workings too banal to merit critical examination (Morrison 1993). However, the ideas, structured practices, and experiences of race and racism are pivotal to European modernity and continue to be lived today, even though they are shrouded in silences, evasions, and forms of invisibility (see Trouillot 1997; Pred 1995; Carter 2010). To understand the workings of power as expressed by race and racism, I offer *Black spaces.* When we move our attention to B/black spaces where race and space converge in the ontological and material borderings of our world, we may discover new, non-Eurocentric ways to read and render our societies more legible. Without this ability to identify and examine these violent social realities and how Black life sustains itself in a broken world, we cannot hope to affect the necessary social transformations in our basic and advanced knowledge and practices (Harney and Moten 2013).

Hannah Arendt warned in *The Origins of Totalitarianism* that the right of every human being to belong to history ought to be guaranteed by humanity itself,

> for it is quite conceivable, and even within the realm of practical political possibilities, that one fine day a highly organized and mechanized humanity will conclude quite democratically – namely by majority decision – that for humanity as a whole it would be better to liquidate certain parts thereof.
>
> *(Arendt 1973, 299)*

Her warning resonates with the present moment in Italy in which people classified as non-European and especially African are being denied historical belonging, dehumanized and condemned to social oblivion through all sorts of spaces and spatialities, from prison-like detention centers, to rural encampments and urban ghettos, to street hang outs after being refused work on the basis of name or skin color, to being psychologically and materially pushed away and even to their death in public domains such as buses, parking lots, hotels, and cafes.[13] The fears and uncertainties gripping societies during this present moment of social-economic transformation are being channeled, to modify Raymond Williams's notion of structures of feeling, into of structures of anti-other feeling.[14]

Political figures have easily capitalized on anxieties about work and the future, directing structures of anti-other feeling into expressions of anti-blackness assembled through centuries of unreflected prejudices and misperceptions of Africa. And while the world is becoming ever smaller, compressing as people interact through actual and imaginary movements of ideas and culture in space and time, B/black spaces are expanding. I focus on Italy, yet this analysis is comparative as anti-blackness is experienced widely throughout Europe, the United States, and beyond (Winant 2004; Macedo and Gounari 2005).

A recent expression of anti-black sentiment is taken from sports, specifically soccer. Soccer is the leading European sport and notorious for acts of violence and other expressions of anti-blackness among fans and players in the stadiums. In April 2014 as 32 teams prepared for the World Cup games in Brazil, an anti-racist Twitter campaign was inadvertently sparked when in the middle of a game Dani Alves of the Barcelona team and reportedly the best third right player in the world picked up and took a bite of a banana thrown at him by a spectator during a match. Dani Alves da Silva, who is Brazilian, born in Bahia, was then thirty-one years old. This photographed gesture was simulated by fellow players, political figures, and other supporters around the world who in defense of Alves took "selfie" photos eating bananas that spread like wildfire, becoming an anti-racist Twitter campaign called, "we are all monkeys."[15] With a certain comical irony, Alves' apparently simple gesture and refusal to dignify the symbolic violence served to negate his own negation as the banana was intended to signal that as a black man he was primitive, animal-like. It is a commonplace that fans express their hostility toward black players by throwing bananas on soccer fields, "Booing" the players and referees, ridiculing and seeking to humiliate with handmade posters.

The Italian player Mario Balotelli, born to Ghanaian parents and adopted by a Milanese family, has been the object of countless incidents of such hostility, confronted in stadiums for instance with signs reading, "There are no Blacks in Italy" (La Repubblica, Crosetti, 30; see Merrill 2015). After being insulted by ultra right spectators, Marco Andre Zoro, the Ivorian player for Greece, began to cry and wanted to relinquish this hard earned position. In an act of solidarity and encouragement, his teammates painted their skins black for the subsequent game. Among Alves' supporters were teammates from his and other teams, for instance Lilian Thuram, the ex-defender for France who was born in the overseas French territory, Guadaloupe. Thuram was quoted in the Italian daily newspaper, *La Repubblica* saying,

Nobody can understand the pain of being called a monkey … Blacks are not born but become so through the perceptions of others. To me it happened when I arrived in France at the age of nine. The banana and the howls are acts of pure violence, and a cultural problem that needs to be addressed from an early age. Racism in the Western world exists, and how.

(29 April 2014 30–31, my translation)

And as the Western ontology of Blackness is disseminated through education, trade, travel, work, housing, popular film and other media including social media, the situation today for most Black people globally remains quite dismal (Lewis 1995; Marable 2008; Winant 2004).[16]

Some Italian scholars and social critics have addressed the pervasive anxiety and fear toward the so-called 'Other.' They have noted the rigid idea of social, cultural difference that African and other non-Italians have come to signify in the geographical imagination over the past several decades (Pugliese 2008; Andall 2005; Pagliai 2009; Grillo 2003). Many Italian church and other voluntary associations of the Italian left, intercultural centers, and social centers for students and youth have fostered acceptance of the changes, embracing multiculturalism or 'interculturalism' as the term is used in Italy (Merrill 2006). Some of these social actors seek to influence local administrations, pressing national and local political representatives to institute mechanisms of integration and intercultural reciprocity.[17] And there is a great need for these anti-racist allies, people who are acquiring what France Winddance Twine in *A White Side of Black Britain* calls, "Racial Literacy"[18] (see Twine 2011). Notwithstanding the positive moves that are taking form especially in some key cities like Reggio Emilia, Rome, Lampedusa, and Torino, the roots of fear and hostility toward people deemed too different to belong structure social feelings and behaviors, or what anthropologists might describe as the habitus of daily life.[19] And there is so much silence surrounding the structure of anti-other and anti-black feeling that more drastic configurations of subversion are needed in order to undermine what are in effect strategies of control. The assertion of imagined yet naturalized and taken-for-granted differences works to divide or fragment and obscure from view interdependent and relational identities.

Black Spaces

Black spaces provides an original and innovative conceptual and methodological tool to make sense of and illuminate the persistent anti-blackness in contemporary Italy and elsewhere. Blackness and anti-blackness are generally unthinkable popularly and among scholars because they are passed over as not a subject of knowledge, beneath notice. After carefully examining the cultural and economic production of knowledge in modernity, Antonio Gramsci and Michel Foucault came to recognize that what counts as valuable knowledge is always entwined with who has the power to name, institutionalize, and define it as such. What we render intelligible is invariably a function of social and economic power. Knowledge of cultural and biological differences, passed down for hundreds of years from the science (fiction) of man to scientific racism, is expressed and re-produced not only in scholarship and popular media but also phenomenologically in taken-for-granted ways through social exchanges in public spaces.[20] The insinuation of power in all that passes for knowledge can lead us to overlook all sorts of information as we filter out what we believe is worth thinking about or not thinking about. That which is routinized and everyday, as Gyan Pandey suggests, is regarded as "trivial," and therefore not of sufficient import to scrutinize (Pandey 2013). Indeed, we see the world through inherited hierarchical cultural-political grids that frequently lead us to recognize and mis-recognize some practices while we reduce others to the silent dustbins (Trouillot 1997). A sort of discursive noise barrier keeps us from hearing and perceiving Black spaces, from re-cognizing the deeply (im)moral presence of black spaces that we have for centuries been blinded from learning from. Western perceptions of space and time promote a structure of refusal on the basis of which, as Pandey puts it, "a discourse is denounced as not being a language, a gesture as not being an oeuvre, a figure as having no rightful place in history" (Pandey 2013). A great deal of racialized violence, direct or in more subtle expressions of microaggression, is deemed acceptable on the basis of a learned inclination to accept it as natural and as something that doesn't concern us. Detention centers, occupied spaces filled with refugees, multiplying urban ghettoes for non-Italians, and non-verbal acts of everyday physical and symbolic violence are for instance generally sanctioned as part of the natural order of things. We may recall Primo Levi's warning about the emergence of the Lager, and how Europeans came to define people around them as Others in such a way that one could slaughter them with impunity:

> To many, individuals or groups, can fall a belief, more or less conscious, that "every foreigner is the enemy." What is more, this conviction lies at the bottom of their souls like a latent infection; showing itself only in uncoordinated and everyday acts and not at the base of a system of thought. But when it happens, when the unexpressed dogma becomes the premise of a major syllogism, then, at the end of the chain, is the Lager.
>
> *(My translation) (Levi, 2015, 3)*

In Italy immigration policies are instituted on the basis of an "emergency" logic to protect national security. The Ministry of the Interior beginning in 1998 has delegated certain exceptional measures of control of immigration under a generic rubric, "centers of immigration."[21] There are three types of structure: i Centri di Accoglienza (Cda), i Centri di Accoglienza Richiedenti Asilo (Cara) e i Centri di Identificazione ed Espulsione (Cie). Protest has emerged especially around the Cie, because of a mandate to arrest and prepare for expulsion migrants whose legal documents may have expired for any number of reasons. However, there is considerable murkiness around what these various centers are doing and a sanitized way of describing them as "Centri di Accoglienza," or "Reception

Centers," a language that tends to normalize and render them more palatable. The centers designed for reception are constructed on the basis of immigration as a national "emergency" and major security risk, with asylum seekers and migrants declared a social threat.[22] Giusi Nicolini, Mayor of Lampedusa and Linosa and others have suggested that these sites can become Lagers when people are forced to remain there for endless periods of time in unsanitary conditions beneath standards of civility and dignity. Asylum seekers are held in these confined sites of prolonged suffering, sometimes for years. Fabrizio Gatti, journalist of the *Espresso* magazine, disguised himself as an undocumented migrant in order to enter the "Centri di Accoglienza" because the Italian government did not allow observers or even physicians to enter.[23] Gatti described the centers as more like the gulags of the former Soviet Union than official institutions of a democratic country (Gatti 2007). He observed acts of humiliation, brutality, and extreme dehumanization (Gatti 2007).

Black spaces of social control and institutionalized violence have been part of Western cultures since the Atlantic slave trade/plantation societies in the Americas and the European colonization of Africa beginning in the 16th century. I liken these spaces to the CIA's "black sites" because like these classified domains of the state where anything can happen without public knowledge, they are located on the material and psychological peripheries, out of bounds, erased from a field of vision; and as Fanon discussed in *Black Skin, White Masks*, rendered systematically un-recognizable. The American CIA's clandestine "black sites" are described in a sterilized language as places out of the public's field of vision, where "extra-ordinary rendition" of suspected terrorists is necessary to protect U.S. citizens. Generic descriptions have become standard currency in media reports that mislead the public, using such terms for instance as "coercive methods," instead of torture, and the deliberate infliction of physical and emotional pain against suspects who lack access to legal representation. Similarly, there is an Italian discourse about migrant communities as the root of social "problems" that allegedly appeared only suddenly when they arrived and defamed pristine local places such as the San Salvario neighborhood in Torino (see Merrill 2006).

Social Bordering

Africans are symbols of pollution to the social order, and employed by the global media to depict the crisis and consequences of immigration. On May 3, 2014, the newspaper *La Repubblica* published a photo of a busload of asylum seekers, with African men front and center. The story was that a group of parents of grade school children scheduled to take a school trip to Siracusa, Sicily complained to their mayor that he must stop the school from taking this visit. The parents had learned that newly arrived migrants not placed in "Centri di Accoglienza" were being transported in these same school buses to various other locations in Sicily or on the mainland. Parents feared their children might contract "tuberculosis, lice, scabies" or even AIDs from these buses that had not been cleaned after the migrants had sat in the seats. The parents lamented that they did "not feel protected" ("non ci sentiamo tutelati").[24] This represents a desire to disinfect the territory of African presence. In Italy, the implicit message is that Africans are illicit. Political leaders and popular media have depicted Africans and other non-Europeans as criminals, seeking unlawful entry into Italy as 'clandestine' or illegal migrants who pose a security threat. The legal structure supported these ideas with its "security package" (pacchetto sicurezza) that sanctioned the arrest and detention of people without legal documents.[25] Cecile Kyenge, former and only Minister of Integration, warned that this threatened democracy: "Italian laws create norms and practices of severe discrimination, and when the rights of one part of the community are ignored, there's a loss of rights for all" (Kyenge 2014, 44).

However, from the vantage point of the people of African descent whose experiences as human beings and creative expressions of dissent and refusal are systemically denied and erased, Black spaces are sites and expressions of social life. A social border stops Black Italians who have lived most or all of their lives in Italy and who may appear to be integrated into Italian ways of life and social networks. There are also people of African origin in Italy who speak a number of languages including that of their ethic group of origin, who maintain diasporic ties with families and other social networks, and do not necessarily wish to be admitted into Italian social networks unless their livelihood is contingent upon them. Whether or not one wishes to be fully incorporated into local social, cultural, and political worlds, most people believe they ought to have the unprejudiced freedom to make that determination for themselves. Social borders persist, and are acutely painful for the second generation and many in the first. But they can also be a source of strength. Knowledge of the refusal to recognize people of African descent as part of Italian culture may be embraced, and alternative resources used to create new subjectivities and communities. Veronica, a palpably frustrated young twenty-four-year-old woman who came to Italy at the age of ten from the Ivory Coast stated that she does not believe in "integration" and wishes to return to the Ivory Coast because she does not feel "Italian." She is a leader and co-creator of an organization for unity among Africans in Italy, with members from the Ivory Coast, Ghana, Togo, Senegal, Bukina Faso, and an Italian woman described as very African identified. As she described it, the organization is intended to help members know "who they are" by maintaining continuity with African cultural practices while building friendship and support networks. Others deal with living in an environment that privileges white Italianness by asserting, "I'm Italian" again and again, which can be viewed as rather revolutionary in a social system that has sought to define itself as part of an imaginary yet impactful Western European, White, and Christian social formation. Even the assertion "I belong here" on the part of people born in Africa who have lived out the bulk of their lives in Italy and have made it their home is an expression of resistance to the status quo that would contain or erase their being. In both instances they are saying in words and actions, "I know your ways and have adopted many of them as my own," while in the same breath suggesting "I see you. I am a witness to your systemic cruelty towards me, towards people like me, towards your own people and to your brutality. I have perspectives that diverge from yours and that you cannot erase even as you try so hard to do so." Many of my interlocutors from the first generation have expressed these ideas and sentiments. For instance, an exceptionally widely and deeply read man from Rwanda who had lived in Italy for over thirty years having been sent there as a child to escape repression and where he was unable ever to return. He taught French to schoolchildren in Torino, but would converse only in Italian with friends and colleagues. He was also a social activist who worked as a cultural mediator with a number of government offices, and who dedicated himself to transforming Italy's social system by teaching and writing about its racism and class oppression. Tragically, this inspiring man died from heart failure at a young age, having lost his battle to create for himself a place of love and belonging. He died from a broken heart.

Achille Mbembe describes the "slave" as "the forename we must give to a man or woman whose body can be degraded, whose life can be mutilated, and whose work and resources can be squandered – with impunity" (Mbembe 2001, 235). Colonists could commit acts of violence on the colonized by consigning them to the animal world of things without human consciousness.

In the colonial mentality, the native had no history, freedom, or individuality, they were like dogs toward whom colonizers were abrogated the right to exercise their will. In that world, and in this world of the "postcolony,"[26] violence and death are normalized, penetrating almost everything and escaping nothing. Conceiving the position of formerly colonized subjects along the same lines as the enslaved in the Americas, Mbembe suggests that formerly colonized Africans are for the most part people who possess life, property, and body as if these were alien to them. European colonial conquerors sought rigorously through ideas and rituals to define the contours and conditions of human morality in order to establish that natives were so radically different from and inferior to Europeans that they were *by nature* excluded from the field of 'the human,' cast in the perimeters of the animal world. How can we in the present truly talk of moving beyond colonialism and racism if the profound effects of colonization in Africa on political-economic structures and minds are so robust in the present?

In exploring the barriers that African nationals and the African Diaspora of Europe encounter today, scholars must move beyond orthodox Western paradigms to understand formerly colonized peoples. One can observe, as reaffirmed over and over again elsewhere, that European culture has a lot of difficulty recognizing the 'strange' or different in persons and cultures that do not fit the ideal image of 'European,' namely 'White' and Christian. This is not merely a question of xenophobia or 'fear of the other,' but instead a deeply rooted refusal to really see and feel common humanity with nonwhites (Mills 1998). As Mbembe argues, "More than any other region, Africa ... stands out as the supreme receptacle of the West's obsession with, and circular discourse about, the facts of 'absence,' 'lack,' and 'non-being,' of identity and difference, of negativeness – in short, or nothingness" (Mbembe 2001, 4). The African continent stands apart as the figure of the null, the absolute opposite of that which is – the very expression of being nothing at all. And it is this imagined signification of Africa that Europe has deployed for centuries to justify its unapologetic exclusionary and brutal practices towards others. For as Mbembe asks, "What does it mean to do violence to what is nothing?" (Mbembe, 2001, 174). You cannot put to death that which has already been deemed as nothing, an empty figure.

In "Stranger in the Village," first published in Harper's Magazine in 1953 and then in the edited collection, *Notes of a Native Son* in 1955, James Baldwin, a distinguished U.S. Black essayist and novelist examines his position as the first Black person ever seen in a Swiss village, where the legacies of colonial history and language weigh heavily. He describes the effort to fit in and be liked while realizing that he is a curiosity, and later that he can't be welcomed there because he isn't perceived as human being:

> No one, after all, can be liked whose human weight and complexity cannot be, or has not been, admitted ... it must be conceded that there was the charm of genuine wonder in which there was certainly no element of intentional unkindness, there was yet no suggestion that I was human: I was simply a living wonder.
>
> *(Baldwin 1998, 118–119)*

With his characteristically brilliant lucidity, Baldwin explains that Europeans respond to him in this manner because they never question their superiority to Africans nor their natural right to conquer them,

> There is a great difference between being the first white man to be seen by Africans and being the first black man to be seen by whites. The white man takes the astonishment as a tribute, for he arrives to conquer and to convert the natives, whose inferiority in relation to himself is not even questioned; whereas I, without a thought of conquest, find myself among a people whose culture controls me, has even, in a sense, created me, people who have cost me more in anguish and rage than they will ever know, yet do not even know of my existence.
>
> *(Baldwin 1998, 120)*

Baldwin is a North American – a native of New York – yet his everyday experiences force him to make sense of his position in Europe in relation to the African continent, the place of his ancient progenitors. Even though he is in Switzerland, which doesn't have a direct colonial history, Europeans have inherited a widely and thoroughly insinuated cultural–historical relationship to Africa.

Baldwin seeks to understand the taken-for-granted perceptions and attitudes of these Europeans, "They move with an authority which I shall never have; and they regard me, quite rightly, not only as a stranger in their village but as a suspect latecomer, bearing no credentials to everything they have – however unconsciously – inherited" (Baldwin 1998, 121).

The taken-for-granted sense of superiority that surrounds Baldwin during his time in Europe is so much a part of common sense as not to be acknowledged as real. For as he discusses, white men have been creating legends about black men for centuries, and these legends are part of language, "The white man finds himself enmeshed, so to speak, in his own language which describes hell, as well as the attributes which lead one to hell, as being as black as night" (ibid.: 122).

And because, "The root function of language is to control the universe by describing it. It is of quite considerable significance that black men remain, in the imagination, and in overwhelming numbers in fact, beyond the disciplines of salvation ..."

Europeans, like many European-Americans have learned not to see racism, have been taught blindess and muteness from an early age.[27] The prevalent denial of racism and its undeniability among those subjected to it takes a heavy toll especially on young, second generation African Italians in Italy. Such youth have begun to ask who they are, and what they should do. Born or raised in Italy and attending Italian schools, they are culturally Italian. Yet there is a sense of disorientation. In the Italian context some of the students whose parents spent their formative years in Burkina Faso, Senegal, Ghana, or the Ivory Coast are not taught anything of substance about African cultures, and even less work written by Africans. These young people may perceive Italian and other European languages and culture to be superior to their parent's country of origin. A pattern emerges in which when these youth complete school, they find that they are not accepted as "Italian," and face confusion about their identity.[28] Many have never visited an African country.[29]

People of African ancestry have begun to talk about how they are racialized in Italy and the discrimination they face on the basis of their appearance and presumed cultural identity. For many, this shared experience generates a social bond with people linked in some manner or other with diverse African countries and ethnic groups. First generation African Italians often carry in their cultural luggage traces of anti-imperial resistance. They are conscious of belonging to pan-African networks. Among the first generation and their children, there is a growing consciousness of what I analytically refer to as Blackness, even though this form of naming is not yet widely used in the Italian context.[30] I adopt this term as a social analyst, interested in the broad patterns of what Denise Ferreira Da Silva refers to as a 'racial analytics' in the making and remaking of the modern West (Da Silva 2007). Italy is characterized by its own history that informs the way race and racism are produced and experienced. Stuart Hall argued that race is a fluid concept with distinctive meanings from a conjunction of historical influences generated in different national contexts. Hall suggested that while there are distinguishing, historically defined black experiences that contribute to alternative ways of seeing, being, and acting, one must always be aware that black experience does not exist outside of representation. We come to know who we are by representing and imagining ourselves. He suggested, "It is to the diversity, not the homogeneity, of black experience that we must now give our undivided attention" (Morley and Chen 1996, 476). Cautioning against essentializing blackness and reproducing misleading binary identities he invoked the British context to argue:

> Blacks in the British diaspora must, at this historical moment, refuse the binary of black and British. They must refuse it because the 'or' remains the sight of constant contestation when the aim of the struggle must be, instead, to replace the 'or' with the potentiality or the possibility of an 'and.' That is the logic of coupling rather than the logic of a binary opposition. You can be black and British, not only because that is a necessary position to take in the 1990s, but because even those two terms, joined now by the coupler 'and' instead of opposed to one another, do not exhaust all of our identities. Only some of our identities are sometimes caught in that particular struggle"
>
> *(Stuart Hall, in Morley and Chen 1996, 475)*

I offer the concept of *Black spaces* to capture the global and deeply historical patterns of race making that are taking dangerous forms, the shared but multiple experiences and intersecting identities within this system that produces creative forms of fugitivity. While Black life has been rendered unthinkable in Europe or North America, it is far less fixed than is commonly imagined, and there is at one and the same time tremendous and diverse social life in the shadows of socially positioned death (Sexton 2010; 2011).

Social Life and Social Death

Because Italian formal education represents all African cultures as empty of value, second-generation African Italians are reconstructing their political and social subjectivity in Italy. This is one response to the lived experience of being rendered socially invisible as a nonwhite 'other' and rejected as members of Italian culture and society. Second generation African Italians may find solace in their parents' cultural practices. Some desire and develop diasporic collectives among their peers. Others take a more radical position. Both first-generation and second-generation people build a sense of place in Italy. In multiple sites of convergence, they gesture toward a geographically and culturally expanded Italian subjectivity inspired by their lived encounters with people from the African diaspora and other parts of the world. Some reinterpret sound and being through fresh, ever fluid expressive syntheses. African Italians assert a sociality that rejects their rejection. They are making common cause with what Jack Halberstam describes as the "brokenness of being, a brokenness that's Blackness."[31] Many make peace with rejection by what they perceive as a deeply broken system. They hold on to what is left out while also embracing what they carry with them. This is being "in but not of" Italian society, a path comparable to what Harney and Moten in their discussion of being a critical intellectual describe as being subversive, living fugitive lives of rupture but also of connection in the undercommons. Moten and Harney write, "Some people want to run things, other things want to run. If they ask you, tell them we were flying. Knowledge of freedom is (in) the invention of escape, stealing away into the confines, in the form, of a break" (Harney and Moten 2013, 51). This is an ongoing call to dis-order that suggests a world within worlds beyond the structures we inhabit and that inhabit us. A place within a place where one takes the dismissive language of colonial othering that continues to render one a nonentity, and while listening to one another unifies with the recognition that "We must change things or die. All of us."[32] Since the first waves of African student migration in the 1970s, many have embraced the grass-roots radicalism in Italian society and its rejection of respectability. They try to preserve themselves in what Moten describes as the "surround" where they remain in a continual state of movement toward and against death. They travel in an undercommon sociality animated by the celebration of Black thought as it intersects other "submarine socialities" (Moten 2013, 742).

In Italy there are many collective places of improvisation and self-expression. Jean-Pierre is a young man born in Italy in 1989, the son of immigrants from the Ivory Coast. He describes the "Zona Stazione" in Reggio Emilia as a site that has been described as the "Ghetto" in local newspapers. He argues that this is a gross misrepresentation, for it is a site of international convergence where one "can meet people from diverse places, with diverse customs."[33] He may find this area at times "irritating" but prefers to live than anywhere else in the city. The people he calls the "ragazzi dello Stazione" live in this zone, and they meet to discover and create syncronicities, mixing West African, Italian, and Moroccan music. They discuss their efforts to diffuse the fear of Reggiani, and work to disseminate it through their musical performances, sporting events, and festivals while also, hidden in plain sight from those who refuse to see or hear them even when they are placed under surveillance, they experiment with fluid forms of life on the outside looking in.

Jean Pierre was born in Italy, and has never visited the Ivory Coast or any other African nation. He describes his life in Italy as, "Not okay. But better than others." When asked about his identity he described himself as "Ivoriano" only because he grew tired of trying to convince Italians that he was Italian. In his words and while touching his arm, "People stop at the skin; they don't go further. They don't stop at what's inside. This is awful; but very real." Laughing, he describes himself as a "citizen of the world" who must carry three forms of identification every where he goes because as a Black Italian he is always at risk of being arrested and deported.[34]

Raciality in the 21st Century

"Raciality" is a post-Enlightenment concept. Scientific theory codified human difference on a global scale. It produced a sort of ontological horizon that operates symbolically, economically, and juridically at all spatial scales. In this logic, the *'transparent I'* is socially constructed as White European or White American,[35] while racial others occupy spaces in a horizon of othering and erasure. Africans and people of African origin occupy the farthest point on this scale.

Analyzing the role the racial plays in modern thought, ontologies, and epistemologies or what she calls "ontoepistemologies," Denise Ferreira da Silva (2007) demonstrates the centrality of knowledge and power to the production of modern social formations on a global spatial scale. Da Silva offers lucid insights to theorize why people of African origin continue to be regarded as superfluous and thus socially dead to the dominant social order by white supremacist discourses.[36] The racial, she argues, is tied to an ontological context of globality that merges particular bodily traits, social configurations, and global spaces, producing and reproducing human differences as immutable. Modern Western philosophies of "Reason" created racialized and spatially located kinds of human beings who stood differently before the concept of universal man. She writes,

> The racial constitutes an effective political-symbolic strategy precisely because the subjects it institutes are situated differently, namely, in globality. While the others of Europe gaze on the horizon of death, facing certain obliteration, the racial keeps the transparent I in self-determination (interiority) alone before the horizon of life, oblivious to, because always already knowledge-able (controlling and emulating) of, how universal reason governs its existence.
>
> *(Da Silva 2007, 30)*

Such notions of racial difference are enduring; they govern current global and state power relations, (re) producing moral regions and bodies (Da Silva 2007).

Nineteenth century naturalists correlated global regions with bodily and social configurations, and various social configurations established across the globe came to be read as instantiations of different sorts of minds and beings. Da Silva unravels the emergence of a profound logic in modern representation that requires the elimination of racially different 'others' for the self-determination of the not-of-color, transparent I. The modern 'analytics of raciality,' or the sciences of the mind, produced Europe as a marker of irreducible difference that could be captured only when placed against 'other' ways of being a man. The modern Western subject created itself by eliminating outer differences, or outer-determined racially different others. As such, the racial has for hundreds of years been constituted as a weapon of global subjection.

Colonization was also justified by the idea that White bodies belonged to civilized social configurations. These bodies were positioned as 'pre-destined' to engulf the *affectable I* in other global regions. They would be subjected to the allegedly superior force of European reason. National borders presupposed the containment of certain irreducible essences. The "others" of Europe are therefore written as affectable but irreducibly different strangers who cannot share the spatial origins of the European white, or 'transparent I.'[37]

The system of racial knowledge and power that is so central to modern social formation is embedded in lived experiences, contributing to space making. The racial is constituted as a weapon of subjection through which the 'transparent I' who is by definition white is a subject by virtue of their given power to eliminate external differences through cannibalization, to affect others without being affected by them. Contact through immigration (enslavement and colonization before this) is perceived as a threat to the social order,[38] because the transparent I cannot help but be affected by the other. Thus, racial separation is performed as a method of social control. Africa, a continent of enormous diversity with fifty-four different nations is homogenized in this Western imaginary. Its descendants are spatially positioned in what is, in effect, a permanent state that prevents them from providing anything of substance to the 'transparent I,' except labor. Within this White ontology, people of African descent may live this logic not as a merely abstract form of reasoning. On the other hand, the white transparent I enjoys, consciously and unconsciously, his and her position as master teacher, knowledge broker, and world leader.

Contact is a technology of power through which Africans and people of African ancestry are perceived as ill suited to enter modernity, which began with European expansion in the 16th century. According to this logic, "contact" via immigration weakens the existing social and moral order, so it must be obliterated. Contact is widely considered in terms of encounter between diverse cultures as one moves from place to place, yet it is far more than this[39] because it carries ontological meaning about how subjects and spaces are constituted in the West. The reasoning is that racial difference must and will by its own accord disappear through assimilation and integration. Today, the strategy taken in Italy is to talk about integration while practicing control and containment of the presumed dangers of contamination via contact with differences by separating 'stranieri/e' in detention centers, prisons, poorly serviced neighborhoods, trade schools, and the like. In Italy there is persistent alarm around the *numbers* of Africans arriving on boats in Lampedusa and Sicily, fueled for instance by hyperbolic predictions by the Interior minister in 2014 that some 600,000 would cross over by the end of the year. There is also fear that many more would enter Italy should the legal structure be altered to allow people born in the country to claim 'jus solis' citizenship rights on the basis of their relationship to birthplace.

Social sciences have reproduced a cultural analytic that configures racial distinction as something that will be eliminated with time as differences are subsumed by the dominant culture via assimilation to the hegemonic social and economic order. What follows is the taken-for-granted belief that all Black consciousness is mediated by whiteness, determined by the outside. This is why W.E.B. Du Bois suggested that black people have "double consciousness," forced to always look at oneself through a white gaze and perceived as inauthentic because Western society precludes being both a citizen and also a black person. Subjecthood in the West is White by definition, and one is white and a subject by virtue of the ability to exercise power over others. Andrea Smith suggests that according to this logic the 'others' are affected by the power of the Western subject, but they cannot affect power themselves. Nevertheless, the Western subject struggles with anxiety, because in practice it is impossible to exercise power without being affected by others. The Western subject addresses this anxiety by separating itself from the conditions of "affectablity," abstracting oneself from affectable others (Smith 2013). This is a fundamentally racial-spatial separation wherein the Western subject is located in the West *in relation to* 'affectable' third world others, *in relation to* 'primitive' others who are believed never able to enter modernity. The Western subject is classified as the universal subject that determines oneself without being determined by others. The racialized subject is particular, but aspires to be universal and self determining. In the general social structure, is difficult if not impossible for white people to accept black people as one of themselves, for to do so threatens their status as superior. In a letter to his nephew, James Baldwin wrote that he would have to learn to accept that white people could not accept black people for:

They are, in effect, still trapped in a history which they do not understand; and until they understand it, they cannot be released from it. They have had to believe for many years, and for innumerable reasons, that black men are inferior to white men. Many of them, indeed, know better, but as you will discover, people find it very difficult to act on what they know. To act is to be committed, and to be committed is to be in danger.

(Baldwin 1963, 22–23)

Moreover, the logic is that if the racialized subaltern wishes to be liberated and included in the dominant (white Anglo Saxon) society, this embodies a fundamental desire for self-annihilation. But as Fanon suggested, the black man has two dimensions: one with his fellow blacks, and the other with whites. This isn't only a question of perspective, but a potential cognizance of the fluidity of the interplay of Blackness and a complex interplay of identities in movement. A radical being that embraces the unfixed relationality and openness of Blackness, and also what is scorned and rejected. Blackness encompasses nothingness and everythingness, representing people who have refused to be silenced and dis-placed and who have survived in spite of the effort to erase them.

In Italy, people of African ancestry are generally not denied their ancestral origins of family, language, religion, and home in comparison with people in the Black diaspora in the Americas and Caribbean who began to form collectively in the hold of the slave ship. Nevertheless, people of African ancestry in Italy whose countries were colonized by Europeans are similarly criminalized, and their histories erased, or trivialized. As a Moroccan-Italian who has lived in Italy for 30 years said, growing up in Africa he was taught that his culture was worthless, and in Europe he has had to re-learn the value of his culture.

The question of how Black people can be self-determining when confronted with pervasive denial of their humanity has occupied the thinking of generations of scholars of Africana Studies. Racialized logic is fundamental in modern Western thought and ontology. It produces Black subjects who live in tension with who they perceive themselves to be, and who others think they are. One is forced to live with the impossible requirement that to be regarded as human one must recreate oneself as White, or whitened. In other words, one must repress cultural differences in order to be self-determining. And the contradiction is that even when people of African descent are culturally Italian, they are routinely misrecognized. It is in this context where anti-blackness is not diminishing structurally that we must seek to make sense of black sociality. Jared Sexton argues that the 'problem of blackness' is one of making sense of a black sociality that emerges when black social life, in all but the most minor ways, is rendered impossible. Confronted by a world that renders one an impossibility, a world that ascribes one to social and often physical death. The spectacle of the death of Black people is as Saidya Hartman argues, bound up with the history of Europe (Hartman and Wilderson 2003).[40] When embraced, Blackness is a symbol of strength, resilience, and rejection of that which is promised but never given. Black social life is very much alive and readily maintained by multiple millions in Europe, Africa, and the United States (Sexton 2011). Consequently, Black social death must be understood in relation to Black social life and vice versa.

Fanon suggested that people of the African diaspora who are constrained to pay the cost of anti-blackness frequently respond by embracing a blackened world. In *Bad Faith and Black Racism,* Lewis R. Gordon argues that in recognizing that the social life from which he spoke was not his own, Fanon was suggesting that the only way to truly reject racism was to be willing to 'be' Black affirmatively. In accepting that he was defined as a social problem, that the world knew itself through that imposed idea, he was willing to pay the costs, whatever they may be, of being Black; to live Blackness and a Black social life in the shadow of social death (Sexton 2011, 27–28).

Living Blackness as a way of life is living in highly porous, fluid, and mobile spaces (Moten 2008). Mobility and creative improvisation are central dimensions of Black social life, in contrast with the state's struggles to control and fix. We can compare the crossing from Africa to Lampedusa or Sicily and experiences in detention or holding centers with the trans-Atlantic crossings in that they similarly led to the production of creative avenues of subterfuge, evasion, flight, or fugitivity. This perspective doesn't posit Blackness merely in relation to Whiteness. Indeed, Blackness has never really been fully captured by Whiteness. As formerly colonized Africans move more directly onto European territory, they are demanding their right to live, frequently in ways that converge with the visions and values of radical Italians and other subaltern peoples.

There is ample evidence of direct and indirect challenges by people of African descent to the Italian legal and social system, to advance human rights, and institute mechanisms of social equality. Countless groups of people, frequently in coordination with Italian associations, social centers, and trade unions, organize demonstrations and acts of subterfuge (Merrill 2006). Ethnic and intercultural associations have also made ongoing efforts to include and represent "new Italians" in multiple public spaces.[41] Their acts of insurgent citizenship challenge inherited grids (Pandey 2013; Holston 2009), transforming un-archived into archived histories.

Harney and Moten suggest that Black, indigenous, queer, and poor people co-inhabit and are inhabited by fugitive cacophonous structures or what they call the "undercommons." The undercommons represent an outside, a sort of "nonplace" of generative and constitutive power linked with the alternative visions and transformative practices of the Black Radical tradition. This perspective seeks to elaborate blackness instead of seeking recognition or acknowledgement in a system of White supremacy. While African Italians work for recognition as Italian, some also embrace forms of anti-colonial dis-order. More than dispossession, the undercommons is the basis of renewed forms of collective consciousness and fugitive paths that by evading state controls produce forms of subversion. Harney and Moten trace these current practices to flight from enslavement and the making of spaces of marronage and Black protest movements. This idea of fugitive undercommons can also be linked with decolonization movements in Africa, with traces in the current flight from repression and war.

There is hope for the present and future in the ownership of a generative and constitutive fugitive power (Moten 2008). Describing the lives of Black people, C.L.R. James wrote that they face "The lived, existential reality of the day-to-day situations of their denied humanity and the historical irony of their emergence in a world that denied their historicity" (quoted in Gordon 2000, 2). This gives rise to liberation struggles in a variety of forms. Scholars of Africana Studies[42] have explored for over a century how Black people experience their lives in the face of an ethos and practices of social erasure. My concept of Black Spaces is in dialogue with these and more recent scholars as I confront the question of what it means to live in an anti-Black world, and what, as Toni Morrison asks, Black women and men become in such a world. How, in an Italian context do people of African descent 'be' when there is a continual production of new ways to render them, as Donald Martin Carter (2010) has suggested, invisible?

Black spaces are those 'unarchived' taken-for-granted spaces at scales both of the state and everyday interactions and practices and that are integral to life yet 'unthought.' They are the spaces where one is taught not to wander in thought or body even when directly within our fields of vision, because they are potentially dangerous. Like the CIA sites of imprisonment, interrogation, torture, and death, black spaces are hidden or semi-hidden from our view but at some level we know they are there "to keep us safe"; where we thus allow cruelty to be inflicted as long as it is inflicted on nonwhite people. The CIA sites are referred to as "black sites" because they *should not be seen.* They are on the peripheries of cities, in offshore desert oases in the Sahara, peripheral zones of urban areas, and other offshore sites like Guantanamo Bay. Black spaces are where the state contains and has license to erase persons, to strip them of dignity and humanity. They are camps where people await possible expulsion and experience degrading prison conditions. They are material and symbolic spaces such as 'ghettoes' that are diffused in everyday psychosocial interactions and places (Mezzandro and Neilson 2003). They are also epistemological sites rooted in social contacts and ways of seeing that are embedded in a system of racial oppression, a 'racial contract' as Charles Mills has put it, that began with the Atlantic slave trade and European colonization of the African continent (Mills 1999). These histories brought about intense and enduring suffering for Black people, and also enduring hope, resilience, and creative genius.

I consider black spaces of the state camps as what Gyan Pandey refers to as 'unarchived,' for they are widely taken-for-granted and trivialized (Pandey 2013). What happens in black and Black spaces is ignored. Black spaces include daily movements and interactions in public spaces where one is subjected to continual forms of microaggression, symbolic and under threat of material violence. People of African descent and coalitions of the willing often embrace Black Spaces with a capital B.

Black/black spaces warrant more scholarly attention because they articulate who we all are. If the state can dehumanize some people and legitimize their erasure and dehumanization in everyday life, the public at large has a de facto license to do this. I am not suggesting this is a top-down system where the state sets the tone entirely for what people do. I am arguing that state policies and practices are both emulated and mocked by those in a polity. People who are being excluded from a polity live in different spaces from the mainstream, materially and symbolically, and may critique the system in ways the presumed beneficiaries of it do not. This doesn't mean they always do this, because they are compelled to negotiate the system as it exists and at the same time reject what it does to them.

Italians are fond of describing immigration of Africans to Italy as a very recent phenomenon, and thus not comparable to the context in France or England where colonization was extensive. However, Italians colonized Libya, Somalia, Eritrea, and Ethiopia even though for shorter duration, and there were massive post-war internal migrations of Italians from the south and northeast to north central and northwestern industrial cities. The legacies of these forms of dispersal and colonization persist in the present (Andall and Duncan 2005; Ben-Ghiat and Fuller 2005).

Italy is part of a European social formation with a lengthy commercial historical relationship with the African continent, and Africans have been in Italy for centuries. Today, Africans are doing the vital domestic and agricultural labor that Italian youth are rejecting. They are picking tomatoes and conducting social care work including taking care of the elderly and children, cleaning and hauling, and working on Sunday. Africans and others classified as "outsiders" are central to Italy's transition in a 21st century of ever-expanding and deepening interconnection and movement. The importance of this social complexity was not lost on Pope Francis, whose first travel as Papal leader was to the Italian island, Lampedusa, the frontier between Italy and Africa, and the symbol of would-be immigration and loss. Lampedusa is the site where the bodies of asylum seekers have been buried in unmarked graves, and where Italian detention centers have literally overflowed with people seeking protection and dignity in Europe. In his liturgy on Lampedusa, Pope Francis said that he felt the need to be on the island after a major shipwreck on October 3, 2013. He was in grief, and needed to feel a sense of solidarity. Criticizing what he called the "culture of comfort" that brings one to think only of oneself and to be insensitive to the cries of others he said,

> In this world of globalization, we have fallen, all of us, into the globalization of indifference. We are used to the suffering of others. This doesn't concern us. This doesn't interest us. These are not our problems. None of us have voices or faces.

Giusi Nicolini, Mayor of Lampedusa and Linosa, is outraged by the normalization of, and deafening European silences surrounding the loss of thousands of asylum seekers off the coast of her islands. Condemning both Italian government policies and the mass hysteria surrounding the arrival of people who are assumed economic migrants and "clandestine" but who usually arrive on Lampedusa fleeing war and political persecution in their countries of origin, Nicolini made the searing comment, "If for these people the voyage on the boats is their only chance to hope, I believe their deaths in the sea should be for Europe a motivation to feel shame and dishonor" (Nicolini and Bellingreri 2013, 13). The Mayor described the unmarked graves that were established only recently following years of leaving the bodies in the sea, and the need to be able to identify the dead,

> If these deaths had been ours, I would want to receive a telegram of condolences for every drowning victim that I was delivered. If they had white skin, if they were one of our children who drowned during a vacation.

Notes

1 The immigration figures are from the European Commission's European policy network (May 2016/19). The UNHCR statistics include refugees, asylum seekers, and stateless persons in Italy at the end of 2016 (UNHCR, popstats.unhcr.org/en/overview).

2 I do not focus directly on anti-Muslim rhetoric and practice in Italy or Europe, but many people of African descent (from North, West, and East Africa) are practicing Muslims. The demonization of Muslims is grounded in geopolitical relationships that racialize Arabs and Muslims as out-of-place. This racialization is nevertheless distinct from the anti-black racism I examine, and in which North African and other Muslim groups frequently participate.

3 I hyphenate to bring attention to the way these systems of classification are like escape proof prisons. Their power is derived from their very invisibility. I thank Gunnar Olsson for reminding me why Allan Pred hyphenated his concept of taken-for-granted knowledges and practices. I employ Pred's theoretical perspective here, which resonates with Gramsci's concept of common sense but is more focused on everyday practices.

4 I use the language of absent presence to refer to a condition of blackness in being and social existence. If being human is in Europe defined as being White, to be nonwhite is to represent the negation of humanness, absent although present.

5 I am referring to the symbolic relation of opposition between Africa and the West that includes the mapping of differences with racial classifications. This has continued into the present. See Henk Van Houtum's discussion of the "global apartheid" of the European Union's border regime (see Van Houtum, 2013).

6 Some people of African descent born in Italy prefer the appellation "Italian African" to "African Italian."

7 As noted by Tahar Ben Jelloun (2005), the word, 'stranger' has the same roots as 'strange' and 'foreign,' indicating those who are 'outsiders,' 'external,' and 'different.' The outsider is classified as a danger, and enemy (see Sniderman et al. 2002).

8 Italy has one of the lowest birthrates in the world, on a rapid descent especially since 2009. On average, Italians have 1.39 children, compared with 1.58 in the EU. However, the demographic picture varies widely between Italian regions. There is also a downward trend in mortality. The Renzi government launched a campaign (2015–2017) to spur women to have more children, offering 80 Euros per month to low and medium income families until the child reached age three. This move, and the government's declaration of September 22 as national "fertility day" in 2016 was met with a public outcry.

9 According to official ISTAT figures, in 2011 babies born to people with at least one Italian parent represented 19.4% of births.

10 See Carter (1997); Ifekwunigwe (1999); Carter and Merrill (2007).

11 There are several explanations for the relative lack of overt hostility toward Africans in Southern Italy. The south has had a fraught relationship with the north, as evidenced in the emergence of Umberto Bossi's "Lega Nord" party in the late 1980s, which began by arguing that Southern Italy was a parasite of the Northern regions of "Padania" and should be a separate country. Much of the south has remained agricultural since the post-war economic boom that led millions to migrate to the northern industrial zones where they experienced systematic discrimination. The idea that southern Italians are a distinctive race and prone to criminality dates back to the 19th century when Cesaire Lombroso and other physical anthropologists conducted anatomical studies. Southern areas record extremely high rates of unemployment and organized criminal activity. Southern regions, especially Sicily, have had a long and complex relationship with North Africa. Some scholars today are deploying the idea of a "Black Mediterranean" to capture Italy's interconnectedness with other subaltern people, and their oppositional politics (see Raemaker's blog; Di Maio 2012; Lombardi-Diop and Romeo 2015; Hawthorne, forthcoming).

12 For a discussion of European ideas and practices around racially mixed relationships, see Twine (2011).

13 For more on the notion of a present moment of danger and for an interdisciplinary approach to its study, see Merrill and Hoffman (2015).

14 Raymond Williams also analyzed the spaces that designated the 'esprit du corps' and power of the English bourgeoisie. He discussed how this social class appropriated space, for instance in the form of luxurious country estates and national parks for their pleasure. (See Williams 1995 (1973)).

15 Maurizio Crosetti and Francesco Merlo, *La Repubblica*, 30 April 2014 pp. 1, and 30–31.

16 Anti-Blackness refers principally to people popularly classified as black on the basis of skin color and the attendant values it is accorded. While blackness is the major archetype of cultural distance from 'pure' Europeans, other archetypes include Arab and Muslim peoples who may or may not also be considered black, as well as Jewish peoples, Roma and Siti, and sometimes Eastern Europeans.

17 Intercultural reciprocity, dialogue, meeting and integration are also terms used and practices encouraged by political figures such as Cecile Kyenge, the first Black member of parliament, and Giusi Nicolini, the first woman mayor of Lampedusa/Linosa.

18 France Winddance Twine, in her pathbreaking *A White Side of Black Britain*, explores how white women may acquire antiracist consciousness and gain what she calls "racial literacy." There are six components of Racial Literacy, including 1) defining racism as a current instead of an historical problem; 2) understanding how class, gender inequality, and heterosexuality mediate experiences of racism and racialization; 3) recognizing the cultural and symbolic value of whiteness; 4) understanding that racial identities are learned instead of natural, and produced in social practices; 5) having a racial grammar and vocabulary with which to discuss race, racism, and antiracism; and 6) being able to interpret racialized practices and codes. Twine argues that white women and men involved in intimate interracial relationships *can acquire a critical awareness of how racial ideologies structure one's life*, but this is not automatically given as a consequence of having close relationships with one or more people who are black (see Twine 2011, 92).

19 This comes from Pierre Bourdieu's (1977) *Outlines of a Theory of Practice*.

20 See the next chapter.

21 This first happened when the establishment of CIE or 'Centro di Identificatione ed Espulsione' (Center for Identification and Deportation) were promoted and approved by the Center Left government. That law that made this possible, called Turco-Napolitano, turned reception camps into detention facilities (see Chapter Five).

22 Under article 12 of law 40 in 1998, the so-called Turco Napolitano law under the more restrictive Bossi Fini legislation of 2002.

23 This absence of permission to enter and observe the sites is challenged by Human Rights organizations, Doctors without Borders, and an Italian group of journalists led by Gabriella Guido called, "LaciaCiEntrare."

24 *La Repubblica*, Sabato 3 Maggio 2014, pp. 20. "Bus di migranti per la gita scolastica: I genitori dicono no," by Alessandra Ziniti.

25 In April 2014, the Italian Parliament voted to alter this law.

26 The Postcolony is a term that Achille Mbembe uses to discuss the political and social conditions in African countries in the shadows of colonization by Europe, the legacies of colonization in the present conditions of life.

27 See whiteness studies on the normalization of whiteness and the denial of white privileges (e.g., Frankenberg 1993; Roedigger 1991; Lipsitz 2006).

28 Students whose parents are from Africa are frequently tracked into professional trade schools instead of toward the university bound route of the Scientific, Classical, and Language Lycees.

29 See the film made by Mondinsieme of Reggio Emilia, "Il paese di papa."

30 Cecile Kyenge, the first African Italian to serve in the Italian parliament, calls herself "Nera" or Black, preferring this to the more commonly used, "di colore" or of color.
31 Introduction to Harney and Moten (2013).
32 Ibid., p. 10.
33 Prevalently with North African, West African, and Chinese origins or ancestry.
34 If at any time he does something the authorities deem against the law, they can take his citizenship away.
35 'White' signifies an identity.
36 For an incisive analysis of the emergence of White supremacy in the West see Charles Mills (1999).
37 As Fanon suggested in *White Skin, Black Masks*.
38 Or as Aimee Cesaire argued in *Discourse on Colonialism*, colonization involved not human contact, but rather relations of domination and submission, or "thingification."
39 Aimee Cesaire describes 'contact' during colonization non-inexistent. Colonization established a relationship of domination and subordination rather than acknowledgement of competitive cultural exchange.
40 See Debra Walker King (2008).
41 For instance, *Alma Mater* in Torino, and *Mondinsieme* in Reggio Emilia.
42 For example, Frederick Douglass (2013); Anna Julia Cooper (1998); W.E.B. Du Bois (1994, 1999); Frantz Fanon (2005, 2008).

3

UNARCHIVED EVERYDAY VIOLENCE

Violence is central to cultural processes of legitimization, normalization, and simplification through which power orients everyday practices (Kleinman 2000). In this chapter I examine black spaces produced in everyday encounters or interactions. I detail the tension between the phenomenology of routine symbolic violence,[1] and the struggle for being. I examine events, words, gestures, pauses, gut-reactions, feelings of humiliation, pain, and inchoate forms of flight registered in bodily acts that can't be easily read or articulated. As Gyan Pandey argues, these so-called "triflling" forms of knowledge articulate human subjectivity and produce spaces and ways of inhabiting space. An implicit power-knowledge is (re) produced in everyday practices that scholars may remake by filtering the "minutiae of everyday life" (Pandey 2013). Only by describing these so-called "triflings" can we gain greater self and collective knowledge (Pandey 2013; Trouillot 1997).

On a cloudy spring day I boarded a bus that runs through the urban center and into the peripheries in the northern Italian industrial city Turin, with Giovanna, 58 years old and of Somali origin. Giovanna moved to Turin in the 1970s after studying Italian language and letters in a Catholic grade school in Mogadishu. She quickly secured Italian citizenship. She enrolled in the University of Turin where she studied Modern Foreign Languages and Letters, and met her partner. She served as an activist and cultural mediator at the inter-cultural women's center, Alma Mater, for a quarter century. While raising their two children, Giovanna was a leader in the Somali women's association that was politically active in Italy and in Somalia through transnational relations. With her acute understanding of Italian institutions and culture, Giovanna played an instrumental role in the creation of Alma Mater.

Passengers were crammed into the bus on a cool spring afternoon. Giovanna was able to find an empty seat in the front. I stood beside her, holding the strap above. The bus had stopped several times before an elderly White gentleman boarded and brusquely asked Giovanna in Italian, "Do you have a ticket?" She understood that he meant she was seated in a spot that gave priority to disabled people. Giovanna responded by quickly and politely rising to vacate the space for him. These seats are not marked as reserved, and anyone may sit in them. However, when she stood up he mumbled, "These people are so rude." He then cleaned off his seat as if she had defiled it.[2]

Giovanna did not respond to this slight with any discernable expression of frustration. She later described his "ignorance," as "typical" of the responses she routinely encounters. For this reason they are "not worth" expenditure of emotional energy. However, as everyday acts of aggression and symbolic violence aimed at people who have visible African ancestry, such encounters are significant, and with an afterlife. Pandey refers to these acts as "unarchived prejudices" that undermine one's sense of personal freedom. They displace the uniqueness vital to emotional and intellectual life that each person is expected to have within a society.

Unarchived prejudices constitute a technology of repression intended to erase Black Italians, and to prevent them from speaking about the everyday racism they experience (Merrill and Hoffman 2015). These black spaces are also culturally embedded narratives of denial. This produces persons who are expected to live with a diminished sense membership in a social collective, or permanent sub-personhood (Mills 1998).

The legacy of such black spaces is multidimensional, for a great many people who are part of the African Diaspora, and the critical scholars who document their experiences, are sanctioned for discussing it. When North American Blacks and others[3] have sought to bring attention to microaggression they have frequently been described as 'over-sensitive' or 'too emotional' (Pandey 2013). This language of power is frequently used against women and persons in weak social positions as a way of silencing dissent. Social valuations go along with access to resources, job opportunities, and dignified treatment. Researchers and non-specialists have rendered routine acts of discrimination as too trivial, or too ordinary to discuss.[4] But they are not trivial. We produce culture in these habits, meanings, and practices during the course of our embodied intersubjective encounters in everyday life, in relation to the events and environments in which we find ourselves (Jackson 2002; 2012).

My goal is to make visible the tacit daily violence of anti-blackness and the effects of this taken-for-granted experience on recipients. In other words, I ask 1) How does racism take place? 2) How are spaces of inclusion and exclusion produced in social experiences? 3) How do people who do not correspond to those to whom I refer as *recognized Italians*[5] respond to routine racism? This discussion is focused on *affective experiences*, or deeply masked experiences that people rarely talk about directly. For those who do not appear to be stereotypically recognized Italian, or 'White,'[6] racialization is a regular experience. Yet for most social actors who are perpetrators and participants, it is so naturalized that one is not cognizant of it. As Giovanna told me, "People don't realize this is happening."

Italian Context

In Italy, anti-blackness assumes specific cultural forms as part of what Allan Pred called, "situated practices" embedded in specific cultural histories (see Merrill and Hoffman 2015). Political leaders, popular media, and educational institutions play prominent roles in cultivating old ideas and stereotypes about people presumed to be of African descent. Derogatory images of Africans have circulated in public discourses and media since the late 19th century when Italy engaged in campaigns of colonial conquest in North and East Africa (Carter 1997; Ben-Ghiat and Fuller 2005; Palumbo 2003). Images of African people were generated and diffused in colonial films, magazines, cartoons, postcards, and other visual representations (Di Carmine 2011; Del Boca 2002; Pieterse 1995).

In Italy blackness is double-edged. It is both hypervisible and invisible (Carter 2010), direct and verbally or physically aggressive, while also more subtle and characterized by "microaggressions."[7] There has been some popular debate about racism in Italy since the early 1990s. A common claim is that Italians do not discriminate on the basis of race or color. In popular discourse, Italy is believed to be different from other places like France, England, or the United States where racism is deeply rooted in historical systems of slavery and colonialism. Italy is instead described as a place where people are good or "Brava gente," where people love the "good life" (la bella vita)[8] and are simply innocent of any substantive experience of interacting with non-Italians. The language of "brava gente" is also employed in relation to Italian colonial histories (Del Boca 2005; 2002; Palumbo 2003). Such perspectives assume an insularity and or variety of localized cultures with a relatively fixed distinctiveness through time, absent of significant impact from cross-cultural movement across place.

In contrast to these perspectives, I begin from the premise that Italians are not as unfamiliar with differences as is commonly assumed. As Maria Viarengo who is Ethiopian-Italian commented,

> Italians have never been monocultural. That's nothing but a myth. They don't know their own history. Do you know how many people with different religious beliefs and speaking all kinds of languages have lived in Italy? Many came to conquer. The Etruscans were here, the Normans, Huns, Turks, the Moors, people from all over the place came here and made what is today Italy. And do you know how many Southern, and Italians from the Veneto migrated to northern Italy after the Second World War? So when they say that they're just not used to dealing with social differences, they're just deluded.

In order to make sense of why she experiences so much everyday racism, Viarengo, a writer who also grew up in Eritrea and the Sudan, completed an unpublished genealogical analysis of colonial images of Africa from the late 19th century to current representations in popular media.[9] Colonial images were diffused in Italian magazines, postcards and other published images, unofficial photos taken by colonial soldiers, fiction, travel literature, and cartoons. Teaching intercultural education to schoolchildren, Viarengo has discovered that children have inherited images and ideologies of the colonial past that inform their perceptions of Africans and African Italians today. There is for example an old tale that describes blacks as wolves that is circulated even today to control and provoke fear in children who are told that if they behave badly, the "black wolf" will eat them up. This image of cannibalistic and beastly black creatures who wish to devour and consume human beings endures in a contemporary context where similar imaginings of African men are reproduced in journalism and other popular media. Viarengo argues that representations of blackness produced by Italians in the mid 19th century shifted toward the late 19th century in relation to the political context.

In the mid-19th century, Italians circulated photographs portraying Africans as primitive yet noble savages, simple, and childlike. One would comment, "Oh, how cute these Africans are with their big feet and big smiles and long earrings!" Such depictions were demeaning in that they elicited paternalistic responses in Italian viewers. However, although Abyssinians held spears and shields in these representations, the women were portrayed working, and the images conveyed the sense that Africans were not so much as "bad" as just primitive and childlike. These ideas are also still in play in the contemporary period, converging with others. The term "Negretta" that was commonly employed in the past continues to circulate today, and Viarengo describes how Italians will say when they see her, "Oh what a beautiful Negretta" and this really irritates her because what they are saying is that she is a black inferior and not a person, not a woman.

When Ethiopians defeated Italians in Adwa in 1886, making them the only European army with technologically sophisticated firearms to have lost a war with a relatively unarmed African group, they were humiliated. Yet Italy continued to pursue colonial rule. A different visual technology developed. Italian colonialists circulated posed images of Abyssinians as morally degraded. African women in particular were photographed, often by amateur photographer-soldiers and officially by colonial officers, as half or fully nude.[10] Many African women in the nude or semi-nude photographs lowered their eyes in shame. This nudity was meant to suggest that African women were erotic and passively waiting to be raped, a metaphor of conquest.[11] African women were compared in Italian magazines with Italian women who were portrayed as morally superior. The poses and accompanying texts were designed to convey the idea that African women were silent, submissive, lascivious, and animalistic, and they did not engage in productive work. Such images were contrasted with Italian women represented as "angels of the house" and "exemplary mothers of their children." The white women were depicted as active, and the African women as waiting to be acted upon, and indeed raped. These negating mis-representations of Africans, Viarengo points out, continue to circulate in Italian advertising and other media, informing the Italian collective imaginary (Viarengo, unpublished personal communication 2014; cf Frisina and Hawthorne 2017). In addition to the ideology of the sexually available African woman, there is also the myth of Africans as servants to Whites.[12]

Current representations of African women in Italian television series are infrequent, and those who appear tend to be peripheral characters living in tent camps, or in caretaking positions.[13] In the *Rai* fiction series, "Butta La Luna" which aired from 2006–2009 and has since been re-broadcast, the protagonist Alyssa Calangida (played by British actress, Fiona May) is a woman from Nigeria who comes to Italy looking for the Italian father of her unborn child, who however refuses to recognize the pregnancy. Alyssa gives birth to a daughter who appears white, and the story revolves around her adult life and that of Alyssa who becomes the virtual caretaker of everyone around her. The story resonates with *The Help*, a novel by Kathryn Stockett that was adapted into a Hollywood film which has been shown on Italian television and popular among Italian viewers. *The Help* represents black women taking care of middle class white women, catering to their every need while caring only part time for their own families. The film diffuses in the 21st century European context the 19th and 20th century myth of the good-natured, black domestic servant, formerly the happy slave that became images of Aunt Jemima and Uncle Ben. In Italy domestic service is one of the few jobs allowed for in immigration legislation because there is a demand for domestic work.[14]

There is now also a pervasive image of Africans as by definition criminals, living in Italy without legal documents or illegitimately on Italian soil because they do not appear to have Italian blood ties. They are alleged to be in Italy to take jobs and social services to which they have no natural rights. Since the Berlusconi administration privatized Italian television in the 1990s, there has been even greater diffusion of American television images in which Black people are typically represented as criminals, augmenting the circulation of stereotypes and stigmas that become part of national common sense and anti-other structure of feeling.[15]

The Lega Nord, Italy's most prominent far-right, populist political party, has earned its reputation for promoting nativist discourse over the past several decades. The party influenced anti-immigration national legislation as part of a 1990s coalition with Prime Minister Silvio Berlusconi (Merrill 2011). The Lega Nord's most recent leader at the time of this writing, Matteo Salvini, whose motto is "give back Italy to the Italian people" with a focus on immigrants, called for preventing refugees and immigrants from landing on Italian shores by pushing them out to sea, and closing all mosques in Italy. However, the emergence of a pervasive anti-other structure of feeling over the past several decades is built upon profound internal prejudices between northern and southern Italy, and its own relationship to modernity and colonization. Public responsibility for fueling the intense anti-other feelings in Italy must also be shared with the political center and left. Beyond some symbolic gestures, the political left has at the very least tolerated official racist policies, doing very little to confront common mis-knowledge and 'ignorance' of Africa and people of African descent (Merrill 2013; Pugliese 2008).

Italian collective imaginaries of Africa and Africans are also fueled by popular political discourses. Populist political parties began to appear in Italy in the 1980s. The originally northern-based Lega Nord, a regionalist party that defines itself in cultural differentialist terms, has worked to stigmatize newcomers to Italian society, spreading false information and demagoguery about Africans and other immigrants for decades. An Italian student at the University of Turin, who is also a volunteer teacher and a political activist in the recently formed *Committee of Solidarity with Refugees and Migrants* (*Comitato di Solidarietà con Rifugiati e Migranti*), put it this way:

> The Lega made people *hate* black people. They don't distinguish between political and economic immigrants; it's just black people. They say, "We don't want these F*****g black people here." Everyone says this is for economic reasons, because there aren't enough jobs in Italy … blah blah blah … but the Lega says to the average voter that we should shoot the boats and send the blacks back.[16]

This young Italian activist was referring to the indisputable influence the Lega Nord has had over social policies and public perceptions of people of African descent even in the Piedmont region where the Italian communist party was born. In this region there is a culture of blue-collar work, trade unions, and an entrenched world of cooperatives. During the past two decades there has been growing influence of neoliberal philosophy and populism (see Ciafaloni 2011).

There are no Italian laws criminalizing discrimination on the basis of color or language,[17] and even when lead by center or center-left coalitions, the government has said or done very little when the Lega has made now countless degrading statements. For instance, in 2013 the Senate vice president Robert Calderoni compared Italy's first black minister, Cecile Kyenge, to an orangutan (Merrill 2015). Even in Reggio Emilia, situated in Italy's "reddest" (Italian Communist) region of Emilia Romagna and with one of the highest concentrations of immigrants in the country, the Italian Left has supported some intercultural initiatives, yet has not taken a leading role to ensure that people of African, North African, and other areas of descent are treated with dignity. Reggio Emilia shopkeepers frequently utter complaints about 'Africans' being in the country to use Italian social services without adding anything to a society they perceive as having already been established.[18] These are ideas deeply rooted in

European mythologies about places and peoples characterized as without histories until the arrival of European colonists.[19]

The Lega and its allies, sometimes including the political left, have inflamed fears and tensions about economic and social transformation by scapegoating immigrants (cf. Pred 1995). They have remade longstanding yet dormant ideas by disseminating a narrative that immigrants and refugees are in Italy "clandestinely" or illegally, are culturally backward and criminally dangerous to Italian identity.[20] Over the past decades the Lega local and national leadership have made enough damaging statements about immigrants for a book of key words, but their comments surrounding the appointment of Italy's first Black minister, Cecile Kyenge have had considerable impact on people of African descent.

In 2013, Kyenge's appointment could have been interpreted as a point of pride and hope among Italians of African descent. Yet her abusive treatment is instead at the forefront of many minds. A lowered shaking head is accompanied with the refrain, "And do you know what they did to Kyenge? What they said about her?" In fact, Italy's Interior Minister, influential members of parliament, elected politicians, and local city council members continually reminded Kyenge and the public of her body and skin color. As Frantz Fanon theorized she was, "overdetermined from without," meaning that she was perceived and classified according to a fixed "epidermal racial schema," signifying nonbeing.

As a Cabinet Minister, Kyenge's blackness and her gender were employed to diminish her as racialized and a woman. She was referred to by elected political figures as belonging "in the house," and needing to be raped so that she might understand the rape of white women by Black men. Kyenge's appointment in a position of influence seemed to threaten the overwhelming myth that Black women are passive, oppressed by men, lacking agency, subjecthood, and intellect. The dominant stereotypes that Maria Viarengo described for the colonial period remain. As suggested in an openDemocracy article, "Kyenge evokes the ghosts in a social and cultural context that has never come to terms with its own colonial past, and where women are struggling with persistent patriarchy" (Meret, Della Corte and Sangiuliano 2013).

How do these growing predispositions towards African Italians translate into a cultural common sense expressed in tacit and non-so tacit feelings and beliefs as people go about their everyday lives in public spaces? How is race made through everyday movements and encounters that Erving Goffman referred to as 'mixed contacts' or daily exchanges between people socially categorized as "normals" and the racially stigmatized with bodily traits that are perceived as discrediting? How are symbolic boundaries produced as black people are 'put in their place' (Merrill 2006; Puwar 2004)? Othering is insinuated in for the most part subtle yet powerful unarchived prejudices in Western racial ontologies and part of what Antonio Gramsci referred to as cultural common sense.[21] These taken-for-granted practices and the knowledge that guides them generate the pervasive everyday violence of microaggression through which hierarchical differences are manufactured.

Not So Trifling

But you must smile through your tears…

Martin Luther King Jr.

To consider knowledge expressed non-verbally is not an easy undertaking in ethnographic work, which generally relies on discursive and visual evidence collected through interviews, surveys, or observations believed to resemble social facts.[22] Nevertheless, we all notice, participate in, and navigate our lives through non-verbal expressions in social encounters. We sense whether someone is in the mood to talk, if they are happy, excited, sad, distracted, angry, confused, or distant. We perceive how other people feel and think through direct observations of their 'body language,' including facial expressions, posture, hand and other gestures. We describe virtual strangers as emotionally 'cold' or 'warm,' based in part on our perceptions of the person's countenance and mannerisms. We read the feelings and thoughts of others as if through a sixth sense, or a synthesis of all our other senses – sight, scent, sound, touch, and taste – that opens us to subtle forms of knowledge, as for instance when we inadvertently walk into a private conversation and someone merely has to ignore and turn a shoulder inward as if to say "you're in the wrong place" – to convey that we do not belong. Or when a teenager in an expensive department store like Saks Fifth Avenue is 'looked at' by the woman at the counter who nonverbally conveys her question, 'What are you doing here? You can't afford anything here, so go away.' Or, "Are you here to try to steal something?' When we enter a restaurant and are greeted by the waiter with a friendly smile and led to a centrally located table, we 'know' we are welcome there. We acquire these and thousands of other unspoken messages without even hearing or being able to record them in a notebook or on a digital recorder. Yet we also believe that what we feel is real, sensing what we are being 'told' non-verbally through bodily gestures, facial expressions, and 'vibes.' These tacit expressions of thought-emotion frequently express gut feelings and sensations that are triggered by cultural mores, ways of thinking, and preconceptions.

In order to make sense of how race works phenomenologically one must pay attention to non-verbal as well as verbal modalities of communication. My focus is on people of African ancestry socially perceived as nonwhite who, as Erving Goffman suggested, are structurally 'stigmatized' as racially different from whitened Italians[23] in a process of ascribing racial identities to people or groups that don't necessarily identify as such for the purpose of dominating them. This stigmatization operates through the application of social categories that include attributes members of each social category believes ordinary and natural (see Fanon 2008). Contemporary critical social phenomenologists like Michael Jackson suggest that in our world where entire populations are written off as expendable, inequality is determined 'horizontally' in the everyday intersubjective expression of prejudices, condescension, and discriminatory gestures that people use to stigmatize and denigrate others. These expressions construct or reinforce the social and material boundaries that separate those deemed to have social value from people ostracized as illegitimately present (Jackson 2012). As Pierre Bourdieu suggested with his concept of habitus, we continually struggle over the 'sense of the social world,' its meanings and orientation, its present and its future (Bourdieu 1977). This is a process of producing the world through praxis, or struggle for place in a world where our being is mutable and unstable and where it is an unremitting task for us to make sense of and if possible control the forces that shape our destiny (Jackson 2012; see Desjarlais and Throop 2011).

By focusing on daily forms of 'unarchived prejudices' (Pandey 2013) and expressions of microaggression, I am not suggesting that *all* social contacts and encounters between people with racialized differences are symbolically violent. Everyday racist aggressions are pervasive and insidious, even in Italy – a place known for its friendly and welcoming people. And symbolic violence is also expressed in different and intersecting ways toward women, the disabled, religious minorities, and others. Identifying and understanding the source of these operationalized attitudes as part of the structural formation of modern social life is crucial for an understanding of the workings of race in the West, and emergent racial segregation in Italy.

Where one is in a variety of intersubjective encounters in public spaces such as public transportation, cafes, restaurants, markets, streets, shops, groceries, department stores, and other spaces, people of African descent are frequently treated as out of place interlopers, or as not even present. Acts of distancing and rejection are expressed directly and verbally, but even more commonly though tacit unspoken signals. They are part of the daily experience of most people of visibly identified African descent, with the exception of very young children. How are these everyday prejudices conveyed by recognized Italians or people who are seen as belonging in Italy, and how do people who are stigmatized respond? These are practices of objectification, humiliation, and discrimination that do not take the form of physical torture, yet torture socially and psychologically they do.

Racial abuse is common and may also be accompanied by words, gestures, and sometimes physical violence. When a petite woman who often wears long colorful African designed pagnes and t-shirts, and has lived in Italy for 26 years, was asked about her treatment by recognized Italians she responded, "They are hostile. And I have the scars to prove it." She then described her experiences walking in a public market in Turin. She was repeatedly shouted at by an Italian man and woman, "Go back to your own country!" This woman being yelled at is from a prominent journalist family critical of the Kenyan administration, and her parents are themselves from two different ethnic groups, Kikuyu and Luo. She became pregnant as a teenager, and although she did not complete her secondary education is self-educated, especially about African culture, art, and history. Her move to Italy was motivated by her interest in Italian culture, unemployment, and patriarchy in Kenya. In Turin she enrolled her daughter in an elite grade school. Her daughter earned a university education, is now married and living in Finland with her family. These types of humiliating experience have become a routine experience of direct verbal assault that African immigrants encounter while within earshot, but assaults not directed towards the target in a way that would allow them an opportunity to respond. As Pape Diaw, leader of a Senegalese association in Florence, Tuscany described, "You hear comments on the bus, in the markets, in schools."[24] Such experiences of daily symbolic violence risk demoralizing the targets, damaging embodied dispositions and perceptions of the world (Jackson 2002).

Another example is derived from my personal experience while walking down a narrow street on a Sunday afternoon in January 2014 in the small town of Reggio Emilia in Emilia Romagna with my partner, an American of African descent. An elderly gentleman riding a bicycle yelled something to us like "Schifo di barca," or "go back to that disgusting boat," an apparent reference to the boats of asylum seekers from Africa in the Southern Mediterranean, and the people on these boats.

A routine form of verbal distancing and humiliation can be confused with lack of knowledge, or as many people of African descent in Italy describe, "ignorance."[25] Nevertheless, and as activists and intercultural leaders argue, if one refuses the common refrain that rationalizes stigmatization in Italy, one must conclude that the patterns of interaction include a refusal to "recognize" as Frantz Fanon argued, those who have in practice become linguistic and cultural insiders as belonging in the Italian polity.[26] An example frequently offered is the comment regularly made to a person who appears nonwhite yet speaks Italian with considerable fluency: "Where are you from? You speak Italian really well. " And the person who may in fact speak Italian better than many Italians if they have had formal training beyond high school and who may also speak a local dialect will respond, "Yes, I am ITALIAN!" And then the next response is often, "Oh, but where are you *really* from?"

In March 2014, a group of high school students attended a discussion in Bologna at the Regional Legislative Assembly building during the annual "Spring without Racism" (Primavera senza Razzismo) week of programming with local schools organized by the intercultural center *Mondinsieme* of Reggio Emilia. The audience, including some political representatives and members of *Mondinsieme*, first viewed a film, "Conversations on the Topic" (Conversazioni sul Tema), in which a group of youth of diverse ethnic origins sat around a table discussing issues of identity, citizenship, work, and education. One of the major points of discussion was that they felt pressured to have a single and fixed identity, and rejected as "real" members of Italian culture and society. The students in the audience were born in Italy or had spent the greater part of their lives in the country. During a brief discussion that followed the film screening a young woman in an aching tone spoke about how she and her friends felt Italian, but were not socially recognized as Italian. She described Italy as "molto chiuso," or "very closed," where people continually convey the message that because her parents were not born in Italy, she was not truly Italian. Other students voiced the feeling that they were placed in an identity suspended between countries, even though they knew little if anything about their presumed countries of origin. In a pleading and frustrated voice, a young woman whose parents were from the Ivory Coast said, "I didn't choose to come here. My mother brought me when I was a child. And yet now, I feel like I don't have a country because I don't know my own country and here they don't accept me as Italian." A local regional councilman who seemed not to quite grasp the gist of their suffering responded by assuring her and the other young people that Italy was much more flexible now, "It's better than many other countries." He tried to offer encouragement by describing how one could talk across differences of religion and culture and race to discover common interests such as a sport or music and that this way, "Hand in hand, we all are becoming more complex, and finding more things that we have in common." The councilman's words suggested that he conceived identities as fixed and essentially different, in contrast with the more complex identities the students, who did not appear buoyed by his words, sought to describe. A woman from *Mondinsieme* in her early 30s whose parents are from Eritrea and who was herself born in Italy then stood up and affirmed the student's experiences of being "classified" and "essentialized" as other because they had not been Italian for 1000 years.

Birth rates among people of non–Italian ancestry are three times higher than among recognized Italians, and this is observable in public spaces in Reggio Emilia, Bologna, Milan, Turin, Florence, and Rome where parents push their children in carriages, carry them on their backs, or walk with them hand in hand. The growing social complexity of Italian society can be observed in grade school classes on field trips in public sites where some 20–30% are children of color. It is also striking that among groups of teenage youth who walk together and gather in piazzas especially on weekend evenings in Reggio Emilia, there is frequently a person of color, usually of African descent. This is something that was not visible in Italy even a decade earlier, and it demonstrates that among some youth there is a growing sense of membership.

Nevertheless, my interviews indicate that while in mixed company with a group of friends these youth may experience a sense of belonging as Italian, when not among their friends they are frequently received as outsiders to Italian society. Moreover, the emergent pattern is that few youth of African origin attend Italian universities, because most are tracked into professional or vocational high schools instead of the classical and scientific high schools that feed into the universities. Parents born in countries such as Nigeria, Ghana, and Albania have told me that often, teachers and administrators do not regard their children as smart and do not encourage them to do well in school. They are instead through neglect, mischaracterization, and criticism given the message that they are not capable of being permanent members of Italian society (cf Keaton 2006). When asked how his children were doing, a man of Nigerian origin who has lived and worked in Italy for 15 years and has three young children in Italian schools responded:

> Racism is everywhere but it's higher here because of the system. When Italians see you they think you're here to take their job so as a foreigner you're always regarded as an inferior person and they think you're here because you don't have any food in your country and your country is poor and that's why you're here. You don't have benefits here unless you're a citizen. For the children it's the same. They are always a foreigner. They are born here but not a citizen so they treat the children the same as the parent (sic).

The issue of holding legal citizenship is extremely significant, and the struggle continues.[27] However, it must be noted that people of African ancestry with Italian citizenship are also routinely perceived as permanent cultural outsiders (see Ong 1996). The sense that Africans cannot possibly be Italian and are therefore socially peripheral at best is experienced regularly.

Phyllis, a woman of Rwandan-Tanzanian origin who works with an organization that places refugees from 18–25 years of age with Italian, Moroccan, Somalian and other families for a year on the model of cultural exchange, spoke with me.[28] Phyllis and Giovanna, who is Somali-Italian, shared their frequent experiences. Italians constantly express amazement at their ability to speak Italian and don't hesitate to 'put them in their place' when commenting on this. Giovanna was given her name while attending a Catholic school in Mogadishu. She has been married to an orthodontist of native Italian origin for 40 years and received Italian citizenship long before her marriage. She refuses to think of herself as "Italian," because people don't treat her or other people with African origins as if they really belong here. Giovanna speaks impeccable Italian and in terms of monetary privilege relative to most of Italian society lives an upper class life style; nevertheless when not with her White Italian husband, she is frequently assumed to be a domestic servant.

That the distancing behavior toward people classified as non-Italian does not distinguish by level of education or material wealth is also demonstrated in the manner in which white Italians regularly direct conversations to persons they perceive as socially of their tribe, giving them eye contact and physically gesturing toward them when people of African descent are also present. This happens even when the White person is a woman, for racialization overwhelms the diminishment of women.[29] A medical doctor of Nigerian origin who lives in Reggio Emilia told the story of an Italian teacher friend who had invited her to dinner at the home of another doctor, and during the several hour visit, he never looked at her while speaking. This is a form of humiliation that White people tend not to see. When the medical doctor of Nigerian origin told her Italian teacher friend about the experience, the friend was astonished because she hadn't been cognizant of any of it. Yet to the woman of Nigerian origin it was as if her male colleague and recognized Italian had not even acknowledged that she existed.

Everyday Geography of Racialized Contacts

In the last chapter I referred to the growing social and cultural diversity in Italian public places, notably in outdoor markets. On market days in Reggio Emilia, Senegalese men walk the area selling books about African cuisine and culture to market-goers. In and around the area there is a certain observable level of comfort with social differences and the women of African descent (including North African) appear to feel relatively at ease, most notably those who are not alone. This can be explained in part by the culture of these mixed markets, spaces in the open and without walls where the practice is to bring a variety of goods often from afar to sell to strangers. Women and men do not by contrast sell goods in or frequent the Saturday "farmer's market" in one of Reggio's piazzas because that is a market for locally produced small batch goods. In the large mixed markets there is very little if any intimate social contact even though it is common to barter over prices.

In Italian markets most stalls operated by people of African, Chinese, or South Asian descent sell non-descript or Italian articles such as housewares, leather purses, or sunglasses. It is uncommon to see items made by Africans being sold in the formal stalls. The exception is in places like the weekend 'Balon' market in Turin, on the peripheries of the largest of the city's markets in Porta Palazzo where 'ethnic' pieces are sold on weekends, concentrated in one zone. In other instances African made items such as art objects are sold along the retail avenues, laid out on cloth. Even among street vendors who have re-appeared in recent years after a period of repression and when many were able to secure formal jobs, most sell items manufactured in Europe. Thus, people of African descent are not seen to threaten the Italian commodity market by offering alternative goods, and even when they do, these tend to be perceived by Italians as exotic curiosities or enhancements to a well-established market system of trade.

The element of moral sympathy for people of African descent who are believed to pursue entry into Europe in order to protect themselves and their families from war or poverty is habitually expressed in Italy with a kind of paternalism linked with curiosity about 'exotic' African customs, and hypersexualized images of African women. The expression "Poveri disgraziati" or poor wretches that is commonly used to describe African immigrants and refugees carries in the weight of old tropes in which people of African ancestry are characterized as child-like, dependent, lacking a social and political consciousness. Many of my interlocutors report that Italian society is interested in no more than seeing Africans perform exotic dances, not in really learning about how they think and how they enhance an Italian social environment. This paternalism mingled with exoticization represents a form of symbolic violence toward the racially stigmatized. It appears for example in the practice among many not-so-young recognized Italians of speaking loudly to people of African descent as if talking with some one with learning disabilities or to a child. Goffman describes how people stigmatized with disabilities such as blindness are treated as if they were also deaf and crippled, and that people classified as 'normal' or without any social stigma are not quite human (Goffman 1986). Well-meaning individuals frequently approach racially stigmatized people from former European colonies by offering a special treatment normally reserved for young and lost children for whom knowledge must be reduced to bare bones in order to be comprehended.

Racial aggression also takes place in the popular privately owned public establishments such as café/pasticcerias, restaurants, and specialty shops. Owners, barristas, waiters/waitresses, and customers deploy indirect forms of communication to discourage people of African descent from entering. In Italy where good manners are important and part of the "bella figura" or making a good impression, it is customary to greet customers who enter a café with a friendly hello or "Buon giorno/Buona sera," a warm "thank you" or "grazie" along with a well wish and "arrivederci" or see you again upon exit. Italians tend to stop in bar/café and restaurants at least once if not several times per day.

It is however unusual to see a customer of African descent in a bar/cafe, restaurant, or specialty shop. One shop owner in Reggio Emilia where 'stranieri/e' originate from over a hundred different countries, a woman of Brazilian origin who is light complexioned, commented on this absence by complaining that a "Negro" had never entered her shop or any of the other shops on the street. When asked if she and her fellow merchants wished that Africans would frequent their businesses, she replied, "No. I don't think so. The people here don't like the Negroes." And I have observed on numerous occasions and have heard from informants about the experience that one is being censored when entering such places, not wanted there, erased before birth, regularly communicated in a variety of tacit ways. There is a common refusal to greet the person of African ancestry with a courteous hello and to neglect all the other mannerisms one would normally deploy to protect one's 'bella figura,' which is discarded because the potential customer is not perceived as a member of the existing social order and his or her perceptions don't count.

Another common microaggression among merchants willing to do business with people of African descent is to address them with the informal and disrespectful or "Tu" form, and to say "Ciao" if anything at all as the form of greeting.[30] The informal form of address is in Italy usually employed by adults when addressing *social subordinates*, and children. Italians know that to use this informal form is to implicitly yet also quite intentionally slight and treat the person as second class or worse. In upscale cafes and restaurants in particular, a method of turning people away is to serve them slowly and with a sense of annoyance, and to serve them less coffee than would normally be given a customer. It is as if the racially stigmatized were being punished for being in a place they are perceived as socially not belonging. And this is actually very out of keeping with Italian cultural preoccupations with retaining a "bella figura" in order never to be humiliated for socially inappropriate or rude behavior.

In Turin, Reggio Emilia, and Bologna I observed people of African descent walking into a café, bread store, restaurant, or any clothing, shoe, or specialty shop and the owners and/or service employees conveying bodily, through a rigid countenance and carriage, that they are not wanted there. In one restaurant in central Turin where I wished to enjoy lunch with two people of African ancestry, the waiters served our table after several other tables of Italians who had entered the restaurant behind us. When we complained about this poor service and treatment, we were given weak apologies and the service remained poor. We had to ask for water and bread while other tables had been served these standard items. A bag of bread was finally handed to us that included a half-eaten piece.

These and other relatively subtle expressions of hostility include a 'look' of disapproval and disdain, a refusal to return a greeting, an angry glare on the street, and even being pushed aside while walking in order to make room for a *recognized Italian*. Neighbors frequently 'look at' people of African descent with an angry demeanor, while service employees at department stores handle the merchandise one purchases roughly, shop owners refuse to offer help, and waiters provide aloof and or perfunctory services (see Puwar 2004). One wonders what they might have done to one's food.

A 60-something Italian teacher described an all too frequent exchange. This happened when she was seated in a café she regularly frequents that is owned by a woman of Southern Italian origin. While enjoying her coffee, a "uomo di colore" (man of color) entered the establishment and as she described:

> He was very well mannered (making flowing hand gestures toward her chest as if to suggest that he stood straight and was cleanly dressed). He came into the store and he spoke very well and he was very polite and he didn't obtrude or he wasn't loud or anything. And you could just sense, without words or anything, that the owner of the café was not happy that he had come into the place. That she didn't want him there. She didn't tell him to leave or anything, but you could just sense that she didn't like that he had entered her café. And so then, this very well mannered man went up to the woman, who is the owner of the café, and very politely said that they were organizing a Latin American cultural program and he wondered if she'd be willing to buy some tickets to the event. And he handed her a ticket, laying it on the counter. And she said to him very brusquely, "No. I'm not interested." She said this even with what I would have to describe as a bit of hostility. And I sat there, not saying a word because I wanted to be very polite. And I just watched. And then after he left, she took it upon herself to talk to me. And tell me her feelings. And with extreme vulgarity she began to complain, "I don't know what these Latinos or these Africans want from me. I never

give them anything. I don't know why they're here. We can't even find jobs for our own." And with a lot of vulgarity about the Africans that I don't want to repeat she went on about this. And it really bothered me because I note from her accent that this woman is herself from Southern Italy. And so finally I said to her, because I just couldn't handle this any more, or her assumption that I was going to be a customer who would of course as an Italian agree with her. I said to her, "Signora, when I was young in Reggio the Reggiani did not want Southern Italians here. They didn't want them entering their shops. They didn't want them living in their neighborhoods or getting work here. They wanted them to go back to the South." And then I got up and walked out.

My interlocutor reported her observation of the racial stigmatization and hostility expressed by a recognized Italian towards a person of color because she knew I was interested in African experiences in Italy. She aligns herself with the Italian political left and doesn't approve of the poor treatment of African or other "*stranieri*" (strangers) in Italy. Although not a member of a political organization that opposes intolerance or promotes integration, she takes an active role by accepting the transformation of Italian culture and treating "stranieri" with respect and in some cases helping individuals. Trained in psychology, her philosophy is to treat others with dignity, and relate to every person as a distinct individual. This recognized Italian expresses considerable fidelity to her Reggiana and Italian identity, frequently describing Italian towns, architecture, historical figures, actors, journalists, and writers with loving pride. She has not taken any interest in African cultures, and expresses some of the popular view that there aren't enough jobs for Italians, especially youth, so these newcomers really should not be living in Italy. However, although she has had little actual exposure to people of color, she makes a conscious effort to be open and flexible in her encounters with immigrants and African Italians.

This is not an unusual position or philosophy among recognized Italians, and important to point out in my discussion of everyday symbolic violence. Even when there is racial stigmatization of a certain kind, based on inherited negative stereotypes and absence of knowledge, some Italians do not begrudge people of color the right to live in Italy. A few, although far less than one would wish to see, go out of their way to be kind and helpful to people of color – offering a warm smile, relatively respectful service, and even a gesture such as paying for his or her coffee as a way of expressing solidarity and human empathy.

The pervasive anti-black and anti-immigrant structure of feeling that has been slowly sedimenting in Italian society is not intrinsic to Italian culture. To the contrary, Italian culture teaches sociality of the kind that I have on occasion heard compared to African sociality: that is, the expectation that one must treat strangers with dignity and even welcome them as potential members of one's inner world. Here I suggest that many West African forms of sociality are based on very different systems of kinship relations and have tended to be much more accepting and welcoming of 'strangers' than in European cultures. However, there is in Italian culture a practice of gathering under one roof, so to speak, of collective and cooperative sociality for common purposes and for building solidarities among people at the local scale which is also practiced in many African cultures (Harney and Moten 2013).

The structure of anti-other feeling, evocative of anti-southern sentiments and practices of a previous era, is dangerous to the very fabric of Italian society. Poverty and unemployment rates in Southern Italy are three to five times what they are in the North, and the risk and writing on the wall here is that black spaces will develop in concentrated forms, that is segregated 'ghettoes' of poverty and hopelessness where people of color will become trapped for generations as in France, the UK, Sweden, Germany, other parts of Europe, and the US.

What effects are normalized expressions of hostility having on African Italians and more recently arrivals? In *Existential Anthropology*, Michael Jackson (2005) suggests that we produce and transform the world in daily practices. He argues that when one is socially erased by racist humiliation or lack of recognition they may feel demoralized and lose some self-confidence. Inequality and social distinctions produce racialization. People are ostracized or ignored, and these acts build or reinforce boundaries separating from and rendering many social groups expendable. To do this is to degrade the entire society by rejecting the human right to basic dignity. Not all violations of human rights involve physical harm. In situations such as these, a person's humanity is violated, for their status as a social subject is reduced or erased to that of an object or nonentity without or at best on the margins of active social relation to others.

Finally, it is also the case that individual whites who through proximity to Blackness of various kinds become what France Winddance Twine terms "racially literate," that is those who have come to be understand and experience stigma and "rebound racism." They are treated as social inferiors or "race traitors," especially in public social contacts (Twine 2011). Twine has demonstrated that white working-class and middle-class women in England who establish families with African Caribbean men and give birth to children from interracial relationships are frequently cast "honorary Blacks." In Italy where intermarriages are not unknown and not gendered in that both white men and white women occasionally marry people of African descent, the white female partner whose status is already low relative to men is in particular stigmatized. Twine argues that in England some of these white mothers gain racial literacy and become important anti-racist allies.

Black spaces are in this context the unthought experiences, situated practices of Blackness in spaces of 'mixed contacts' that are part of everyday common sense, expressed through tacit, more or less subtle verbal and non-verbal gestures whose underlying intent is to control the movements of people socially identified as having African descent. In the process, these encounters produce social and material distance between white and nonwhite, and reduce the life chances of post-colonial people in Italy. Black spaces are also substantive spaces of experience, of "body-mind-world" and as such, dialectical spaces of conflicting perspectives and positions: on the one hand that of the dominant modern Western subject informed by an ontology of superiority and an inability to be affected by 'others' in any more than the voyeuristic ways; and on the other hand that of the postcolonial African subject who manages to survive and create, affect and influence the West even when as is often the case this is not recognized. Italians, as part of the West and a now globally racialized terrain, uncritically inherit this ontology, rendering it a culture much colder, more parochial, insulated, less flexible, and even cruel in everyday encounters and consent to symbolic and actual violence. The making of Black spaces is thus a complex process that involves engagement with social death and its rebirth.

Empowerment in the Face of Social Erasure

How does one respond to such systematic efforts to condemn one to social erasure or at best at the spatial margins to the dominant social order? The question of how people in the African diaspora manage to live with dignity and pride and create social life in the face of anti-blackness has preoccupied activists, writers, and scholars of African studies for centuries, from Olaudah Equiano and Harriet Jacobs to W.E.B. Du Bois and Anna Julia Cooper, to Frantz Fanon and C.L.R. James, James Baldwin, Audre Lorde, bell hooks, and a wealth of rich contemporary scholar and artists. The kind of social and political subjectivities one develops while living in a world in which blackness is perceived as by definition "a problem," where one is cast as second class and treated as such, is of paramount importance to any understanding of Black experience in the modern world. In *The Bluest Eye*, Toni Morrison (1993) explored the interaction between the social and personal feelings of shame one experiences when treated without human regard or respect, and the way one's sense of self can become fixated on removing the stigma that one's body has been assigned and internalized. Everyone knows what it means to expect to be respected as a human being, and everyone wishes to avoid any experience of being scorned or debased.

There is also the question of what purpose the stigmatization fulfills in any given social order. Social classifications that assign meanings and roles to social groups and inform perceptions of what is 'normal' or 'untouchable' because marked with an intrinsic pathology are not really aimed at individuals or persons, although they are often certainly experienced as if they were. As Erving Goffman (1986) has argued, people assigned as normal or stigmatized are not persons, but rather perspectives generated in social situations during mixed encounters where roles interact. The stigmatization of Blackness and the denied prejudices and expressions of symbolic violence it inflicts in the everyday are the architecture of a technology that works to erase the presence and experiences of certain perceived racialized, ethnic, and religious groups from various spaces of competition. It is common sense that when one is classified as a subordinate and permanent outsider, one will be easily discriminated against while a student, when applying for work, housing, or receiving health care (Twine and Gardener 2013). And when work is secured, the forms of employment will generally (based on this cultural logic) be among the dirtiest, most dangerous, and most precarious that serve the interests of persons believed naturally entitled to their superior social position. So there is an economic or market logic underlying anti-blackness that is intertwined with the racial ontology that has positioned the perceived power to affect others as paramount to the White of European descent, or the 'transparent I.'

Although people gain a sense of their own identity through various intimate and public social experiences, skin color as a symbol that conveys social information has distinctive and fluid meanings among diverse social groups.[31] Even though people build images of themselves from the materials they're given to convey personal and social identities, they also exercise certain freedoms in defining their selves. bell hooks has deployed the spatial term 'margins' to describe the position of Black American women in professional settings dominated by Whiteness in a generative instead of static sense of the margins. The margins are Black spaces of past and present experiences of self-making dialogue and converge, where collective memories become the foundations of alternative forms of critical knowledge, forms of social solidarity, and productive opposition to power (hooks 1992). As Fred Moten suggests, present and historical practices among enslaved, colonized, and now stigmatized as criminal are a Blackness that has turned away from social rejection and negation by the 'transparent I,' focusing energies on creating ways to survive and thrive collectively (Harney and Moten 2013).

A number of my interlocutors of African origins have suggested that Italians fear that if they give people of African descent the opportunity to speak in public symposiums about immigration or Africa, discussions from which they are routinely *talked about* but not invited to participate, Italians will be shown to know less than people of African descent. The critical point is that there is a perhaps tacit or unconscious fright that if nonwhite Italians are really treated equally to White Italians, Italians will lose their monopoly on symbolic and material power (Ahmed 2012). In other words, nonwhites would openly and freely 'affect' White Italians and the global racial hierarchy would be broken. There are also frequent related comments about how Italian parents worry that African Italian school children are bright and may even learn their materials more rapidly than their own children. This sort of consciousness of whiteness as systemic can help shield people of African descent from interiorizing the many slights and forms of symbolic aggression they experience in everyday encounters.

There are a variety of responses to experiences of violence, social erasure, and social marginalization in Italy, including diverse productive and creative expressions. A pan-African Black consciousness across ethnic, linguistic, and religious differences among people from vastly diverse places in Africa is emerging. While collective expressions tend to be focused on the needs of people from specific countries such as Somalia, Burkina Faso, or Senegal who maintain transnational ties and allegiances, regional diasporic solidarities across international borders, for instance of people from the horn of Africa (Ethiopia, Eritrea, Somalia, and Sudan), Anglophone areas in West Africa (Nigeria and Ghana), or among practicing Muslims from West and North Africa are appearing with greater frequency and intensity. Among the youth of the "*seconda generazione*," diasporic collectives are even more transnational and intercultural; they may include people with parental ties all over the African continent. These various groups in ethnic and inter-ethnic associations, recreational or entrepreneurial cooperatives, often express implicitly or explicitly the assertion of one's right to live in Italy and be accorded human and or full citizenship rights. Expressed in the collectives are everyday "moments of being" in Black life, strivings and resilience (Jackson 2002). For example, the Association of Burkina Faso, "Abreer", in Reggio Emilia proposed a project to the municipal government and was has been given a plot of land on the outskirts of town where they grow vegetables and spices, using bio-dynamic agricultural technologies. The Association has since used a larger plot of land to produce a greater abundance and variety of products for the local community. Members of Abreer were trained in the latest agricultural technologies at the Italian Forestry School, and have generated a detailed plan to build an agricultural business in Burkina Faso, for which they have been given land that would produce for local consumption in a region of the Sahel with a scarcity of nourishing food production. Abreer is the first Burkinabe association in Reggio and comprised of older members, which also has an offshoot association of younger people (under 30) of Burkinabe origin called UGIORE (Unione Giovane di Reggio Emilia) that has a soccer team and generates dance and theatrical performances in order to advance positive images of their culture. Like Abreer, UGIORE members are active in politics in Burkina Faso and seek greater representation of the diaspora in Italy. A member of UGIORE in his 20s told me they were working to be accepted and more visible members of the local Italian world. When he first arrived, 13 years earlier, "At first they (Italians) would curse and spit at us because of our skin color. They called us 'Black' and told us to go away. But now they are better, more accepting of us. Little by little." Martin Luther King and his non-violent protests for civil rights, he added, inspired him and his cohort. "We are struggling or our rights here and to be accepted because at this point we are in fact ourselves, Italian. But there need to be more Africans and people like us visible in public places, in stores and banks, and so on." In the face of obstacles to their existence in Italy, members of both associations seem to be aware of their power and its limits, and to emphasize 'we' instead of 'I.'

People of African descent are claiming their right to belong, expressing in word and deed, "We're here," and by this very act enacting Black sociality in the face of social erasure. Visible on bicycles and foot, alone and with friends or family members, in multiracial groups or not they are an active presence in Reggio Emilia and in other Italian cities. However, their comfort level is palpably low in almost all observed instances of mixed contact. A woman of Eritrean origin, who has lived in Italy for 40 years, secured a good job at an elderly home, and retired with a pension, claims that Italians are just "ignorant." She knows that many Italians simply do not want Africans in the country. The sense of not belonging registers in one's body and mind, whether or not one is able or permitted to give voice to these experiences. People respond to daily rejection and offense in a number of different ways.

People who are ostracized usually define themselves as no different from other human beings who routinely conceive them as essentially different and from whom a distance needs to be vigilantly maintained (Goffman 1986). Although people of African origins or ancestry have been interconnected with Europe in an accelerating manner for hundreds of years, most living in Italy today date their genealogical relations at one or at most two generations. So while they may have been influenced by anti-colonial politics in their countries of origin, by their parents and grandparents, experiences of anti-blackness are relatively new to them.[32] When regularly vulnerable to racist humiliation or erasure, they make their way out of this dilemma in a number of ways. In Italy it is common among people of African descent to simply blink and keep going as if the offense were not happening, to avoid openly responding to the racist aggression. I am told that this is because by taking "the high road" one retains a sense of dignity and avoids the pain of further acknowledging the slights. Open confrontation would place one in the position of trying to teach the recognized Italian that he or she is racist – a job many consider far too great and perhaps impossible. So one frequently simply and often stoically walks away, and if feasible avoids further encounters in that place. Some people invest considerable energy in ignoring the hostility and even cooperating with recognized Italians, as if the differences between them were irrelevant.

A variation on this happens when for instance one is in a restaurant and receives poor services. When with my two lunch mates of African descent we were not served while recognized Italians who preceded us were, one of them brought this to the attention of the waiter who apologized, but did not alter his behavior. Later when our table was not given bread, I asked the waiter to bring some and he gave us a bag that included a half-eaten piece. My companions, both highly accustomed to this treatment even though it is always painful, expressed disgust about the event. Giovanna, who speaks impeccable Italian, told the restaurant owner about this in a direct but half-joking way, using local idioms. When the owner realized she was in effect an 'insider' who was shaming his poor public presentation, he apologized and brought us a token chocolate by way of apology.

The most common response to such daily insults is to avoid and voluntarily withhold oneself whenever possible from contacts in which one is likely to experience discomfort or humiliation. People of African descent seldom enter café/pasticcerie, bread stores, small shops, or restaurants. They tend rather to shop in the open markets or large grocery stores. Many remain in small groups with co-nationals, either familial or social or both, and participate in church or mosque sponsored activities. Some gain sustenance from these collective supports where they identify with others who are also stigmatized in Italy yet agree to strengthen each other through mutual cooperation and support. In these small groups one can create protective circles.

It is very difficult or even impossible to avoid micro-aggressions and overt racism when one resides, works, shops, and travels in close proximity with White Italians. African Italians and more recent arrivals express the feeling that they are constantly being observed, and this can create considerable anxiety. In such situations, many feel they must perform in an unobtrusive, un-self conscious manner even as they know they are being scrutinized to an even greater extent than native Italians scrutinize each other. Not knowing how recognized Italians will receive them, it is very challenging not to be conscious of the impression one is making on others. Many African Italians feel they must behave in an exemplary fashion in order to in effect prove themselves worthy of being treated with dignity and respect. Others, as I have suggested, try instead to avoid stressful social contacts and flee to safe spaces within their own ethnic, religious and peer groups or neighborhood pockets. For instance, on any given day during the mid-day siesta hours there are twenty to thirty people of African descent, primarily exclusively male, standing and sitting in the piazza in a neighborhood near the Reggio Emilia train station.

There is a certain degree of fluidity and slippage in relations between people perceived as outsiders or newcomers and recognized Italians. An African Italian member of an intercultural organization encouraged unemployed African Italian youth to extend themselves into the Italian world as volunteers. As she put it "Racism is stupidity. People will judge you on your skin color until they become familiar with you and then they'll treat you like a human being. That's how it works." Scholars have adopted the term "exceptionalism" to explain this practice where the "transparent I" is able to accept as human individual members of denigrated groups especially when they are not asked to accept more than one or a few (Gordon 2000). When for instance a Black person or family moves into an apartment complex or neighborhood, the neighbors may initially express hostility by withholding everyday courtesies. However in time and with growing familiarity, the Black family may come to be seen as "alright," different from others in their ostracized group. Unfortunately, this does not transfer to fundamental transformations in racial structure, and the exceptional perceptions do not diffuse and render less potent systemic practices of erasure. It can be argued that treating some individuals as acceptable exceptions to social norms only further fuels anti-blackness by suggesting that some people can *earn* the right to be regarded as (white) human beings. They must only conform fully to dominant social expectations either by acting as 'model immigrants' or by performing the role of the seemingly fully assimilated person who remains, in spite of this, a permanent outsider as member of the stigmatized group even if he or she may be accorded the status of honorary White person.

Black spaces are not unambiguous, nor are they binary. Another way that people of African descent respond to expressions of repulsion and rejection by white Italians is to internalize to a certain extent the dominant idea that Black people who do not appear to assimilate to Italian social norms are outside of modernity, and identify themselves with ethnic enclaves that they see as exceptional. There is in this strain of thinking a tendency to adopt notions of fixed national and ethnic differences, and their attendant stereotypes. A woman who hails from Brazil, a country that has promoted the practices both of cultural and phenotypical 'whitening' and also of multiculturalism describes her own community as "Acting very correctly in Italy; never stealing anything or doing anything wrong. And they have learned Italian culture." She adds that the immigrant community from Cape Verde is also above reproach, whereas, "The Senegalese and Ghanaians are by comparison not to be trusted."

There are other divisions, for instance through the adoption of insular and fixed notions of African-based ethnic community that protects itself against a hostile outside by rejecting all but the necessary contacts with White people. The exclusionary ethno-nationalist beliefs of Italians are turned inward toward the community, and there is a certain amount of border policing. Inter-racial couples seen walking in public places, for instance, are sometimes scorned through non-verbal glares by women and men of African descent. However, as Twine suggests, white allies can be pivotal and even crucial in an anti-black social landscape as long as they acquire the necessary racial literacy: recognizing that racism is a contemporary and not an historical problem mediated by class, gender inequality, and heterosexuality, that Whiteness has considerable cultural and symbolic value, and the ability to interpret racial codes and racialized practices (Twine 2011). For recognized Italians *can be affected* quite strongly by African derived cultures in their creolized or African forms, even adopting ethnic practices believed important to particular African group identities. The various forms of alliance between the recognized Italians and people of African descent can, with considerable effort on the part of the recognized, help undermine the formation of stigmatized segregated communities where access to resources are so limited that residents can become systematically disabled.

To what extent, if any, are my interlocutors creating spaces that transform the anti-black social order? Do they negotiate and seek reform? Can their actions be characterized as embracing spaces and lifestyles that challenge the existing social order? Living in the context of anti-black racism is stressful, and it can be deeply demoralizing, when combined with the challenges of finding employment, housing, supporting family members under neoliberal policies of privatization and precarious employment. The range of responses to anti-blackness in Italy represents various forms of incipient consciousness and politics, some more reformist than radical, some symbolic and indirect, and others directly oppositional. The very act of being in Italy can, as I've suggested, be interpreted as radical and transformative. These are ways of living with brokenness. Yet as Wilderson, Sexton and other Afro-pessimist theorists have suggested, it will take more than presence, persistence, and even a broader social cognizance and racial literacy to displace fundamental anti-black ontology, Western system of knowledge, power, social and cultural structures, and ways of being. In the next chapter, I turn my attention to the death of a young man in Reggio Emilia and to the formation of Black identity, collective consciousness and solidarity across ethnic differences.

Notes

1 Pierre Bourdieu introduced the concept of symbolic power to describe indirect, subtle, often unconscious and taken-for-granted expressions of power and domination. Symbolic power involves disciplining social subjects to accept their place in the social hierarchy of distinctions. See Bourdieu (1977) and Bourdieu (1989).
2 Over the past two decades, the Lega Nord has made public comments about the need to cleanse public trains and buses that Africans, by their very presence, have been contaminated.
3 This treatment is comparable to other socially ostracized people, for instance the Dalit of India.
4 Anthropologists might call this 'cultural knowledge,' or 'habitus' (Bourdieu 1977).
5 See George Lipsitz (2011), especially his discussion of white and black spatial imaginaries in the United States.
6 I am qualifying 'white' here because in relation to much of Europe Italians as a whole have been considered 'almost white,' not quite as white as the French, Germans, Swiss, and so on. Northern Italians tend to see themselves more in terms of whiteness than Southern Italians (see Pugliese 2008).
7 Donald Martin Carter theorizes an "Anthropology of Invisibility" in which he examines these issues in relation to African Diasporic peoples. See Carter (2010).
8 The notion of Italy as a place for the good life or "la bella vita," a phrase taken from Fellini's film of the same title, is a popular representation that tourists frequently repeat. However, Fellini's film, like Paolo Sorrentino's 2013, "La Grande Bellezza" (the Great Beauty) is actually a critique of Italian and generally upper class decadence and superficiality. Sorrentino is parodying much of the reign of Berlusconi. Both directors caricature elite Italian society.
9 Maria Viarengo, personal discussion, Turin 2014.
10 Viarengo argues that at this time women would not have been walking about uncovered.
11 Conquest by the European, and in this case Italian rape of African lands and cultures.
12 Jan Nederveen Pieterse outlines diffuse representations of the Moor or African in Renaissance and Enlightenment iconography, suggesting that portraits of dark skinned servants signified the hidden sexuality of the white women whom they served (Pieterse (1995) See also Sander Gilman (1985) on representations of women in medical discourse.
13 See Fred Kudjo Kuwornu's documentary film about representations of Blacks in Italian film, "Blaxploitalian: 100 Years of Blackness in Film" (2016).

14 The Philippina woman has to an extent displaced the iconic the black woman servant. However, the trope of black woman who is submissive and nevertheless the principal caretaker in the family persists.

15 There are some exceptions in these representations in television fiction especially Canadian, German, and English productions that are also shown on Italian television. In some of these programs, many crime dramas or SciFi, people of African descent are represented in work that requires intellect and as actively contributing to problem solving.

16 In the 2014 European parliamentary elections (May 25) populist, anti-immigrant parties made considerable gains or held on to a significant number of seats in France, the United Kingdom, Switzerland, Austria, Hungary, Denmark, Sweden, Finland, Belgium, Lithuania, Greece, and the Czech Republic, and Italy. Some of these countries, including Switzerland, Austria, and Denmark, are thriving economically, thus economic woes cannot explain the populist vote. Indeed, Spain and Portugal whose economies are in shambles did not vote widely for right wing populist political parties.

17 See 2016 Report on Italy by the European Commission against Racism and Intolerance.

18 May 2014 Interview with shopkeeper of Brazilian descent with Italian citizenship married to an Italian and who has lived in Italy for 30 years. She also said that Africans were "furbi' a rather derogatory way of describing someone as 'clever' for untoward purposes. She said they come to Italy, get residence, and then bring their 75-year-old parents here so that they can collect pensions they did not earn. Others, she claimed, had children here because Italian social services give money to people with children. In fact, most immigrants pay into pension plans while working, and never see this money because are forced to leave the country after losing their jobs. So they pay taxes and into pension accounts they never enjoy. Moreover, for decades immigrants have been working in jobs Italians did not want, dangerous and dirty jobs with low social status. They have taken these jobs and others that require skill, and have paid taxes and into pensions that have helped keep the country afloat. They have paid rents, and purchased all sorts of consumption items including automobiles, supporting and fueling the Italian economy. What is more, very few immigrants from Africa bring their parents to live in Italy, so this is simply slander.

19 See Anne Mcklintock (1995).

20 Interview, May 2014 with man of Nigerian origin who has lived in Italy for over 10 years.

21 Gramsci defined "common sense" not as native intelligence, but rather as the embedded, inchoate, and taken-for-granted beliefs and perceptions characterizing conformist thinking among the mass of people in any place and society. This generally involved superstition, folklore, religious beliefs, and inherited ideas. For Gramsci, common sense is intrinsically tied up with power and therefore with his concept of hegemony, established through a process of consent to knowledge and interests of the dominant class accepted by society at large as being in its own best interests. That which is cultural is recognized to the point of being accepted as 'the way things are.' Common sense helps maintain economic and political hegemony because it profoundly penetrates the psychology and practices of a society. See Crehan (2002; 2016).

22 In geography there is a growing literature of emotional and affective geographies (see e.g., Pile (2010); Jayne et al. (2010); Tolia-Kelly (2006); Davidson et al. (2007); Thrift (2005); Gress and Seigworth (2010); McCormack (2003)). There have been considered two separate theoretical explorations, respectively of how emotions are embodied and located in everyday lives, and how affect is expressed through texture, tone, imagery, and so on. To date, scholars interested in emotional and affective geographies have not studied how racialized identities and places are produced through affective interactions. However, there has been attention to how power engineers collective emotions and affect, and to the conceptual underpinnings of emotional, embodied and affective geographies (Pile 2010; Thrift 2005; Jayne et al. Valentine 2010).

23 Elsewhere I have described Italians as 'almost white' because of their discursive place in relation to the rest of Europe (Merrill 2013). Here I describe them as whitened

because this is what seems to be emerging as Italianness is remade in relation to the growing presence of people of color. This fashioning of whiteness is exhibited in descriptions of people of African descent as "Neri," and in the ways people of African descent increasingly employ the term, "white" as a gloss to describe Italians with deep generational claims to belonging.

24 "Il Portavoce dei Senegalesi "Vogliamo solo la Verità," 13 Dicembre 2011, *La Repubblica*, Firenze; "Chiudete Casa Pound" L'Appelo di Pape Diaw," 14 Dicembre 2011 *La Repubblica*, Firenze

25 When asked about Italian racism, many people of African descent have responded that Italians are "ignorant" because they don't know anything about Africans or people outside of their own immediate spheres so they treat one in very demeaning and offensive ways. This reluctance to use the term "racist" I believe stems from a number of sources, prominently from the denial of racism in the Italian press and public at large, and from fear of offending recognized Italians. Italians often explain their rejection of people of African ancestry as simply a matter of "cultural differences," namely that Africans are "too different" from Italians. Theorists of recent racism in Europe have argued that older forms of biological racism based on hierarchical beliefs and prejudices based on skin color have been supplanted since the late 20th century with "cultural" "differentialist" or "new" racism. This new racism is articulated in a language of difference and an alleged natural human incommensurablity of cultures (see Stolcke 1995; Pred 2000; Merrill 2006). There is a lot of debate about whether this so-called 'new racism' is really so new at all, but what is important is that the language of differentialist racism, or what has come to be described as a 'natural' xenophobia felt toward people with different appearances, was taken up by the populist political right since the 1980s and is now part of common sense. That people of African descent in Italy are sometimes reluctant to openly describe Italians as racist is partly a reflection of the dominance of this culturalist discourse, and also a fear of further distancing themselves from Italian culture, in which they participate. I have found that certain categories of people of African descent tend to suggest that Italians are more ignorant than racist: those who are married to Italians, those whose children have never lived in any country outside of Italy, those who have held stable jobs for many years, those who are interested in working in politics, and those who work in politics. Many others, especially the most recently arrived as refugees and immigrants, and in the second generation are describing Italian society ever more frequently as racist. Young Italian intellectuals and activists are also using this language.

26 In his critiques of Hegel and Sartre, Frantz Fanon discusses the problems of the refusal of reciprocity and recognition of colonized populations by Europeans in *Black Skin White Masks*.

27 See the group, "Italiani senza Cittadinanza" that has been mobilizing for years to press the government to create an easier path to citizenship especially for the so-called 'seconda generazione.' Camilla Hawthorne, a graduate student in Geography at the University of California, Berkeley, is completing dissertation research on this topic.

28 I met Phyllis (a pseudonym) at Turin's intercultural women's center, Alma Mater where she works as a Cultural Mediator (see Merrill 2006).

29 See Alison Blunt (1994) for a fascinating historical discussion of intersecting gender roles, imperialist projects, and racism in colonial Africa.

30 This is similar to the pre-Civil Rights Southern United States, where Black men were called "Boy" and never "Mr."

31 See Stuart Hall's (1993) "What is this 'Black' in Black Popular Culture?" and his presentation, "The Floating Signifier" (on streaming) at Goldsmith College in London (Hall 1997).

32 In her study of Ghana, Jemima Pierre (2012) suggests that anti-blackness and the cult of Whiteness have not escaped the African continent itself.

4

THE DEATH OF SYLVESTER AGYEMANG

Can You Be BLACK and Bear This?

No one dies if they live in the lives of those who remain.

A sign held in a street following Sylvester's death

At the Viale Piave bus stop on a major arterial ring road surrounding the small city of Reggio in the province of Emilia Romagna is a large portrait of a young black man, Sylvester Agyemang. The leader of a local group of street artists painted the image adjacent to the site of his passing at the request of a group of African Italian youth and the family. On Monday January 13, 2014, Sylvester Agyemang was killed while stepping off a bus on his way to school. The eldest child of a family of Ghanaians, Sylvester was just days shy of his 14th birthday. According to the official story, the driver of the jumbo and overcrowded vehicle operated by the Italian firm Seta spa closed the rear door on Sylvester as he descended at 7:30 am at a stop along one of the belt roads encircling the city. The closing door entrapped his backpack and as he frantically sought to pry himself from the moving vehicle, his body was flung violently toward the pavement where he landed headfirst. While Sylvester lay motionless in a pool of blood, fellow students reported screaming at the bus driver to stop, yet he drove on as the young man lay dying in the street near the sidewalk. Moments later another Seta bus driver witnessed the crisis, yet drove on without stopping to assist. Failure to assist in the face of an incident involving injury to someone's body is a criminal offense in Italy.

Days after the tragedy, the local newspapers reported that the man believed to have been the driver of Sylvester's bus was under official investigation for "Omicidio Colposo" by the assistant district attorney for the equivalent of manslaughter or negligent homicide, and also for "Omissione di Soccorso," or wrongful death based on his failure to stop, assist, and report a street accident.

The second driver who passed and did not assist or rapidly report the incident was also under investigation for *Omissione di Soccorso* which translated legally into *Cooperazione Colposa* or accessory to a criminal act. The driving license of the man presumed to have driven the bus was suspended and he was removed from his driving position at Seta, while he however remained on Seta's payroll in an office job.

At the time of his death, Sylvester had lived on the outskirts of Reggio Emilia for nine years. He had moved to Italy from Ghana at the age of five. He and his mother joined his father once he had secured steady employment. The eldest of Augustina and Emmanuel Agyemang's three children, Sylvester was on his way to the Italian high school he attended, a professional training school for white-collar office work such as accounting where he was the only student of African descent in his class. Many children of parents born outside of Italy attend vocational or professional schools in Reggio. Sylvester was an avid music fan, and he played several instruments. The day before he died he had played piano at the Pentecostal church in Reggio that his family attended. The newspapers reported that he dreamed of becoming a policeman in order to protect and help others. At his funeral, a family member described him as a young man who so strongly wished to communicate with others that he had learned Italian very rapidly. One said, "Sylvester had the desire to learn, and to be accepted by others."[1]

When Sylvester's shocked and heartbroken parents learned of the incident, they and other family members and classmates transformed the site of his death into a small memorial and expression of outrage. They laid flowers, candles, and notes, hung a large banner with a school photograph of the young man reading "Ciao Sylvester" (Figure 4.1). Students strung a second banner (Figure 4.2) reading, "Killed like animals. These things only happen here in Reggio!"[2]

Although the local newspapers reported that Sylvester was trapped in a closing door and had fallen to his death, Sylvester's parents believed there was evidence that the bus had also ridden over their son. After the tragedy, local Reggiani complained of the overcrowded jumbo buses operated by Seta that place their children in peril every day. Many people of African descent asked, "*Why did the bus driver close the door on Sylvester?*" "Why hadn't he been more cautious and waited to be certain that all the children had descended before closing the door and driving off? Why had he not stopped and assisted at the scene, and why had the second driver been indifferent to the scene?"

Local students and parents in particular expressed a sense of outrage over Sylvester's tragic, unnecessary death. But the loss of this promising young life seemed to have touched a place in the large Ghanaian community that was shared across the ethnic distinctions, especially among African Italian youth whose parents grew to maturity in various parts of West Africa and who saw themselves in Sylvester. The event ignited a deep sense of mourning and collective actions expressing support and African diasporic solidarity for reasons that are not self-evident. What might explain the outpouring of collective empathy in response to

FIGURE 4.1 "Killed like animals. These things only happen here in Reggio"

FIGURE 4.2 A makeshift memorial near the bus stop and site of Sylvester Agyemang's passing. Translation: Killed like beasts. These things only happen in Reggio!

the image and knowledge of Sylvester's untimely death? How and why does it suggest group recognition and relatedness across the African diaspora beyond the sign or 'fact of blackness' by skin color and other bodily features?

Witness, Memory, and Loss

My goal here is to explore how people who witness scenes of violence against Black people feel themselves implicated in their fate (Alexander 1994). How do these facts or realities of blackness awaken a sense of group identification, recognition, and knowledge among people in the African Diaspora in Italy across the vast diversity and differentiation of their historical and cultural experiences as black subjects?[3]

Scholars of the African Diaspora in Europe have adopted the terminology "Black Europe" and more recently "Black Mediterranean" in order to signify the profound and yet largely unacknowledged and intense interweaving of Blackness and Europeanness. Allison Blakely argues that Black identity is being forced upon individuals and groups of people of African origin in Europe, an emergent and heterogeneous Black consciousness inflected by place of origin and settlement, ethnicity, social class, religion, and other elements of multiple identities. As Blakely suggests, all share a common background rooted deeply in the history of European colonial empires and their engagement in the transatlantic slave trade (Blakely 2009). But there is no language to represent the inchoate way someone who may or may not self-identify as "Black" might understand themselves as part of a larger group, or an African Diasporic "people." How do incidents like the death of Sylvester Agyemang signal common experiences, memories, and relationships between people of vastly different African origins living in Reggio Emilia, other parts of Italy, Europe, and across the diaspora more broadly today? And how might they also leave opening for creative self-knowledge and self-understanding?

Race is a biological science fiction, and there are huge differences in language, religion, customs, and class on the African continent and in the Americas. Yet during the long era of European colonialism, racial ontologies have consigned those outside of "Whiteness" to a subordinate status, structured the polity, and produced a pattern of violence, blackness as pain, and loss, for public consumption from Europe to Africa and the Americas. Sylvester's death was not digitally recorded and broadcast in the Italian press, yet his was a very public passing. The newspapers covered the story for weeks and described his death in some detail and a memorial was rapidly constructed at the site. What shared histories, memories, and experiences might Africans and African Italians have brought to the loss of Sylvester? And how did his death consolidate collective relationships by making Africanness-as-also-Blackness an irreversible site of abjection and loss, as well as an opening for struggle and inspired membership in the Italian-European polity?

It is worth considering first that images of black victims of suffering and pain have served as rallying points of Black collectivity and nationalist thinking in the

United States since the Civil Rights Era. Debra Walker King, in her poignant book *African Americans and the Culture of Pain*, describes the dynamic of how the black body is a memorial to African and African American pain, and the cultural rendering of Black people into abstractions. A symbol of the legacy of racist white violence, and the Black people, the only ethnic group whose skin color has continually been associated with objectification, alienation, disfranchisement, and racially motivated brutality, organized to break this vulnerability and produce more security. King explores how images of black pain and defenselessness, which are culturally very 'unAmerican' experiences, are important to the white racism that inflicts and denies it, serving as vehicles for the disappearance of black *people* who become victims, symbolic scapegoats, images of racially motivated hatred, and icons for calls to activism instead of full and complex human beings whose pain elicits compassion and empathy (King 2008, 2). Such sensitivity to the loss of a full life in its complex lived experience is reserved for representations of White victims of brutal crimes whose pain and cruel deaths are not displayed for national consumption.

In the US, the unprotected "black body" in pain has been a national spectacle for centuries, from public rapes to lynchings and mob violence, to police beatings and murders watched as a perverted form of entertainment (Spillers 2003; King 2008). While commodified in the national imagination, these are actual Black collective experiences that began with the original rupture from Africa. The systematic violence experienced, witnessed, and described is part of the long history of enslavement that is inscribed in the bodies of formerly enslaved. Linda Brent's autobiography of her life as a slave girl, which had to be 'framed' and introduced by a white woman, describes a searing and relentless vulnerability to sexual assault by white men. This was such an integral aspect of plantation culture that raping enslaved Black and mixed-race (multiracial) women was a rite of passage for young White men of all ages.[4] The brutality of enslavement, Hortense Spillers argues compellingly, is written into the flesh of African Americans (Spillers 2003). In the post slavery historical context, the public spectacle of black men being lynched was an American pastime that James Baldwin portrayed with heart-rending eloquence in his short story, "Goin'to Meet the Man," as a normalized arena of perverse pleasure for White spectators and consumers (Baldwin 1995). The killings of Trayvon Martin (2012), Michael Brown (2014), Eric Garner (2014), Tamir Rice (2014), Sandra Bland (2015), Walter Scott (2016)[5] and many others recorded in sound and or image resonate with the historical display of the violent lynching of Black men and women, a reminder that Black lives are always vulnerable to premature death. These killings also suggest that violence against black people does not end with overt acts of injury or murder, for the perpetrators are almost never brought to justice.

White viewers, Elizabeth Alexander eloquently reminds us, tend to watch these scenes as participants in a system coded to produce their sense of superiority and security while distancing themselves from the empathy that would suggest true witnessing, and, I would add, loss (Alexander 1994). Public lynchings were social events (see Baldwin 1995). By contrast, African Americans receive displays of violence against Black women and men with a sense of profound familiarity, empathy, loss, and mourning (Rankine 2015). The ghosts of ancestors, both victims and survivors, whisper in all the racial killings, and the aftermath of injustice. Memories of systemic, targeted, racial violence constitute an amorphous collective identity that resonates with a sense of profound loss across social class and ethnic differences (Spillers 2003; Hartman and Wilderson 2003; Rankine 2015; Coates 2015). Black spaces almost always involve rewounding and seemingly endless, deepening loss. Media, politicians, and many scholars habitually contribute by lack of concern and/or cognizance to the prevailing social denial that Black spaces are integral to a social order, an order built on the habit of trivializing Black losses while affirming its own gains and tenuous hold on power.

How do African and African Italian experiences and memories of trauma and loss compare and intersect with African American collective histories and memories? How is a tragic event like young Sylvester's death experienced by Africans and African Italians in Italy? In Europe, black bodies in pain for public consumption only recently became a national spectacle. Late 20th century images of starving children in Ethiopia, the AIDS epidemic in Africa, violent military dictatorships in places like Uganda, and brutal ethnic genocides in Rwanda, Sudan, Congo, and elsewhere circulated in newspapers and television have informed Italian knowledge of Africa and Africans, superimposed on old romanticized images and discourses of a 'primitive and exotic' land and people. When immigration from Africa and other parts of the economically underdeveloped and postcolonial world emerged as a significant phenomenon and was named a national 'crisis' beginning in the late 1980s, narratives and photographs of black prostitutes, disease carriers, street sellers called 'vu cumpra,' drug dealers, long lines of people represented as desperate and potential criminals awaiting entry, and currently of boats filled with destitute or dying immigrants and refugees came to represent Africa and Africans along with people from parts of the Middle East and South East Asia. These now regularized spectacles of black bodies in pain are usually presented by White men and consumed by White audiences, suggesting a code in which blackness is to be understood and metaphorized as trauma and anguish. Yet Black people have also been watching and interpreting these images and discourses. When Sylvester Agyemang fell off a bus and was left in the street, what collective versions of African Italian and African European history might they have brought to bear on this tragedy? What ideas about black lives informed particular readings of and responses to the incident? What historical memories and experiences constructed by White Europeans did Africans in Italy also understand?

Understanding how Africans and African Italians might perceive and experience Sylvester's death necessitates historically situating their current accelerated and more visible presence. In comparison with North American Black and African-Caribbean experiences the transatlantic slave trade deeply affected modern African history. However, the direct experience of violent forced removal from the homeland and enslavement as chattel is not part of African collective memory (see Hartman and Wilderson 2003; Hartman 2006). The several hundred-year period of the transatlantic slave trade did however disrupt and spark immense transformations in ways of life, systems of value and beliefs that came to be intertwined with much of Europe and the Atlantic colonies. The slave trade helped set the stage for the recent movements of people into Europe, the Americas, and the United States, a stage that was more fully furnished by European imperialist colonization from the late 19th through the mid-20th centuries, representing another and more directly impactful rupture. Colonization was by and large based on a relationship of force involving in some cases extended brutality, physical displacement, and corvee labor.

In this context that extended and accelerated processes of European industrialization (part of a pattern that intersects North American and Caribbean experiences of enslavement), colonization was a form of violence that precluded any reciprocal intersubjective recognition between colonists and colonized subjects. There was generally no empathy in the colonial situation, as the colonists knew virtually nothing of and were indifferent to the colonized's culture, its people. This was not true among Native Americans in relation to British colonists. The early colonists only survived because Native Americans taught them about local crops and other survival strategies.[6] Colonizers did generally not mingle with the colonized, so their only point of reference was with other colonizers with whom they shook hands, drank coffee, and exchanged commonplaces (Fanon 2008; also see Memmi 1991 and Pierre 2012). In front of Blacks as objects, white colonizers did not wish to feel or experience anything except to see a reflection through which they might derive pleasure through power or a notion of mission to spread their knowledge. For a white colonist to treat colonized as human in the colonial situation (or in American slavery and apartheid (Jim Crow) systems in the United States and South Africa) was tantamount to being a "race traitor," punishable by diminished social prestige or even complete ostracism.

Colonization in 19th and 20th century Africa is likely etched in collective memory, yet in quite varied ways according to particular place, history, culture, and experience. There are significant ethnic, political, and religious differences in Africa that intersect distinctive relationships with specific European colonizing countries. Nevertheless, shared memories of systemic violence, impoverishment, exploitation, and loss that continued across the African continent after independence are part of the long afterlife of both the slave trade and colonization.[7] The experience of racism in the United States that Ruth Wilson Gilmore (2002) described as "state-sanctioned or extralegal production and exploitation of group-differentiated vulnerability to premature death" is expressed in inter-ethnic rivalries inherited from European colonization as well as anti-black racism.[8] In some places the experience of war, repression, and poverty due to unemployment along with poor health conditions and government corruption that cannot be disentangled from the political and economic interests of foreign governments, are so life-threatening that vulnerability to premature death is a prominent feature of life. Once in Italy, the danger to premature death does not entirely abate, and as I discuss in Chapter Five, is frequently reinforced by precarious living conditions, deliberate neglect, and social erasure.

People of African descent who witnessed Sylvester's violent death and experienced the agonizing process of litigation that followed brought to this event the histories of colonization and more recent experiences of loss that have contributed to in this context what we might describe as incipient understandings of what Michelle Alexander designates as a "bottom line blackness." The communal experience of Sylvester's death was by no means the first instance of a violent death that was interpreted by sympathetic white Italians as a tragic, but not racially motivated event in Italy.

The thousands of Africans whose lives have been lost literally or via social erasure in the Sahara desert and Mediterranean Sea, in on- and offshore detention facilities inform and should help us to understand the unspoken experiences people of African descent bring to this loss. There are unfortunately numerous instances of anti-black violence in recent Italian history that have been widely covered by the national press. These stories can help us comprehend what African Italians bring to Sylvester's tragedy. One was the shooting of Senegalese traders Samb Modou and Diop Mor in Florence described as a "Caccia dei Neri" or "hunting of blacks" in December 2011. Another was the beating to death of Nigerian Emmanuel Chidi Nnamdi in Fermo in September 2016. These cases speak both to a sense of vulnerability and also the experience of being classified as spectacles of pity instead of participants in the Italian social body. The journalistic responses to Nnamdi's murder even among Italian antiracists, as Camilla Hawthorne and Pina Piccolo argue in their article "Antiracism without racism," is to diminish the experience of anti-blackness as part of a deeply global and local system by attributing such incidents as the acts of fringe individuals (Hawthorne and Piccolo 2016).

In 2001 I was attending a conference in Padova when I saw television news coverage that an Italian man had killed two Senegalese merchants and wounded a third in Florence's Piazza Dalmazia market in the morning and then fled in a car. As police sought to identify the killer, he reappeared in San Lorenzo market in the afternoon, wounding two more Senegalese and threatening to shoot an Italian stallholder who tried to stop him. When police approached him, he shot himself. The two men killed were 40-year-old Samb Modou and 54-year-old Diop Mor, both Senegalese of origin. I was unable to find any biography of these men in the Italian press beyond their ages, or any information about the wounded victims. Mourners and demonstrators in Florence displayed photographs of Samb Modou, his wife, and 13-year-old daughter. The then Mayor Matteo Renzi expressed his outrage against the killings, stating that they had shaken the city to its core. And the President of the Republic Giorgio Napolitano denounced it as a "blind explosion of hatred" and called on Italian society and authorities to "Nip in the bud every form of intolerance and reaffirm the tradition of openness and solidarity in our country."[9]

A placard was erected on the street expressing 'solidarity' with the street traders. And the lower house of the Italian parliament observed a minute of silence. Images of Samb Modou and Diop Mor's bodies lying in the street covered with white cloth were front-page news. However, national and international viewers and readers did not learn who these men were or how they came to Italy, and were therefore unable to participate fully in the public mourning of their loss to the Italian community and the impact on the human lives they had left behind.

The killer was described in detail as 50-year-old Gianluca Casseri, an accountant, science fiction writer, and far right sympathizer affiliated with the far right *Casa Pound* association and a person who 'lived in his own world but was not insane.' Some union representatives and other Italian citizens described the killing spree with a sense of shock and embarrassment, but the general position adopted and promoted by Mayor Renzi was that this was not a racist act, but rather the act of a lone mad man. Senegalese traders and other Africans reported by contrast that they were regularly verbally abused on the streets, told for instance to leave the country, and accused of 'stealing' Italian jobs.

While I was staying at a hotel in Pavia, I walked daily through the center of this small city to reach the conference site. I met a Senegalese man, Mamour, selling books. I saw him frequently during my week-long visit, and he talked with me openly and unsolicited about how upset he was about the killings in Florence, how the Africans in Pavia were organizing a demonstration to protest the injustices of racial discrimination. Mamour described his own experiences in Italy as having begun well while he worked 'under the books' at a factory in Milan. When he asked to be 'regularized' so that he could receive documents to remain in Italy legally, he was fired. He was in mourning over the loss of Samb Modou and Diop Mor. And he was also in mourning over the recent loss of his brother who had been ill and had died in Senegal. He regretted not having seen or been able to help his ailing brother by sending more money. He described a profound pain and empathy for the victims of this ultimate expression of corporeal anti-black and anti-African violence, adding that he received such violence symbolically and in microaggressions on a daily basis. Mamour's experiences suggest that the killing of Modou and Mor can be taken into one's own experience of being from the knowledge of one's own vulnerability to similar violence. It also suggests that awareness of the violence to which Mamour and others are vulnerable can lead to individual and collective efforts to create paths out of this sort of existence.

I attended the protest demonstration in a small piazza near the central open market in Pavia. Participants expressed outrage and frustration over the absence of humanity exposed by the killing of Modou and Mor and the wounding of other Senegalese. The Pavia chapter of the Senegalese Association and the trade unions

Cgil and Cisl organized the demonstration to denounce what to them were undoubtedly acts of anti-black violence. People wore signs hanging around their necks written, "No Al Razzismo. Vogliamo Chiarezza"/"No To Racism. We Want Clarity," and "L'unica razza che conosco é quella humana"/"The only race I know is the human race." Others held signs that expressed frustration over their exploitation in informal work, "Cittadini del Mondo. É Proprio Vero Chi Sfrutta il Lavoro Nero"/"Citizens of the World. It's really true that we're exploited in Lavoro Nero," calling on "Citizens of the World" to pay attention to the exploitation of human beings working in the underground economy. There were demonstrations in cities all over the country. In Florence, groups from the Senegalese Association, the Immigrants' Collective, and the Movement of Asylum seekers marched to the Prefect's office, demanding justice and to meet a representative. One told a guardian reporter, "Don't tell us he (the killer) was a mad man because if he was he would have killed whites as well as blacks."[10] Police set upon the protesters, arresting many for speaking out against the injustices they face.

In another incident, Emmanuel Chidi Nnamdi, a 30-year-old Nigerian refugee, was beaten to death in Fermo, Italy on June 5, 2016 after he responded to racist insults against his 24-year-old wife, Chinyere. Emmanuel and Chinyere had escaped Nigeria after their parents and 2-year-old daughter were killed by Boko Haram. The couple had survived the precarious trip across the treacherous Libyan Sahara desert and the Mediterranean sea, but not before losing another child along the way. They arrived in Italy in 2015. As they awaited word on their asylum application they were housed in a shelter run by a Catholic organization in Fermo.[11] While strolling near the seminary where they were living, 39-year-old Amedeo Mancini who was sitting on a bench with a friend began to shout racist insults at Chinyere, calling her a "scimmia Africana" or an African monkey. When Emmanuel tried to defend his wife, Mancini beat him with a steel bar that left Emmanuel in a coma and then gone a day later. Mancini was known to be associated with ultra right groups including the Casa Pound association, and had been banned from public sporting events for his violent behavior.

While officials, even among the Left, refused to describe the brutal beating as a racist act, the murder of Emmanuel Chidi Nnamdi was interpreted as an act of dehumanization that, along with daily acts of verbal aggression, are leading to the emergence of independent Black organizations. In September 2016, lawmakers voted against seeking charges against senator Roberto Calderoni who had likened Cecile Kyenge the country's first Black minister,[12] to an orangutan. During her term Kyenge (2013–2014) was continually subjected to a far right campaign that included nooses being hung up around a city she visited. So a system that legitimizes actions of anti-black verbal abuse is more than complicit in Emmanuel Chidi's murder. Mancini's racist expressions were neither aberrant in Italy nor more widely in Europe. People who suffer the consequences of a global system of racism may witness these incidents with an empathy and mourning conditioned by the violence it inflicts that is passed on for generations.

The death of Sylvester meant for his family the opening or re-opening of a great abyss of suffering and loss that resonated with centuries of the deliberate exploitation and careless disregard for Black life in the West. For Black Italians and Black residents in the politically Left and always progressive Reggio Emilia where there was an intercultural center directed and co-directed by a Moroccan-Italian and Italian-Eritrean, Sylvester's death meant the loss of innocence. It dashed the hope that this time, in Reggio Emilia, their troubles might have been attributed to the economy and job market, that their difficulty finding secure employment and their frequent treatment by Italians with extra iciness might be caused by Italian anxiety about their poorly performing economy and their inability to keep their businesses afloat or to survive on their small pensions. The loss of Sylvester signaled the end of this innocence. His death meant that all people identified as other and especially with blackness were vulnerable. If Sylvester could die while going to school, and his death be virtually sanctioned by the local police and administration, Black Italians knew that they too were potentially disposable, that Sylvester could have been, might have been, and might be, them. The authorities were not acting to defend the family against the loss of an innocent Black life, and it was widely believed among black youth and members of the Ghanaian community that had Sylvester's name been Poggioli, had his skin color been light, his death would have outraged the local community and those responsible would have been brought to justice. Many suspected further that had Sylvester been called Poggioli or Ferrari, he would not have died that morning while getting off the bus.

Community and Africanness-as-also-Blackness

As James Baldwin (1998) suggested, the persistent racial prejudice, racial profiling, and racial violence in the United States are rooted in Europe. Their growing presence in Europe has been transformed from an exotic, childlike abstraction to a threat. Italians who can no longer look upon Black people as mere travelers from another world perceive and act on the basis of a swell of racialized anxiety and an anti-other, deeply anti-black structure of feeling that for centuries existed for them almost entirely in the mind. As people of African descent have become living, material beings, Italians are beginning to embrace some of the hostility long present in the United States, reproducing blackness as otherwhere.

In the aftermath of the death of Sylvester, Black youth began to unify around the common identification with this young man whose life appeared to them to have been recklessly taken, another tragedy of the Italian society that sees people who appear to be of African origin as permanent 'strangers.' For the Ghanaian community of Reggio and many second generation Africans, the premature loss of Sylvester, a young Black Italian, became a symbol of social injustice toward people of African ancestry in Italy, the limits on Black freedom and equal access to public resources, and the need for solidarity among diverse Black or African communities and empathetic like-minded individuals. While most people in Reggio expressed sympathy and outrage about Sylvester's death, their interpretations of how the incident might have come to pass and whom to blame diverged from the perceptions expressed among many people of African descent. Some secondary school students, teachers, and other community members understood Sylvester's passing as an example of the outrageously poor management of the public bus transportation system, Seta. Residents express ongoing frustration about an urban bus system that has worsened in recent years as services have been cut back and students are literally packed into buses or unable to board. The vehicles taking children and teenagers to and from school each day are grossly overcrowded and therefore unsafe. When weather permits, many older students ride bicycles to school instead of cramming themselves into the small spaces.

But Sylvester lived at too great a distance from his school to have ridden a bicycle. Beyond this, especially for the family and African/African Italian community, there was the question of culpability and responsibility. What *really* happened? Why did the driver close the door on the young man and then not realize he had made a fatal error? Public transportation is widely used by Italians and hosts of visitors in Italy where tens of thousands of trains and buses are carefully regulated in order to avoid accidents. And if Italian drivers know they are legally obligated, that they have a duty to assist if they participate in or even witness an accident, why didn't the driver stop? Why didn't the second Seta driver who passed stop his bus to help this young man who was in need? Some believe that had an ambulance been more rapidly called to the scene, the young man's life might have been saved. The Agyemang family and members of the Ghanaian-Italian and African diasporic communities asked if the driver had in fact committed a deliberate crime. Italian bus drivers frequently behave with hostility to passengers of color by passing them by at a stop, not responding to their questions about directions, and closing doors on them as they exit. I have witnessed this behavior in Reggio Emilia and Torino.

By the time of his death, Sylvester had lived in Italy and attended Italian schools for almost a decade; he had acquired considerable cultural knowledge of Reggio and Italian culture, adopted many Italian mannerisms and tastes that are popularly (although inaccurately) assumed to be "European," such as piano playing. If he was not yet legally an Italian citizen, Sylvester had by this time developed a complex and multifaceted identity that was in considerable measure culturally Italian.[13] However, Italian laws and customs do not yet accept and legitimate Black Italians as authentic insiders. Formal citizenship is awarded with great difficulty if at all, and cultural citizenship is rarely recognized. As Minister of Integration, Cecile Kyenge campaigned against Italy's "security package" policy (law 94/2009) based on the Bossi-Fini legislation that scapegoats, represses, criminalizes, and incarcerates African and other migrants. Instead of developing methods of integration, Italy identifies "strangers" as the primary cause of all the country's ills, reducing their rights and augmenting institutional humiliations and obstacles to recognition and representation. Kyenge argues that for years, Italy's inadequate and repressive laws have generated institutional racism, "There have been standards and practices that have produced serious discrimination injuring many people guilty only of originating from an other country" (Kyenge 2014, 71). As a Black woman who advocated for a policy of jus solis (right of the soil) to replace the jus sanguinis (right of blood) practices in Italy, Kyenge was ridiculed by political figures from the Lega Nord party who caricatured her as a primate, using her race, gender, and African origin to discredit and silence her (see Merrill 2015; Hawthorne and Piccolo 2016). Humiliated but not deterred, Kyenge argued that Italy was in violation of human rights conventions for practicing discrimination and denying rights on the basis of skin color. She suggested that through its policies that criminalize and hold migrants in a state of illegality, the country was supporting the diffusion of a new form of "slavery," producing a "new poor" vulnerable to exploitation because deprived of representation or rights in many economic and social sectors. Her interviews with people on the receiving end of these injustices reveal testimonies of the suffering of individuals who have adopted an Italian life style yet who are not legally recognized with Italian citizenship. A 16-year-old born in Morocco who has spent the bulk of his life in Italy wrote to the Minister in his appeal for recognition,

> I feel Italian, but according to the bureaucracy I am not. Sometimes, when I happen to travel outside the country and meet people in these places who ask me what nationality I am, I want so much to respond "Italian," or rather I want to scream the fact that I am Italian, but I can't do so. It may seem childish, but when a foreign film cites Italy I feel proud of the country that I consider my own.
>
> *(Kyenge 2014, 75)*

Such youth are developing a sense of collective identity based on similar shared experiences of social exclusion, invisibility, and erasure (see Carter 2010; cf Keaton 2006). This deeply spatialized Black ontology is grounded in the hierarchical division between Europe and Africa that asserts rights and belonging and contests marginalization in Italian society while affirming the self as a being and subject. Even the star soccer player Mario Balotelli, who was adopted by an Italian family at an early age and grew up speaking Italian with a Milanese accent, has been faced with continual hostility to his classification as a 'real' Italian.[14]

Days after the tragic event in Reggio an association of university students and other young people called "Studenti Autorganizzati," which communicates via blog posts, along with the family and other community members, spontaneously organized a demonstration in Reggio's piazzas and streets in order to demand that the municipal authorities investigate Sylvester's death. They also called for the resignation of the Seta officials responsible for the jumbo buses that were said to have ignored recommendations to upgrade the security mechanisms on the back doors. Holding umbrellas to shield them from a cold winter rain, over three thousand people stopped Saturday morning traffic while walking through the major arteries of the city at the time and past the site of Sylvester's death. They held signs: "One can't die going to school" and "Don't trample on our lives. The city must act. Responsible parties at Seta must resign. Justice for Sylvester!" And perhaps most compelling, "No one dies if they live in the lives of those who remain."

At the head of the movement Sylvester's parents, family members, and friends walked arm in arm with other African and African Italians, students, teachers, and parents and cried, "Justice!"[15] Their march ended in the city center, in front of the municipal administrative building in Piazza Prampolini where they shouted to authorities, "Come out!" and "Shame! Shame!" The student organization, family, and an extended community that included many Italian students and parents had taken to the streets and raised their voices, demanding their right to have justice for Sylvester's death. They also insisted on their right to travel safely, a basic human right recognized by international conventions. The Ghanaian and other local communities of the African diaspora inhabited and pressed for their right to live with security as members of the Italian community and citizens if not juridically than at least in cultural practice.

As the Agyemang family waited for the prosecutor's office to return with their investigative results and charge both drivers with manslaughter and failure to stop and assist, they were supported by members of the Ghanaian community in the region, among whom many are members of a Pentecostal church of the Reverend Charles, and the group Studenti Autorganizzati.[16] The tragedy also prompted a number of youth associations of African origin to gather collectively across ethnic lines, led by UJARE, or Union de la Jeunesse Africaine di Reggio Emilia. Jeunesse Africaine is an inter-ethnic youth association created by a group of people who were born or who arrived in Italy at a young age and whose parents are originally from the Ivory Coast. The association began as an ethnic youth group for people of Ivorian origins, but transformed into a multi-ethnic youth association that includes members with ties to other parts of Africa, and even an Italian member who is according to my interlocutors considered an "honorary African."[17] The young women and men between 19–25 years of age experienced Sylvester's tragic death as a loss not only to his family, but also to diverse people of African descent in Reggio. They identified and empathized personally and collectively with Sylvester, and his tragic death. Jeunesse Africaine worked with ASNOCRE, or Associazione Studenti non Comunitari di Reggio Emilia, an association comprised of predominantly Cameroonian university students, and ASPAI mosaic d'Amore, a volunteer charity association that works in Africa. Together they organized a dinner to honor Sylvester and express their solidarity with the Agyemang family, held on a Saturday night in March in the

Mondinsieme intercultural center building. Sylvester's family was seated at the head of the room. The leader of ceremonies, Adama,[18] was a 25-year-old man born in Italy whose parents were of Ivorian origin. The room was filled with people of Ghanaian origin or descent, others from Nigeria, Senegal, Ivory Coast, Congo, Burkina Faso, Eritrea, Cameroon, and five people of non-African origin (including myself), one from the Mondinsieme staff, and two Italian women. Also present for a brief time was an 'Assessore' (councillor), member of the center–left government who worked with the Mayor.

Adama introduced Sylvester's family. On several occasions he stated that this dinner was organized to demonstrate "collective support and solidarity among people in the African community of Reggio." He explained that the meal included dishes from the Ivory Coast, Togo, Cameroon, and Morocco that had been prepared by the members of the sponsoring associations. Sylvester's father sat with his head down before speaking for a few moments, introducing his wife (to his left), his wife's mother (to his right), and his younger brother (to his right at the end of the table), and pointing to other members of the family seated in the audience. Speaking in Italian, he thanked those who were there and expressed his family's profound grief, and the senselessness of this tragedy. Then the Assessore spoke. He wore jeans and appeared very disheveled, which I interpreted as a statement that he was of the political left yet inappropriate in this cultural and human context. He explained that the mayor couldn't be there, but had sent him as a representative. He held that the passing of Sylvester was a loss for the entire Reggio community, and the young man would not be forgotten. He acknowledged the anger people felt about the incident, and agreed that one should not die going to school, which is one's right. He added that the community was going to heal from this deep pain, and the city government supported the family in their grief. The Assessore stayed for just a short period of time, departing before dinner. An Italian woman who appeared to be in her early 60s then spoke briefly, describing herself as Sylvester's teacher. She described Sylvester as a young man well liked among his classmates, and said that his empty desk remained in their classroom as if Sylvester were still among them. She expressed how extremely upsetting this was for all the students in the class, adding that many of these students had actually witnessed what happened, making the healing process even tougher.

After everyone had eaten the delicious meal, the tensions in the room seemed to abate. Adama asked us to stand up for a minute of silence for Sylvester. It was an emotionally wrenching moment, and the family sought to hold back their tears. A collection box for the family was placed in the middle of the room. A young man in short dreadlocks who appeared to be in his 20s then began to sing while strumming a guitar. He first sang a religious melody invoking Jesus, while continually referring to Sylvester as with us here in spirit. At one point Sylvester's father exhibited a photo of his son on an iPad that he placed in front of some soda bottles in the middle of the head table where the family sat. As the singing continued, Sylvester's spirit was called upon. Another young man with longer dreadlocks accompanied the young man with the guitar in song. They sang about Jesus, in Italian, and many in the audience who knew the lyrics sang with him. Then the young man intoned in an African language. At one point he told the audience that the language was Lingala from the Republic of the Congo, his place of origin. When he sang another song in Lingala, many in the audience were familiar with the lyrics and joined him. I asked how they knew the song. A Nigerian woman told me that everyone recognized these tunes because they were popular, and had been performed by several different artists.

Adama ended the ceremony by referring to the collective solidarity between Africani Reggiani and the Aygemang family. He expressed a pan-African and African-Reggiano common culture, based on shared histories and experiences. At one point a Ghanaian woman seated behind me spontaneously mentioned that she had enjoyed the food even though it wasn't from her country and that, anyway, African cuisine was very similar. There was a sense of belonging and unity in the room. The recognized Italians departed before the music had begun. The room felt saturated with deep empathy for the family, and the spirit of a child lost far too soon. There was also an expression of love of African cultures that crossed national, ethnic, and even religious boundaries, and a sense of collective unity based on faith, and hope.

A few months after the dinner, Jeunesse Africaine in collaboration with Mondinsieme and the local chapter of UISP sportpertutti (Italian Union of Sports for everyone) organized a soccer tournament in honor of Sylvester and his family, inviting all the African associations in Reggio Emilia to take part. Jeunesse Africane hoped to collect enough funding to open a space in honor of Sylvester, where Africani Reggiani and others could gather together to exchange knowledge, and build collective solidarity across national origins. The family told Adama that their solidarity helped sustain the family through a prolonged period of distress.

Weeks after the incident, no progress seemed to have been made in the investigation. The Agyemang family's lawyer, Andrea Pelligrini, had written letters to the District Attorney and directors of the Seta spa company asking for information. The daily paper *Gazzetta di Reggio* reported his questions as follows: Did the telecameras inside the bus work? What had they recorded? What did the cameras around the bus stop record? Did the door buzz to let the driver know that the door wasn't completely closed before he began moving? Neither the government office nor the private company officials responded to these inquiries. A month later, the newspaper reported an interview with Sylvester's father, Emmanuel Agyemang. He expressed the need to clarify whether the bus driver had been able to see the back of the bus with his mirrors. He also stated, "I want justice for my son; I want to know exactly what happened that day." He told the press that no one from Seta spa had contacted the family, but that the family had found a lot of solace in solidarity with the Ghanaian community, not only in Reggio but also in Germany, England, and other parts of the world.

Over two months following Sylvester's death, the story became even more bizarre. In late March, the district attorney's office announced that the municipal police, who had been assigned charge of the investigation, had sequestered the wrong bus. Two jumbo buses had proceeded from Rubiera, an area just outside of the city where Sylvester had lived: one at 7:01am and anther at 7:10am. Sylvester, it was determined, took the second bus and yet the first bus had been sequestered. In the interim, the vehicle that had transported Sylvester had been circulating the city for months, and had been twice serviced – erasing all traces of evidence. The municipal police reported that it was not their fault, but instead Seta had given them an erroneous bus.

They sequestered the wrong bus. The logic that had to follow was that they had also suspended and taken the driving license of an erroneous driver. Was this true? The district attorney was investigating. The newspapers also reported that identifying the incorrect bus was not a crime. Nevertheless, there was some question of possible foul play by Seta that the district attorney's office claimed to be in the process of determining. The newspapers then reported that it had become clear that the wrong driver had been identified. So in May, the accusation of manslaughter was dropped. The district attorney's office then relieved the police of their role as head investigative office, transferring responsibility to the caribinieri or national military police generally in charge of public security.

A month later, in May, stunned members of Studenti Autorganizzati, family, and some of the African-Reggiani community organized another demonstration march in order to convey to the city government that they would not submit to their "anti-social politics as business." They would not accept this injustice. They demanded their right to the truth about Sylvester's death. On May 11 they marched from the city's Piazza Martiri Del 7 Luglio, (after their plans to march from the Commune Piazza dei Tricolore had to be cancelled because an event was already taking place there) and through the main central avenue to the Pentecostal church, shouting, "Justice!" and "Truth!" in Italian and English. They held signs also in Italian and English reading, "You can hide a bus, but you CAN'T hide the truth" and "The Strong must protect the Weak." This gathering drew around 100 people, compared with the thousands who had marched just after Sylvester's death in January.

By July nothing more had materialized. The newspapers had reported that the district attorney's office was investigating the 'real' driver, that the case against the mis-identified driver was dropped, and that he had just married after his good name has been libeled for months. Tensions on the buses intensified, with conflicts between drivers and young passengers of color leading to confrontations and even arrests. One Seta driver reported telling a journalist, "Five or six years ago, it wasn't like this. The situation has changed a lot and has gotten worse. Especially after the Sylvester tragedy …" (26 May).

Three years after Sylvester's death, in spring 2017, the 32-year-old bus driver, Giuseppe Picone, the ex-administrator of Seta, Filippo Allegra, and the director of the office of motorvehicles, Maurizio Coli, had not yet been tried. A hearing had taken place and testimony heard, but the next meeting scheduled for April 17, 2017 had been canceled due to a technicality about consistent audiences.

In April 2017, a judge ordered Seta's Catholic insurance company to pay 800,000 Euros to Sylvester Agyemang's family in damages. The family and their lawyer, Andrea Pellegrini, had asked for 1,5 million Euros. The judge's ruling in the case was that 80% of the guilt for the incident belonged to Seta and their driver, and 20% to Sylvester himself. Judge Chiara Zompi ruled that the driver had made a fatal mistake when he left the door open before driving on, and that Seta had made an error by ignoring the requests by its security officials who had several times before the event signaled that the security mechanisms on the doors were damaged, below standards, and in need of repair. She also imputed 20% of the guilt to Sylvester whom she labeled "imprudente" or careless. Sylvester's father, Emmanuel Aygemang, responded that he did not accept that his son bore any responsibility for what had happened, "He was dragged for meters and his backpack remained on the bus. My son did not make any mistakes. The mistakes were made by the driver and Seta."[19]

Alternative Stories

Sylvester Agyemang was loved deeply by his parents, siblings, and extended family. His loss created a gap in their lives that can never be filled. In an effort to illustrate a reverence for his life and being, and to remember him as a beautiful young man with direct and searching eyes who enjoyed reading and playing instruments, the family tacked to the iron rod fence behind the bus stop a plastic, rectangular poster with the words "Ciao Sylvester" and an image of Sylvester wearing a white t-shirt with a circular blue image of the world and an airplane flying into it, above the logo the word "JESUS." Sylvester held a book under his arm against a background of African-style patterned orange-brown-yellow tapestry behind a musical stage. We see Sylvester in the frame before a standing microphone and set of drums. In the left corner of the large poster is a small cartoon drawing of a pale skinned yellow haired figure with a halo, in front of a white broken heart with black colored blood, all before the sun and the words in "Le Persone Lions Volano in Cielo" or the Lion person flies in the sky.

It is difficult for me to see this image, which is surrounded by bouquets of flowers and small stuffed animals, without looking into Sylvester's large searching eyes, and feeling his energy without being filled with enormous sadness and regret that he is gone. I feel for the family and the community that lost him, and for the world that will never gain from this young man's contributions. This is not a story about me, but I cannot ignore my own social and historical position in witnessing and writing about it. As a white anti-racist woman scholar, even though I have Black family, friends, students, and colleagues and was raised as largely culturally Jewish with an acute awareness of anti-Semitism, I do not have any known African or Black ancestors and have never fully shared the history and ongoing experiences of vulnerability to assault and death that my family and friends continue to endure. I have a hyper-awareness of this as experienced by people I love, as well as strangers who represent them. Yet while I empathize with their vulnerability and feel a passionate sense of outrage by it, I am not the direct recipient of these constant threats. But what I do know, and feel, is that I have a responsibility for Sylvester's loss. As a person born into a world fundamentally structured by racism and where I am identified by the outside as White, I cannot be a witness in the same way as my Black family members and friends who may carry the cultural memory of such suffering in their own flesh. My own act of witnessing – even though my extended family was murdered in Nazi death camps because they were Jewish, and even though my mother's parents were immigrants from Hungary and Romania so they did not have any direct connection with European colonialism or the transatlantic slave trade – is heavy with a sense of disgust, shame, and responsibility.

Sylvester's loss was to me clearly and unequivocally a heinous act of anti-blackness that is increasingly experienced in Italy. Blacks in Italy are vulnerable to physical and symbolic violence, discrimination in housing, education, the job market, transportation, and in any public spaces. The bus driver did not respect the life of this young Black man, nor did the second bus driver. The first bus driver closed the door on Sylvester and began moving the bus before he had exited. As I've suggested, I have witnessed this behavior as a regular act of physical aggression toward black passengers in Italy during my countless visits. It is an expression of hostility, even hatred toward Black people, and a disregard for their safety that should be recognized and named as morally corrupt and criminal. But is it not, because the ubiquity of anti-black racism is systematically denied, silenced, and sold as a relic of the past. The myth of Italian and White goodness is purchased as a commodity to make White people feel better about themselves, yet always against a Black background that is not even acknowledged as there.

In vivid contrast, the portrait of Sylvester painted by a street artist presents a counter-narrative to Black social erasure and physical death (Figure 4.3). One cannot miss the image of Sylvester's young brown face and large bright eyes when passing by the bus stop in this highly traveled route in Reggio. He is present at the site. In this painting, a young man of African descent becomes a living expression of Blackness and belonging in Reggio Emilia. He was, and will remain, part of Italian history and culture. Does his image convey a radical overturning of established racial constructs? I would say that it does, because by placing it there for all to see it represents is an act of reversal, a rejection of the rejection, expressing what it is – not a turning away from reality, but rather, a facing of the reality that Sylvester was there and he and others like him will remain, because he belongs there. Sylvester's portrait speaks. It says that he is

FIGURE 4.3 Painting of Sylvester Agyemang by a local street artist near the Viale Piave bus stop

Black *and* Italian, turning the essentializing anti-blackness and binary logic that erases him into what Fanon described as a "yes" response to life, love, and generosity, and a no to oppression, silence, and social erasure.

Notes

1 "Sylvester aveva voglia di imparare e di farsi accettare dagli altri." 14 January, *Gazzetta di Reggio*.
2 My translations.
3 I am greatly indebted to Elizabeth Alexander for her moving and incisive essay, "Can you be BLACK and look at this?" (1994).
4 See Deborah Gray White (1999); Darlene Clark Hine and Kathleen Thompson (1998).
5 There have been hundreds of these killings, and with few exceptions, police have been exonerated. See Gray et al. (2014); Lamont Hill (2016); Lowery (2016); Taylor (2016).
6 See Jordan (2012).
7 See Hartman (1997).
8 Many who spent time in Libya or are from the Sudan carry bodily and emotional scars of anti-black hatred in North Africa.
9 "Killing of 2 Senegalese traders- a third injured." December 14 2011. www.bbc.com/news/world-Europe-16175877.
10 www.theguardian.com/world/2011/dec/13/florence-gunman-shoots-street-vendors. "Florence Gunman shoots Senegalese Street Vendors Dead." December 13, 2011.
11 Fermo is located on a hill in the Marches province in Italy. The province is in Central-Eastern Italy, bordering the Adriatic Sea. It is popularly classified as in the northern part of Italy.

12 Kyenge was Minister of Integration in the Letta Cabinet. The Ministry was eliminated with her departure. She was elected to the European Parliament on May 25, 2015.

13 See Fred Kudjo Kuwornu's film, "18 IUS Soli."

14 Over one million people live in Italy without official citizenship, 800,000 under the age of eighteen. They learn the national anthem in schools. They are Italian in practice. A bill to give them citizenship status was put before the Camera di Deputati, the legislative assembly that along with the Senate makes up the Italian parliament in October, 2015. But the reform continues to be stalled. The Lega party presented an amendment to block it, and there is a lack of political will in the other political parties. There are two active social movements involved in protesting and bringing attention to the right to be recognized as Italian citizens, #ITALIANISENZACITTADINANZA and #ITALIASONOANCHIO.

15 "Giustizia!"

16 The Ghanaian community does not have an active ethnic association in Reggio. Their collectives are church-based.

17 Like the other ethnic associations in Reggio, Jeunesse Africaine receives administrative and spatial support from the intercultural foundation, Mondinsieme. Under the leadership of Adil El Marouakhi, Mahta Woldezghi and an energetic staff, Mondinsieme became an important resource for migrants. Ethnic associations hold their meetings in the Mondinsieme building. The organization does outreach in local schools, teaches Arabic, conducts a tutoring program, organizes an annual week of anti-racist activities, and produces educational films.

18 I use pseudonyms for all research participants in non-public roles.

19 "É stato trascinato per dei metri e il suo zaino é rimasto dentro l'autobus. Mio figlio non ha commesso errori. Li hanno commessi l'autista e Seta." "Maxi riscurcimento alla famiglia di Sylvester," 12 Marzo 2017, *Gazzetta di Reggio*.

5

GRAMMAR AND GHOSTS
Refugees and Migrants in Italy

In this chapter I examine the spatialracial formation of African refugees, produced through a number of black spaces, including occupied spaces, the Mediterranean crossing and the Italian border, and the camps or detention centers. My discussion is purposefully multidimensional. I examine Black/black spaces from a number of different angles. Conceptually, I navigate between explorations of black ontologies and structured anti-blackness as crucial features of Black lived experiences in Italy. My ethnographic work profoundly informs my exploration. I hope to give justice and voice to the many who shared with me their stories of anguish and triumph and toward whom I feel a profound responsibility to write and disseminate knowledge that will help facilitate their freedom.

The group of Somali refugees I first interviewed described Somalia as a place that "everyone knows" is in a state of conflict. Yet Italy is doing little to help them. They could not remain in Somalia and hope to have the ability to support their families. One stated with visible emotional hurt, "You go to sleep at night and don't know if in the morning you will be alive." These women portrayed treacherous journeys of escape from Somalia while crossing the Gulf of Aden into Yemen or even more precariously through Ethiopia, Sudan, and Libya. Yet in Italy they were in a state of limbo. As one put it, "We don't exist." Several other women shook their heads in agreement.

Hearing these women describe experiences of being met with general indifference in Italy, I found it difficult to remain composed and certainly impossible to be a detached social analyst. One declared, "We are women. We have problems others don't have. We are trying to find peace." Another maintained that they had already grown weary of telling their stories, having agreed to speak with me only because they hoped I'd be able to inform the public of their suffering, to bring international attention to the fact that their lives in Italy were as wretched as they had been in Somalia. Some had lived in Italy for months, while others had been there for two or more years. None of the women spoke more than a few words of Italian, so a cultural mediator and advocate who worked at Alma Mater and had been in the country since the early 1990s translated from Somali to Italian for me.

These were not young women. Their ages ranged from early 20s to around 60 years. One described how her mother had been murdered in front of her, and her 21-year-old daughter remained in Somalia without anything to eat. Another woman had left ten of her children behind her and anxiety over their well-being weighed heavily on her heart. A third woman didn't know where her family was, and constantly thought about their safety and whereabouts. She showed us shrapnel wounds she'd received when Ethiopian and US military had bombed the market where she'd worked. Two of her children had been killed, and a third was hospitalized for six months. She added, "I'd go back to my country if not for the war, because in my country you don't go hungry, and they don't chase you from one place to another." Another woman tearfully stated, "The police tell us to leave, and they're supposed to be the ones to help us. If our country were in peace, we'd never have gone anyplace else. We don't want to be here. We never did." In one homeless shelter, the police removed a woman while she was sleeping. They threw her out at midnight. "When they do this, they put on gloves because they say we are beasts that they can't even touch." When I asked, the women did not know why the woman had been expelled, but they guessed there was no good reason for it.

In a period of intense conflict in Somalia beginning in 2008, some refugees managed to survive travel overland and sea, crossing several international borders to arrive on Italian territory. Many were first placed in 'reception' centers in Lampedusa, Sicily, Crotone, or Bari for a period of months and when released were reportedly told by Italian carabinieri (military police) who guard the camps that they were now "free" to do as they wished. They could choose either to remain in Southern Italy where they were at the time (2010) unlikely to find help from voluntary organizations, or travel north to urban post-industrial areas like Turin and Milan in search of institutional support. Turin is known to have a plenitude of voluntary, Christian, and lay organizations, a place where they would also be close to the border of other European countries.

Somali and other Africans who escaped war, political repression, and desperate economic conditions in their countries of origin only to find themselves caught in another kind of hell in Italy are among today's most abandoned populations (see Pratt 2005; Wright 2006; Golash-Boza 2015; Mbembe 2017). As anthropologist Barbara Pinelli suggests, the suffering and vulnerability of political refugees in Italy is an extended experience – from the drama of flight, to the forms of social exclusion they encounter in the arrival countries where they are exposed to prolonged and systematic "processes of subjection" (Pinelli 2011). These are the fortunate people who made it to Europe before drowning or falling prey to another kind of demon while crossing the vast terrain linking their countries of origin to Europe.

Life is for us all a struggle to make sense of the social world and to transform one's position in it; and as we all live in social relationship with others, our lives encompass deeply engrained structural inequalities that we may embrace or reject. Power orients social practices, but we do not all respond to it in the same way. Black subjects in Italy as in the West more generally are framed in a system of being classified outside the established social matrix, and as superfluous. Yet, as I have explored in previous chapters, people of African descent often know, even if only intuitively, that as Africans they are a central part of the Italian-European assemblage. This is apparent among refugees whose struggle for personal and familial survival against enormous odds, crossing some of the same routes of the enslaved who were deported to Europe centuries ago. They represent a most recent iteration of courageous fortitude and survival among people of the African diaspora.

There is a commonly held assumption in Italy, reinforced by the pervasive images of black pain and dying, that African refugees and immigrants are symbolic matter 'out of place' in Italian society (Douglas 2002; Puwar 2004). As I have suggested, this sense of un-belonging is also experienced by other nonwhites classified as outside the social order and to a certain extent Eastern Europeans. However, Africans are the only people in the world who have been systematically and persistently discriminated against on the basis of skin color. Charles Mills suggests that Blacks experience a unique sense of alienness, strangeness, and invisibility in the West because they have been classified as such in Western taxonomies in ways that overlap with but are not equivalent to classifications of other nonwhite 'populations' (Mills 1998). Sadly, many[1] who are compelled by history and circumstance to share this social position have a private African refugee living in their own heads: that unloved part of themselves.

James Baldwin's insights about the global condition of blackness in his essay, "Many Thousands Gone," can be usefully applied to the Italian context, where being accepted as a full person may require a complete overturning of social taxonomies as we now know them (Baldwin 2012). To live, it is assumed that the black man "to be truly human, must first become like one of us," acquiescing in "the obliteration of his own personality, the distortion and debasement of his own experience, surrendering to those forces which reduce the person to anonymity and which make themselves manifest daily all over the darkening world" (34). But not everyone, not even James Baldwin himself, follows this path of distortion, moving instead as fugitives, and/or subjects with inner lives toward their "own human vagary" (Quashie 2012, 17), and who reject not only being rejected by the West, but also the old binarisms of us and them, black and white, African and Human.

African Refugees

I learned from research participants working with the women's inter-ethnic organization, Alma Mater, that hundreds of African refugees principally of Eritrean, Ethiopian, and Somali origins had occupied the Olympic Village apartment buildings constructed for athletes before the Winter 2006 games. Turin's political leaders had invested a great deal of money preparing to host the prestigious Olympic games, and had removed one of the city's oldest and largest markets, the "Mercato Centrale," in order to create a place for the Olympic village. The apartments, named the "Ex-MOI," were built rapidly and poorly, contracted through private speculation and special government contracts to friends. When the Olympic games were over, the apartments had remained vacant while the municipal government debated what to do with them. They had just reached an agreement to sell half of the buildings to private investors and retain the other half for 'casa popolare' or subsidized public housing, when in 2013 African refugees occupied four of the residences.

The buildings were located somewhere on the other side of the bridge across the railroad tracks from Fiat's old Lingotto automobile factory. The largest car factory in the world in the early 20th century, in the 1990s Lingotto was remade into a sprawling complex that included a shopping mall, large grocery store, convention center/hotel decorated with a line of national flags, a concert hall, and 'Eataly,' the original slow Italian food mecca and a new symbol of Italian innovation of Turin/Piedmont that draws on-the-go young professionals without time to cook and has since been exported to other cities in Italy and in New York, Tokyo, Sao Paolo, Munich, and elsewhere. But I had no idea where the African refugees lived. I wished to see them with my own eyes, to document their presence in the former Olympic complex. Accompanying and supporting me were my partner, anthropologist Donald Carter, and our seventeen-year-old daughter, Eliana. We began at the Mall, exiting through doors at the back end that open up to two distinct foot and bike bridges with Olympic arches framed by a stunning view of the majestic Alps (see Figure 5.1). The bridges run over the train tracks, and like a large artery they connect a commercial center to a residential area. It was nearing dusk, and the sun was setting slowly along the horizon. Lovers lingered, holding each other and whispering as if not to disturb the serene peaks. As we walked across the bridge with its graffiti marked cement sidings we noticed just in front of us a very slim African man in his 20s, and thought he might be going back to his home in the occupied buildings. We crossed where the two bridges emptied out via winding stairways onto a few commercial enterprises like an agricultural supply store, and saw a neighborhood with tall apartment buildings surrounding a piazza lit with strings of lights slowly filling up with people, the vast majority pale skinned. Along the piazza's periphery there was a church, bar-café, and some restaurants. A man's voice bellowed in Italian through a microphone, and then traditional Italian music.

FIGURE 5.1 Olympic Bridge from the repurposed Lingotto factory complex to the
residences across the railroad tracks, including the Ex-MOI Olympic Village buildings occupied by hundreds of West and Africans from the Horn
of Africa

Credit: Author.

Left of the piazza on the side of the street adjacent to the railroad tracks the
pastel colored buildings appeared relatively new, constructed with pre-fabricated
materials that contrasted with the 1950s and 19th century construction styles of
the other structures. Nevertheless, I initially thought we were in the wrong place,
for I didn't see any people of African ancestry. Then we asked three young men
walking toward the piazza if the pink, tangerine, and blue building were in fact
the Ex-MOI, and the man in the middle responded with a bit of irritation, "Si,
Sono i Ex-MOI" ("Yes, they're the Ex-MOI") as if to say, "What of it?" "Why
do you care?"). As we walked further, it became clear we were in the right place,
because there were posters and announcements about a language school for foreigners on a glass door. Then as we reached a fenced area adjacent to one of the
apartment buildings we saw what appeared to have been a basketball court yard
without hoops where seven men milled about, glancing toward us. Another
young man spoke on a cell phone while resting on a concrete barrier in front of
the building space that appeared to be used as a school and information center.
He wore white earphones, and spoke English. He was of medium height and
build, and dark complexion, wearing a sweatshirt that read "St Diego," and
appeared to be around thirty years of age. Wishing to document the place for my
research, I asked Donald to request this gentleman's permission to take some
photographs. He responded with an emphatic, "Yes, you can take. You

SHOULD take some photos of this place," and introduced himself as Brent[2] from Nigeria. His face, gestures, and way of speaking reminded me of the Spanish actor from the Canary Islands, Javier Bardem, whom I admire. Brent declared:

> Take the photos. Take them. You can even take them of the inside of the building if you want. People should see this. It is important. We are African, but you can see that we are clean. We take care of the place as best we can. We have organized things inside. I built, with my own hands, one of the rooms. I took the wood piece by piece, and I built it.[3]

Before inviting us to follow him inside the building, he told us a bit about his own passage to Turin. Brent is from Nigeria, where as he explained with visible anguish and using hand gestures, "There has been war for many years. People only know now that there is warfare in Nigeria, but for a long time this has been happening. They put, they found the oil in the country. And one group is fighting with the other group for the oil." I was instantly drawn to and moved by Brent. I sensed his suffering and struggle, and also that he was deeply genuine, intelligent, and complex. He used expressive hand gestures to convey the situation in his country of origin. He said he'd spent a long time in Libya, adding that many others in the Ex-MOI had also worked in Libya. When he arrived Italy he was sent to a reception center in Cuneo (southwest of Turin) while awaiting a decision on his application for refugee status. He told us they had closed the center around six months ago, giving some of the people there 500 Euros and telling them to make their own way, without any kind of guidance or direction.[4] With frustration he said, "They thought we should just go to Hell." Some people weren't given any money, including Brent. He mentioned that in spite of this, the newspapers reported that *everyone had been given some money*. He then spoke of the problems he was having with his documents, explaining that the government awards three different types of refugee status: a) full recognition of five years, providing them with their passports and residence permits which enable one to travel outside Italy; b) fixed subsidiary status for three years; c) fixed humanitarian status for one year. He was given humanitarian status, requiring him to renew his documents at the end of one year, which he said was very difficult because one must have evidence of employment in order for the renewal to be given and official employment is extremely difficult to acquire. Most people can't find formal employment, and are therefore compelled to become 'clandestine' migrants. Brent had taken a course in metal-mechanics, but hadn't found a job.

He led us into the building, he said, to see the school,"Scuola Ex-MOI" (see Figures 5.2, 5.3, and 5.4), a large room with paper announcements and schedules of Italian language classes and lessons in mathematics and English taped along the walls. There were announcements of an information desk offered at designated times, and of a general meeting. All the messages were written in Italian, English, and French. There was a chalkboard, table, couch, and some chairs. Education is clearly of central importance in the social life of refugees who try to ensure that their children receive schooling, so they will not be left out. Many of the adults are taking classes to acquire a trade. Everyone needs to learn Italian, and gain knowledge of the local social economy. But that will not be enough. Brent explained that some "whites," whom he described as young people from the University and Social Centers, helped them teach the children, and to organize politically in order to advance their rights. The schoolroom and other building spaces expressed a sense of collective engagement and solidarity.

After showing us the school and meeting room, Brent decided we needed to see more of the interior, so he led us up some stairs and through corridors lit only by the fading natural light. I felt very uneasy. I didn't wish to intrude. But we followed him. I was struck by the scent of mildew mixed with thick stagnant air and cooking spices. It was heartbreaking to listen to Brent talk about the building, and challenging to keep from falling into emotion without thinking about what I was seeing as a critical ethnographer and my responsibility to represent these people. I wanted to hold the people I saw in my arms, and to stay there with them. I continually told myself that I was there for a reason, at this most vulnerable human moment and with my own family. I was there on invitation in order to be a witness and analyst, to report and write about what I saw in order to help them.

FIGURE 5.2 Street entrance to the Ex-MOI common rooms. Announcement of school hours for training in Italian, Math, and English. Announcement of a general assembly meeting, as well as a teller machine and stock room hours
Credit: Eliana Carter.

FIGURE 5.3 Communal room where classes, meetings, and other gatherings are held. Sewing machine and table. Refrigerator
Credit: Eliana Carter.

FIGURE 5.4 Communal room with Happy Birthday wishes and balloons from a previous celebration. Notices of strategic action plans, laws, and procedures for receiving asylum, refugee status, and international humanitarian protection status
Credit: Eliana Carter.

The white walls were marked with hundreds of small and long dark nicks. Two bikes leaned against a wall in the corner next to a stairway along with some large sheets of plywood. As we ascended the stairway to the second floor I saw a corner with a pile of tires, and some blue and yellow bags filled and tied. Atop a makeshift shelf sat a children's pull-toy dog and some children's books. Along the walls machine parts, lamps, boxes, a baby carriage. Drying clothing hung over the railing. Brent told us numerous times that the building wasn't well made; it had been constructed hastily and without care. The residents did the best they could, but he described it as a "mess." There were no showers. No hot water.

We saw the rooms they used to wash themselves. In the larger of the two were large plastic basins for such purposes. In one of the bathrooms a ceiling corner had caved in and was deeply darkened from apparent water damage (see Figures 5.5 and 5.6). It smelled strongly from the visible mold. Brent told us that water continually leaked. There was no heating in the apartment buildings, so winter was very difficult and also nights during most of the year when it is quite chilly. He also described how they'd used space heaters, but these proved dangerous and also tripped up the power.

A child who appeared to be 8 or 9 came from around a corner wearing a white t-shirt with a large green smiling face with 'x' marks for eyes (Figure 5.7). Brent presented mattresses lined up against more mattresses, and led us into a room. It was dark. A man was sleeping. Brent showed us the apartment area that

FIGURE 5.5 Storage area leading to showerless bathrooms. A rack of jackets, two non-operative washing machines, some pots and pans

Credit: Eliana Carter.

FIGURE 5.6 The facilities have degraded. The ceiling of a bathroom, with mold spores Credit: Eliana Carter.

he'd built as his own private space. There were many other people, including two children. He told us many times that groups of young people had built the interior rooms with wood and other materials they'd collected themselves (Figure 5.8). I reflected on the contrast between this space and the apartment buildings on the opposite side of the street from the Ex-MOI, which I had visited some years before. The other area had housed Fiat factory workers before the plant closed in the 1980s.

Brent described between 500–600 people from Eritrea, Ethiopia, Somalia, Nigeria, Ghana, Gambia, Senegal, and other African countries in the four buildings. We passed piles of clothing, bags, and storage containers along the corridors. Near the bathrooms were two washing machines with damaged frames on opposite sides of the hallway with pots and pans on their surface. Neither appeared to be functional. There was a coat rack covered with piles of jackets, a bike, more plastic bags, and a brown pair of shoes atop a fire extinguisher in the wall. Brent led us to the rooftop from where we could see the adjoining colorful Ex-MOI buildings with satellite dishes, and balconies covered with drying clothing, as well as the apartment complexes on the other side of the street, and train tracks below (Figures 5.9–5.12). All sorts of odds and ends, Brent explained, were gathered by the young residents and used in whatever way they could, repairing and selling and using parts of things with which they could offer their services for some remuneration. He said they found things and just sold them in order to purchase food. "We pick things up, we carry them. We sell things. We do what we can to get money for food." There were piles of tires, a box spring, a couple of Persian rugs, a broken table, pieces of wood, scrap metal, piping, a broken chest of drawers. They did day-work when they could get it.

The acts of scavenging parts, remnants, and broken but perhaps reparable electronics in a system of barter and exchange of goods and services signal that these refugees have intimate understanding of and integration into Italian society. They practice their knowledge of a deeply local Italian customary way of doing things in order to survive. Within these economic practices are the ghosts of an Italian past where goods and services were bartered in what has been called a second or "doppio" economy for people who required more than their salaries to survive. In Italian culture in Piedmont there was also a deep attention to conserving things that were customarily preserved, and repurposed. Nothing went to waste. African refugees are engaging with Italian cultural and economic practices that may also share elements of cultural and economic practices in their countries of origin.

As we followed Brent down to the courtyard, there was artwork on some external walls. My daughter, Eliana Carter, whom I'd enlisted as photographer because of her interest, photographed the drawings (and all the other Ex-MOI images). At this moment, another man approached us angrily, asking in Italian what we were doing. Brent confronted him, switching into Pidgin English,

FIGURE 5.7 A young girl exiting a private space constructed by residents. Stacks of personal belongings such as children's toys, a portable sound system, clothing for different seasons, and a makeshift umbrella rack
Credit: Eliana Carter.

FIGURE 5.8 Partition in room for privacy, this one constructed by Brent from plywood and plexiglass. In the background, seated child, and a man on the phone
Credit: Eliana Carter.

FIGURE 5.9 Rooftop, with adjacent non-Ex-MOI residences. A pile of scrap metal and other material occupants re-purpose and sell. Bicycles for transportation. A rack of clean clothing drying in the air
Credit: Eliana Carter.

FIGURE 5.10 View of the courtyard from inside an Ex-MOI building. The city
        removed the basketball hoops
Credit: Eliana Carter.

FIGURE 5.11 View of a yard and community garden. Men on their phones
Credit: Eliana Carter.

FIGURE 5.12 An adjacent Ex-MOI apartment building with residents. Satellite dishes, bicycles, rugs, and other personal items are stored on porches
Credit: Eliana Carter.

"Why you do that? Why you talk in that way?" He told the man that we were taking photos because he had authorized us to do so. A third man entered the dispute, apparently to mediate. It was all over in a few minutes, followed by apologies, smiles, and hand shakes. Brent explained to us that he and these men had been in the Cuneo camp together. The second of the two, Henry, was from Ghana. Henry then joined us for the rest of Brent's tour, adding his own comments. Henry told us that every day except Sunday "the white people" brought them food, pointing to the bins they were brought in. But there wasn't enough food for so many people. They also received blankets, used clothing, and other things such as mattresses. Brent described the refugees' engagement with Catholic charities that have long played a political role in the cultural landscape of Turin and most of Italy. Brent also mentioned several times that some Italians had helped them organize a number of protests, including the ones that initially brought them to occupy the Ex-MOI, "Some white people help us. They are helping us to do the protests."

These refugees are engaging in unexpected ways with youth from Social Centers,[5] employing everything in their power to survive. With these Italian collaborators, they have protested the absence of a formal address and zip code for people living in the Ex-MOI apartments, which would enable them to have access to social funds and resources. They had recently protested in front of the Mayoral building, struggling to redefine the Ex-MOI as a residential site where they could be served. They achieved tremendous success with the Italian bureaucratic system.

Along one of the internal walls of the courtyard are two handwritten signs labeled "Residenza Collettiva" with sub categories about creating an association that must be officially recognized with a residence, which is a human right. At the bottom of the second caption is a statement that begins with an exclamation point that a residential address guarantees that one really exists in this territory. The fact that the refugees won this battle with the city government represents an immense triumph in the assertion of their social life over the effort to assign them a social place fated to permanent social nonbeing.

When he ended his tour, Brent and two other men, one from Gambia and the other whose origins we did not learn, told us,

> This is very very stressful for us. We have a lot to deal with. It's hard, very hard. We're alright (pointing at the building). But it's hard, especially because of the documents. And many people lose, lost their minds. They can't take the pressure. It's too much.

We observed rail thin men who were clearly physically injured and/or disabled; one was in an electric wheelchair. With a sense of urgency, Brent remarked, "We want to work. These people want to work. They can do it if they just have a chance."

Black Fugitives

I reflected on Brent's chronicle of his journey from Nigeria to Italy. I thought about the chapters in his ongoing struggles and the tour he gave us of the occupied Olympic village. He also described collaboration with Italian activists to oppose and transform the system that consigns them to social non-persons (Goffman 1986). I realized that all of these stories and actions expressed reworked and rejected systemic efforts to erase and repress Black life. Brent's struggles for freedom can be understood within a logic of what has been referred to by Fred Moten and Stefano Harney as "Black fugitivity," an acting with energy and imagination against conditions of anti-black racial governance (Harney and Moten 2013; Hesse 2014; also see Kelley 2016). Fugitive action is potentially transformative (Sexton 2016). Through their physical movements, spoken words, and artistic representations, Brent and thousands of others who claim their lives by taking perilous journeys across the Mediterranean, and who occupy public and private property, critique the institutional power that would render them placeless, and assert their belonging in Europe. Building living and social spaces that the state classifies as illegitimate, fighting for their right to live with dignity, and constructing social networks that subvert established ways of being, they both push against and insert themselves as members of the Italian polity.

The notion of "fugitive justice" is inherited from traditions of slave narratives that formulated black fugivitity as the enactment of escaping from and speaking out against repressive racial laws including prohibitions on literacy, using written and spoken word to speak one's truth (Harney and Moten 2013). Brent's words and gestures implicitly condemn an anti-black modern governance structure that sustains the privileged status of liberties ascribed only to White or whitened persons who are led to believe they have some power, and or hold positions of authority. To occupy buildings in Italian neighborhoods is to reject the logic of private property for the privileged.

Brent and his peers have been excluded from the very concept of liberty, and as Charles Mills suggests are caught (along with everyone else) in an unrecognized "racial contract" in which all Whites agree as signatories or beneficiaries to oppress nonwhites (Mills 1999). Yet by occupying the Ex-MOI Olympic residences and asserting their belonging in Italy, they refuse to participate in the system that seeks to normalize their own erasure. They engage in a sort of contemporary marronage by building a space within a space, where survival is contingent upon and critical of the established social order.

There is tremendous symbolic power in the occupation of an Olympic residence. The Olympic games represent one of the only opportunities for a nation state to gain international prestige by collectively out-playing or individually performing a sport better than people from other nations. By occupying the Olympic Village, Brent and other Africans reject membership in a modern polity founded on anti-blackness and repression of transformative critique and alternatives. These refugees claim their universal right to live, sustaining themselves and each other in conjunction with young Italians who are highly critical of the existing social order. In their occupation of these spaces, they embody the ghosts of local histories, where inadequate housing has been a persistent problem in post war Italy (Carter 1997). The ghosts of this problem haunt the present with growing evictions. This also resonates with Frank B. Wilderson's compelling description of Black life in which every gesture and every performance of blackness, every act or action either critical or creative, rhetorical or aesthetic, is haunted by a sense of grammar and ghosts, with a structure and memory of its coming into being through violence (Wilderson 2009).

Brent's story and the estimated 750 sub-Saharan African refugees who have occupied the Ex-MOI Olympic village residences is replicated in other parts of Turin, and Italy. The suffering and homelessness of Somali women refugees whom I first met at Alma Mater in 2010 first impelled me to write this book. Until 2008, there were few African or other refugees and asylum seekers in Italy, but today somewhere between 32,000–70,000 have officially applied for or have been awarded asylum in Italy.[6] The refugees and asylum seekers are notably of Eritrean, Ethiopian, Somali, Nigerian, Gambian, Ghanaian origins, but also from Senegal, Mali, Rwanda, Sudan, The Democratic Republic of Congo, and other conflict-ridden zones. Like Brent, many who now live in abandoned buildings and makeshift camps throughout Italy were working in Libya when civil war erupted and they were compelled to leave (Pastore et al. 2006; Pastore and Trinchieri 2008; Albahari 2015).

African refugees who occupy several other buildings in Turin frequently concentrate according to national and or regional identity. A predominance of Somalis and Eritreans live in the San Paolo clinic, while Eritreans, Ethiopians, and Sudanese are in the old factory building on via Bologna. In 2008, hundreds moved into the former San Paolo Clinic (ex-Clinica San Paolo), where most remained for a year living in unsanitary conditions with neither heat nor electricity.[7] In 2009, they were to be removed by the Turin authorities and transferred to the Barracks of Via Asti (Caserma di Via Asti), formerly the investigative site of the Republican National Guard (Guardia Nazionale Repubblicana) where people suspected of participating in the Italian Resistance against fascism had been interrogated, tortured, and killed. In the summer of 2010, dozens of African refugees were still living in the former clinic, situated in one of the city's residential quarters. When I visited this site I noted that although it was situated in a residential area passers-by did not seem to notice the many Africans continually walking in, and out of the building. These refugees from the Horn of Africa were there, in this residential neighborhood, by this time part of the daily life, yet not legitimate in the eyes of many.

Along via Bologna in another quarter of the city, an additional fifty or so still lived in an abandoned building in front of a small park where several, unable to find work, sat on park benches during the day. These informal settlements of refugees in occupied buildings represent the assertion of the most basic human right to a home, part of the public good that is being denied them. Alice Rossi describes the occupations as part of a new urban infrastructure, "urban intra frontiers" that represent an important aspect of contemporary daily life as an element in the re-functioning of urban spaces in the wake of global economic restructuring (Rossi 2014).[8] A 2014 law criminalizes people who occupy buildings ("piano casa" = amendment decree law 47). The occupants must be constantly on alert. They are targeted as criminals, and vulnerable not only to police stops but also to an array of 'looks,' stares, hostile comments, and other interactions that leave many feeling despair.

Refugees tend to be portrayed as undifferentiated masses of people, obscuring the multiple and layered differences between them that affect their experiences. Jennifer Hyndman argues that the 1948 Universal Declaration of Human Rights is limited by being race neutral and gender blind in its assertion that 'we are all just people,' suggesting that all refugees will be handled in the same manner when there are noteworthy variations in treatment based on gender biases and racism (Hyndman 2000). The racial classification of African refugees in Italy is significant. Many speak openly about being discriminated against because they are "Nero" or "Black." A man living in the via Bologna building who was holding a Koran and appeared to have been in his 30s explained that he and the others had been living in horrible conditions for so long with nothing being done for them that his spirit had turned toward a focus on his home, in the Sudan. Pulling up a sleeve and pointing to the outer part of his forearm, he spoke with frustration and mourning, "Here in Italy they treat me badly, because of my skin." A migrant from east Africa told me, "We are the excrement of the society."

The occupation of the Ex-MOI and other spaces signify a struggle to take back one's own life. The refugees express in their narratives and protest movements a civic consciousness and politics of the present that is improvisatory instead of self-conscious. A Black subjectivity and fugitivity that as Moten and Harney suggest, steals "back the life stolen by the enlightenment" (Moten and Harney 2013, 28) (see Figure 5.13).

The graffiti art by refugees in the ex Olympic village conveys their critique of the normalization of a racial frontier that seeks to erase their centrality to Western history, politics, economy, and culture. A drawing painted on the face of a building internal to the courtyard of an Ex-MOI dwelling depicts a naked, goddess-like Black woman with blue eyes, a white mouth, and a forest green sprawling head of hair shaped like a tree, clutched by a small round-faced light brown child with east Asian features and a big smile, a leaf growing from their head, and snowflake arms (Figure 5.14). The image conveys a sense of an origin story in which blackness is opulent, inventive, and generative. Black women are at the center of this broad scale of productivity that seems to interconnect the

FIGURE 5.13 Announcement of a demonstration on a glass door in the courtyard Credit: Eliana Carter.

natural and human world in a unified tree of life of intersecting differences written into one's very bodily being, sustaining the young and their own emergent resourcefulness.

Another prominent image in this Ex-MOI courtyard illustrates a muscular brown man wearing a sleeveless white t-shirt and blue pants, his head a bird house with a circle and upward pointing zigzagging arrow in the middle, his arms extended as if pleading, and his right arm hung with deep pink netting and the words painted boldly in aqua, "Humanity is Not For Sale" (Figure 5.15) Like the image of the woman, the painting of the man expresses vitality and autonomy. The message directly criticizes human trafficking and the implicit smuggling manifest in the commodification of refugees when state and UNHCR contracts are awarded to organizations and individuals for providing room and board to asylum seekers. The practice of making a profit from asylum seekers and refugees has become a business. The image communicates what Moten might call a Black fugitive assertion of the basic right of being human, to live with freedom and dignity, anywhere. If these building occupiers break the laws of private property and the state, they do so because such systems of governance have abandoned them. The graffiti art conveys a sense of moving against, instead of within, the hegemonic modern conventions of anti-black epistemic and ontological violence that normalize and render taken-for-granted and unspoken the systematic suppression and refusal of liberties and equalities.

FIGURE 5.14 Mermaid-tree painting in courtyard
Credit: Eliana Carter.

FIGURE 5.15 Humanity is not for sale painting in courtyard
Credit: Eliana Carter.

It was dark when we parted with Brent and his friends, and I was reluctant to leave them there. Walking slowly and without speaking, we made our way back across the bridge where our rental car was parked. We hadn't eaten dinner and were quite hungry, so we decided to stop for a bite in Eataly. I stepped into the brightly lit space that was once the country's symbol of industrial progress and leadership and currently of its crafting as the 'postmodern' and avant garde of slow and healthy food for a wealthy, professional middle class consumer. Eataly is a gourmet restaurant-store founded by Oscar Farinetti, son of the creator of the electronics firm UniEuro. He is from Alba, Italy, a medieval town an hour from Turin, reputed to be the gourmet capital of Italy and known in particular as the home of Gianduia chocolate. Eataly's mission manifesto is to unite people all over the world by providing and creating the highest quality of food and beverages produced by local farmers and artisans. The contrast between this site at the renovated Lingotto factory, a consumer heaven that suggests incredible excess and waste, and the African refugees in the Ex-MOI apartments, was so startling that I could barely contain my grief and desire to scream. I understood that the Italians there with friends and families who were enjoying meals in comfort were not consciously thinking about the privilege they enjoyed, their access to this niche market and its kitchens and dining areas of specialized meals (fish, pasta, pizza, cheese, meat) made to order. Yet the presence of this mecca of modern niche pleasure and symbol of Italian market innovation just across the railroad tracks from occupied buildings with such overwhelming social neglect left me feeling frustrated and sad (see Figures 5.16 and 5.17). You can literally see the Ex-MOI from Eataly, and Eataly from the Ex-MOI.

Refugees and Race

In her study of women in Italian detention centers, Barbara Pinelli describes the problem of cultural perceptions, and the continual suffering of women who are racialized even by administrators designated to 'help' them. Their perceptions are filtered through an epistemological violence in which they are, as Fanon described, "over-determined from without" via epidemiological and other bodily features associated with attributes that for Africans translate into time worn characterizations as childlike victims. The refugee women shared with Pinelli their experience of 'the look,' "They look at you like, you know, you're just a black immigrant." The women explained that they entreat people to instead see who they are, "I am … Look!" The capacity to really look, and see, requires a process of re-cognition and racial literacy that necessitates re-cognizing and discarding culturally sedimented classifications based on colonial ideologies and calculated mis-recognitions (Pinelli 2011). It necessitates transforming what Fanon in *Wretched of the Earth* argued was the foundational formulation of Western colonialism, the tenet that tells the colonized he or she is not fully human, even as the colonized finds him and herself constantly struggling with human responsibilities against life and death, freedom and the lack of it, virtue and vice (Fanon and

FIGURE 5.16 Italians shopping and eating pasta in Turin's, Eataly
Credit: Author.

FIGURE 5.17 Italians ordering seafood dinner, and eating dinner at a counter
Credit: Author.

Philcox 2005). Lewis R. Gordon suggests that Fanon's search for recognition fails, because neither the Hegelian master nor the structural white man desires recognition from Blacks – each wants instead work, bodies without points of view, bodies out of view (Gordon 2000, 79):

> Consciousness is embodied. It's in the flesh. In the flesh, one is not merely a point of view but also a point that is viewed: I see, hear, and smell; and I am seen, heard, and smelled. The one who witnesses me is the other, and I do the same to him. Sociality is an achievement.

However, the reciprocity that forms sociality does not as a rule happen between Whites and Blacks. Charles Mills suggests that the Modern world is formulated on the basis of a 'racial contract' between whites, an agreement that racism is the political system and power structure of rule in which material wealth, opportunities, benefits and burdens, duties and rights are differentially and hierarchically distributed on the basis of race. Mills writes,

> The Racial Contract is that set of formal or informal agreements or meta-agreements ... between members of one subset of humans, henceforth designated by (shifting) "racial" (phenotype/genealogical/cultural) criteria ... as "white," and coextensive (making due allowance for gender

differentiating) with the class of full persons, to categorize the remaining subset of humans as "nonwhite" and of a different and inferior moral status, subpersons, so that they have a subordinate civil standing in the white or white-ruled polities the whites either already inhabit or establish or in transactions as aliens with these polities …

(Mills 1999, 11)

Legal scholar Clelia Bartoli argues that Italy is being legally engineered as racist through state policies and discourses, even if most Italians believe racism is immoral, and they are not intentionally racist. Bartoli invokes the US racial system, warning Italians that the legislation of racial classifications for instance in the US Supreme Court's Plessy v. Ferguson decision that legislated 'separate but (un)equal' had an enduring hold on subjectivity and group identity, conditioning how individuals learn to perceive the world, others, and themselves (Bartoli 2012, 50). In her evaluation of current practices in Italy she draws from Stokely Carmichael and Charles Hamilton's discussion of the rise of the Black Power movement against a Jim Crow system of racial apartheid in the late 1960s United States. Bartoli warns that a similar system shaped by White supremacy is becoming intrinsic to the architecture of Italian bureaucracy, produced in everyday institutional practices. People of non-Italian origins or who are perceived through what Fanon called a 'racial epidermal schema' and or as being Muslim face continual obstacles and violations of their rights. The Italian state legislates racism in immigration policies that create illegal status, criminalizing even people who have lived in Italy for many years but who work in an informal economic sector that prevents them from verifying their employment and hence renewing their residency permits. The majority of so-called 'clandestines' or irregulars are overstayers, i.e., they entered the country legally, but their permits ran out. When one lacks formal permission to live in Italy, one is deprived of fundamental rights, inhabiting an "exceptional status." One can be contained in a detention center, refused health care, denied the right to public education, refused the right to marry, prevented from obtaining housing, and denied the right to take judicial action for instance against employers who assume them in the informal economic sector or may dismiss them at will and even withhold their wages. The mark of irregularity – real or imagined – which is defined by a *racially configured* legal status, symbolizes danger to the social order. A form of social erasure, it is conflated with blackness and treated as an unbridgeable alterity that renders one vulnerable to being rejected at the national borders (see Garelli and Tazzioli 2016) and or confined in segregated, enclosed in spaces or urban peripheries, and in practice to become socially invisible (Carter 2010).

Barnor Hesse (2014) describes "foreclosures" as the discursive contexts in which certain words or references become impossible to articulate because the means of their enunciation have been exorcized from our discursive frameworks. The routine evasion of colonial racial histories and legacies in the treatment of refugees and migrants is one such foreclosure, a "colonial–racial foreclosure" that has nourished the preclusion of consideration of anti-blackness in the reception and management of migrants, asylum seekers, and refugees. There is however ample evidence that Europe employs racial classifications to filter people it considers desirable from undesirable migrant populations. In his essay, "Human Blacklisting: the global apartheid of the EU's external border regime," Henk Van Houtum discusses the "external difference-producing border regime" the EU produces by composing a 'white' Schengen list, and a 'black' Schengen list to represent the countries whose citizens do or do not need apply for a visa to visit or transit Schengen countries. He argues that this system of classification inscribes an unambiguously racially exclusive borderline divided by 'black' countries whose inhabitants are unwelcome, and 'white' countries whose inhabitants are welcome (Van Houtum 2013)[9].

Through policies and practices, the EU is fabricating perceptions of migrants and refugees from Africa as 'alien' and threatening to national security, reminding us of the polices applied in colonial Africa to divide 'natives' from colonists and to give the state the power to employ extraordinary, extrajudicial measures against categories of people deemed 'undesireable' (Mbembe 2009; see also Mamdani 2012). Aiming his critique in particular at France where state policies have led to the appearance of racialized 'ghettoes'[10] of concentrated poverty and the repression of people of African and Arab descent, Achille Mbembe (2009) argues that these spaces are consistent with policies that separate "French of pure stock" from persons who are legally French citizens, yet "not quite like the others." Defining people largely of African and Arab descent as a threat to French cultural lifestyle and values, the French state has supported the application of colonial methods of repression via social isolation along with daily threats and forms of harassment of the most vulnerable members of society who are represented as an undifferentiated mass (see also Keaton 2013). David Theo Goldberg has made a similar and quite powerful argument that "urban geometry," the definition, reproduction, distribution, and experience of space, is a trope in terms of which identity is fashioned, not only a matter of a demographic statistic or parcel of property. Goldberg suggests that colonized peoples were first excluded in urban planning within the colonies, and this was later insinuated into racialized urban segregation in the West. Nation states have intentionally manufactured the confinement of formerly colonized people in separate, circumscribed, and frequently peripheral spatial locations where they lack access to rights, goods, and services in a secretive mode of social exclusion designed to keep them from "polluting the body politic, or dirtying civil(ized) society" (Goldberg 1993, 92). Racialized former colonial populations have been warehoused in stigmatized zones and spaces connoting moral depravity, natural inferiority, and degeneracy.[11] The taken-for-granted idea that essentially different "races" belong in their proper places, geographically and socially, and the idea that everyone must 'know one's racial place' has a formative relationship in the discursive and material formations of racial space (Goldberg

1993). In Italy the material and symbolic separations are more diffuse, and, as I will discuss below, at the same time quite contained.

A hierarchy of privilege based on racial classificaiton took root in the very declaration of universal human rights that followed the French revolution. As Hannah Arendt argued, in spite of this declaration, the definition of 'human' in the modern West required that one be recognized as a member of a polity, one of "the people." Only people with full citizenship would be awarded human rights. Thus, the League of Nations and later the UN had to build a 'law of exception' for refugees, stateless people, and people of diverse national origins with a right to asylum. The declaration of the 'Rights of Man' that appeared to apply globally to all human beings, in practice asserted only the inalienable rights of 'the people' who were part of a polity to sovereign self-government. Accordingly, the loss of home meant the loss of one's place in the world, including the loss of a political community (see Malkki 1992). After the Second World War, stateless people believed to be at risk also became important because without a 'state' or nation one essentially lacked social standing.

The refugee is defined as someone who has lost everything except the pure fact of being human, and there is no space in the political order of the nation state for the pure human (Agamben 1995; 2008). Refugees therefore represent disquieting figures in the nation state, dividing the identity between human and citizen. Peter Nyers describes contemporary refugees as "Not so much humans" as the site "where the human stops" (Nyers 2006, 124).[12] This is because in the classic Westphalia regime of sovereignty, only members of a territorially bounded polity, i.e., citizens, had rights. So there has been a practice, even following the UN Charter on refugees in 1948 and 1967, to conceptually erase asylum seekers and refugees as members of a polity; their 'abstract nakedness' as visitors in a nation state have rendered them effectively alien and to an extent immoral, because they are outside the collective moral order of the nation state (see Malkki 1992).

Neglected in this formulation is that refugees, and the division between human and citizen, are profoundly racialized. As Charles Mills suggests, during the rise of Western modernity, the population of the planet was ontologically partitioned according to race. The single most important conceptual division historically is the racialized division between whites and nonwhites, whiteness as signifier of expropriator and colonizer, nonwhiteness as signifier of expropriated and colonized (Mills 1999). Yet these formulations have been "*foreclosed*," essentially excluded from the hegemonic discursive context.

The Mediterranean Crossing

On May 29, 2016 in an interview with the BBC, the Southern European spokesperson for the UN High Commissioner for Refugees, Carlotta Sami, pronounced migrant deaths in the Mediterranean as the "new normal" in Europe.

Over the preceding week alone, an estimated 700 men, women, and children fleeing war and poverty in Africa and the Middle East had suffocated, been burned to death, or drowned after their boats sank, disappearing into the deep waters. Many had been pushed from the Libyan shore onto flimsy boats and into the Central Mediterranean sea. Sami explained that during this period of just one week, 15,000 migrants were forced onto unseaworthy vessels, the majority rescued by the Italian Coast Guard, the European border patrol's Triton, or other entities. The fact that Sami characterized the deaths of at least 700 people as *normal* tells us that such losses of life are acceptable and/or invisible to the collective European social and political will. Although seldom highlighted or even mentioned in the American press, the vast majority of refugees and migrants who embark from Libya and perish in the crossing are West and East African. The Italian news has by contrast made it clear for over a decade that most victims are African, regularly broadcasting a spectacle of images of underwater or sinking boats and lifeless corpses.

With thousands of migrants perishing in shipwrecks between the African and Italian coasts as they attempt to reach Europe, the southern Mediterranean has become a "liquid tomb" (Carter 2010) for would-be refugees and immigrants, their indomitable will to rebuild their lives forever whispering in the currents. Their struggles to escape hardship, reach Europe, and thrive there are routinely depicted in terms of what Sylvia Wynter (2003) describes as the "master code of symbolic life and death," which since the 18th century has inscribed in blackness the symbol of death and what is evil; whiteness what is life and good. Newspaper headlines and photographs produce and diffuse spectacles of brutalized black people in vessels overflowing with the symbolically excluded and mythically diseased 'new poor' – racialized refugees and economic migrants principally from various parts of Africa. Colonial narratives, reinvented in the present yet taken-for-granted as unquestioned truths, convey messages of social dysfunction and death in Africa along with the threat of a dystopic world of decadence and decay through contagion, a topsy-turvy world where the Manichean cultural, class, and racial distinctions through which Europe formed itself would become uncomfortably murky and more challenging to control (Fanon 2008).

Some 2,400 people perished in the Central Mediterranean Sea in Italian territorial and adjacent waters from January to June 2015 alone. Many were never recovered.[13] This is not a new story. Thousands of Africans have succumbed while en route to Europe for over two decades. As Maurizio Albahari (2015) suggested, between 1993–2003 at least 10,000 people died in an effort to reach Europe by crossing the Mediterranean from African ports. In 2010, a network of 560 European NGOs (UNITED for Intercultural Action) documented from 1993 a total of 13,824 refugee deaths. These figures are likely modest, given the challenges of collecting accurate accounts. Beginning in August 2013, a consortium of twelve journalists from six countries has taken up the difficult task of assembling data. With the help of sixteen students they formed the "Migrants'

Files," documenting names, ages, genders, and nationalities of the perished and missing, and creating what may be the most comprehensive data on the losses available today. The group documented at least 25,000 deaths and missing persons between 2000 and late August 2014 (Albahari 2015, 104–105). This is a laudable and important contribution, but it is also worth noting that enumeration favors state and UN discourse that conceals the scope of institutional failures to act. The double death of the disappeared is horrifyingly counted as mere 'bodies.' We will never really know the scope of these losses, for the enumeration projects tend to efface the human tragedies, the loss of loved ones with full and complex lives.

The Mediterranean crossing signifies desperation and tragedy for many people compelled to leave their homes when their environment is destabilized by goverance policies and actions of the continuing past in the present, including international European and US policies. While reminiscent of the transatlantic slave crossing that also formed the basis of collective experiences and memories both actual and through an imagined community, the Mediterranean crossing is by contrast an expression of the choice to move in order to survive and flourish, a claim and assertion of freedom in the very act of movement to Europe. In the context of an anti-other structure of feeling in Europe, the struggle to escape hardship and create a better life for oneself and one's family is a radical act of individual and collective self-assertion, and an anticolonial struggle against what Aimee Cesaire referred to as "thingification."

This message is poignantly conveyed in the video art exhibit, "The Mapping Journey Project (2008–11)" by Bouchra Khalili, a series of videos on display at the Museum of Modern Art in New York in 2016. In these moving images, she details the stories of eight individuals who narrate their clandestine journeys through the Mediterranean basin en route to Europe, a voyage that takes as long as five years. Khalili's vision represents an act of counter-mapping where individuals are given the chance to communicate their complex network of migratory movements by marking out their trajectories in thick permanent marker on a geopolitical map, their voices and hands tracing the routes while their faces remain unseen. Taken together, the videos represent an alternative geopolitical cartography defined by the lives of people born in parts of Africa and South Asia. Khalili's work rejects the technologies of visibility invoked by systems of surveillance, the news media, and militarized border controls. Border control is investing in and deploying 'high technologies' of surveillance informatics to identify 'bodies.' These technologies for instance of biometrics use facial recognition, retinal and iris scans, hand geometry, fingerprinting, and DNA that recall racializing 'epidemermalization' to determine who is and is not authorized to enjoy movement, security, and other rights (see Browne 2015; Mezzadra and Neilson 2013; Andersson 2014).

In another compelling work of art that documents the lived experiences of people who have crossed the Mediterranean, documentary filmmakers Dagmawi Yimer, Andrea Segre, and Riccardo Biadine in "Come un Uomo sulla terra" (Like a

Man on Earth) record women and men describing their harrowing journeys from Asmara, Eritrea through Sudan and Libya, in order to reach the coastal city of Benghazi and from there, cross into Europe. Senait, Mimi, Tighist, Fikirte, Dawit, and Tsegaye describe their lives in Ethiopia and how they were compelled to leave. Mimi had led a quiet, happy life with his wife and daughter until war erupted. With deep sadness, his eyes filled with tears, he explained that he didn't want to leave; his escape was narrow and he would have been killed had he stayed. Tighist tells her story of having first moved to Libya in order find work, having heard there were opportunities there. From Libya she was led to believe she could in time set aside enough money to get to Europe. And Senait described the good life he had lived in Ethiopia until her family broke up during the Ethiopian-Eritrean war,[14] her father was expelled to Eritrea, and her mother died. She narrates the story of how she was forced to leave her home in order to survive.

Similarly, the Somali women I interviewed in Turin described tormenting social conditions especially after the Ethiopian government, with aid from the United States, bombed Mogadishu in 2008 and the city was thrown into utter chaos and violence. Roaming warlords terrorized the local population, and explosives were dropped on homes. One woman told us, "In Mogadishu, you go to sleep at night and don't know if in the morning you will be alive."[15] These words are telling.

Since the 1990s, Italian authorities have ratified a series of stringent measures to control the admission and internal movement of immigrants and asylum seekers. External borders have been militarized, particularly maritime borders. Detention centers have been established to warehouse the newcomers. Reforms as in a "rapid expulsion policy" are aimed toward improving the rate of expulsion or repatriation and preventing access. Principles and discourses of national and European security take precedence over human rights. Well before the international media rendered visible the influx of refugees to Europe from Syria, one analyst remarked, "Italy's becoming a caricature. It's becoming the example of a very extreme political discourse framing migration as a security issue, and justifying the implementation of very restrictive policies, having huge implications for human rights, fundamental rights, and social inclusion."[16] Europe, with Italy on the frontline, is waging a war on immigrant and refugee movements as a threat that should be contained offshore.

Libya is the first destination country and a central country of immigration in the Maghreb. In 2000, Italy first signed an agreement with Libya's former military dictator, Muammar Gaddafi, ostensibly for the purpose of combatting terrorism, organized crime, and illegal immigration. This accord has been repeatedly extended since the Civil War erupted. The agreement included the training of Libyan police and border guards, and Italian funded detention and registration programs for irregular migrants in Libya (Andrijasevic 2009). It authorizes the Italian coast guard to intercept foreigners at sea. Italy's "rapid expulsion policy" sends potential asylum seekers to Libya where they are subjected to human rights abuses. In October 2004, for example, the Italian authorities deported to Libya approximately 1,000 asylum seekers from Eritrea who were allegedly first herded into groups of 30–40 and in the scorching sun made to stand for long periods. Most were later repatriated to Egypt (not their countries of origin) on flights financed by the Italian government. Since the time the agreement was signed, Libyan authorities have targeted sub-Saharan Africans with arbitrary arrests, detentions, and deportations of even people who have been working in Libya for over a decade.

The expansion of state borders to off-shore detention centers is an increasingly widespread phenomenon in the post-911 era, representing the application of state violence against an ostensible external threat. Such sites where human rights are suspended are multiplied in the internal black spaces that contain asylum seekers, refugees, and immigrants in Italy. These "zones of exception" as the Italian philosopher Georgio Agamben described them, evoke comparisons with Nazi concentration camps, but are received by the public with relative apathy (Agamben 1995). This may in part be explained by their relative concealment. As geographer Alison Mountz has demonstrated in her work on off-site detention centers in Canada, such spaces of detention are hypervisible during crisis but otherwise obscured from popular view and human rights monitoring (Mountz 2010). Deploying discourses of security, states manage and manipulate space, subverting access to human rights. Inflammatory narratives of crisis, emergency, and the need for securitization articulated by political leaders and the media ignite feelings of panic, anti-otherness, and nativist sentiments. With some important exceptions, the pattern is silent consent and stasis regarding questions of the humanity of such state actions and their implications, part of the prevailing zeitgeist. This is no widespread heeding of Hannah Arendt's warning that the right of every human being to belong to history ought to be guaranteed by humanity itself, and if it is not, a highly organized, mechanized humanity could (in times of 'crisis') democratically conclude that it would be better for humanity as a whole to liquidate certain parts (Arendt 1973).[17]

In March of 2016, the European Union signed an agreement with Turkey that stipulates that all migrants who arrive on a Greek island or are intercepted in the Aegean Sea will be returned to Turkey.[18] Only a select number of Syrians are to be resettled in Europe. As Glenda Garelli and Martina Tazzioli argue, the Aegean Sea is being transformed into a "migrant container belt" (Garelli and Tazzioli 2016; De Vries et al. 2016). Seven NATO warships, along with the Turkish coast guard and the EU's Frontex, have been patrolling the Aegean between Turkey and Greece since February 2016. On April 15, 2016, Italian Prime Minister Renzi presented his "Migration Compact" to the EU, modeled on the EU-Turkey agreement for Libya. The Libyan coast guard's capacity will be enhanced in the Central Mediterranean through their "Operation Sophia," first established by the European Union Naval Force Mediterranean in May 2015. At an estimated annual cost of 11.82 million Euros, naval units and aircraft survey and divert boats. The mission is painted as 'humanitarian' against human smugglers, but has been operating to transport migrants and refugees, not as is claimed to thwart 'human trafficking.' As Garelli and Tizzioli argue, Europe has not established any humanitarian path for safe passage. Instead, they impede legal passage of people who have been forcibly displaced from their countries. Through the EU-Turkey pact and 'Operation Sophia,' Europe has established a military blockade along the only routes away from the violence (Garelli and Tizzioli 2016).[19]

Border Work

> And that is the great thing I hold against pseudo-humanism: that for too long it has diminished the rights of man, that its concept of those rights has been – and still is – narrow and fragmentary, incomplete and biased and, all things considered, sordidly racist.
>
> *(Aimee Cesaire 2000)*

The psychic life of European-African culture is underwritten by violence, taking new life and meaning in the haunting memories and ghosts of the present. In his article on human blacklisting in Europe's exclusionary border regime, Van Houtum (2013) describes the constant "border work" the European Union deploys in an effort to "separate the wanted from the unwanted, the barbarians from the civilized, and the global rich from the global poor in the territorial society." The ontological multidimensionality of the border that was central to the cosmopolitan vision of the European Union has especially since 9–11 and the international "War on Terror" given way to a renewed focus on protection, security, and state border legislation. Maurizio Albahari argues that what happens at the border should be understood both in its military and humanitarian facets, as a *single* spectacle. Along the Mediterranean frontiers and the Italian interior for over two decades the border has included:

> batons and stretchers, guns and surgical masks, military trucks and ambulances, gates and hospitality, fences and food, armed forces, uniforms and health workers' uniforms, the coast guard and the finance guard, salaried bureaucrats and unpaid volunteers, smugglers and victims, refugees and trespassers.
>
> *(Albahari, 2015, 111)*

The movement from West and Eastern Africa through the North African Mediterranean regions and the sea itself is treacherous, packed with experiences of violence and suffering that cannot but mark a new generation in ways that resemble and are continuous with Europe's historical relationship with Africa.

Parallels between the contemporary Mediterranean crossing and transatlantic slave trade come into sharp relief in the 2008 documentary film written and directed by Dagmawi Yimer, Andrea Segre, and Riccardo Biadine, *Come un Uomo sulla Terra* (*Like a Man on Earth*) where women and men describe in some detail their experiences trying to cross the land and sea between Ethiopia and Italy. Once they've reached Sudan, they must pay to be loaded into Land Rover trucks and driven through intense heat by Sudanese or Libyan smugglers while being threatened with knives if they are ill or complain, and given no water or food. Fikirte and her group were dumped in the middle of the desert for fourteen days until the smugglers returned with other migrants from Darfur and loaded all forty-five people into a single truck. She described people she knew personally from Addis Ababa – "Tasfae and Yared" falling off the truck, and being left to die. The passengers were forced pay more money to be taken to Bengazi and if, like Fikirte, they did not have the funds they were tied up, beaten, and raped.

Women are especially vulnerable to sexual assault while traveling.[20] The women and men interviewed in the film described brutal treatment by police who are even more corrupted than the traffickers.[21] Police knew the smugglers, and they systematically allowed, two truckloads to pass through toward Benghazi. Passengers in the third truck were imprisoned in Benghazi and then Kufrah, described as one of three detention centers financed by Italy between 2004–2005. After a period of weeks, these refugees and migrants were transferred from the Benghazi prison to a long almost airless container, reminiscent of the ship holds in the Atlantic crossing, where they stood for days with over a hundred other people from Ethiopia, Sudan, Somalia, and Eritrea, all seeking a route to Europe. The containers were occasionally hosed down from the outside with water, creating an experience of asphyxiation from the steam generated within the chamber. They were then taken to the Kufrah prison-like detention center, where women and men were kept in separate spaces. Women were raped and beaten.

Locked in Kufrah for days or weeks, they were eventually picked up by a police vehicle and told they were being expelled, but were instead escorted by police in Land Cruisers and then 'bought' by Sudanese smugglers for 30–35 dinars each (the currency used in Bahrain, Iraq, Jordan, and Kuwait). The asylum seekers were then asked to pay $400 to be taken to Tripoli. When they arrived in Tripoli they were rearrested and deported back to Kufrah detention center where they spent another month or more before being 'bought' again by a different trafficker for 30–35 dinars. One man described having been sold by Libyan police to traffickers seven times – always for 30 dinars. "As human beings we ought to have been granted at least a shred of dignity," he stated. Some reported that while they were being held in Kufrah, international observers from the European border control agency Frontex visited and asked questions about conditions. The prisoners were assured not to worry about anything, because they were under United Nations protection. Yet when a film-maker who had himself made this journey from East to the Central North African coast visited the Warsaw-based Frontex, the director, Ilkka Latinen, claimed he couldn't remember if they'd visited Kufrah while touring Libya.

The Italian government is reported to have gifted to the Libyan government the containers used to transport people traded by the Libyan police. This exchange was part of the bilateral agreements between Italy and Libya first orchestrated clandestinely by former Prime Minster Silvio Berlusconi in 2003. Rome set aside millions of dollars annually to help the Libyan government control human movement from Africa to Italy. In the early years Rome also provided motorboats, off-road vehicles, blankets, mattresses, and body bags. In 2007, the Italian oil companies ENI and NOC signed an agreement for the production of gas in Libya worth 28 billion dollars over ten years. And in 2007 Italy's center-left Prodi government ratified the agreements made by his predecessor, Silvio Berlusconi.

Formal agreements between Italy and Libya began in 2008 with the "Treaty of Friendship, Partnership, and Cooperation." This contract financed the construction and human policing of Libyan detention camps, along with the technology required for repatriations. Libya's former dictator, Muammar Gaddafi, traveled to Italy to celebrate the ratification of the Italian–Libyan treaty in which Italy agreed to give Libya $5 million to establish electronic surveillance along the Libyan coastline. Prime Minister Silvio Berlusconi described the intentions of this surveillance system as a "Battle against slave traders," masking the dawn of another major movement against Africans on the part of Europeans that recalls the dawn of colonialism' in the 1885 Berlin Conference through which European governments carved and ingested Africa for their own interests in international prestige, economic, and political profit. The Italian government also negotiated Italy's practice of returning would-be immigrants to Libya, and in gratitude Italy would invest $2 million annually in Libya over the following 25 years.

Satellite detection systems, financed jointly by Italy and the European Union, were erected along Libya's maritime borders. The Friendship Treaty, which went into force in March 2009, called for annual disbursements by Italy of some $250 million for 20 years to help Libya beef up its surveillance infrastructure and police the Mediterranean waters. On April 4, 2011 following the uprisings and civil war in Libya, the Italian government suspended the Friendship Treaty, but Italy recognized Libya's National Transitional Council (NTC) and the objectives of the Friendship Treaty were not altered. On June 17, 2011, the Italian government endorsed a Memorandum of Understanding with the NTC in a short document focusing on measures to reduce "illegal immigration," promote bilateral exchange of information on migration flows, and provide mutual assistance to combat illegal immigration. Since that tie, other agreements have been consolidated to assist Libya with technology, for instance by providing nautical training of Libyan police to patrol the Mediterranean and for DNA identification.[22]

In 2012, Italian Prime Minister Mario Monti and his Libyan counterpart Abdurrahim El-Keib signed the "Declaration of Tripoli" encompassing the foundational principles of the first agreement signed by Silvio Berlusconi. The focus is on strengthening the capacity of Libyan authorities to intercept migrants hoping to reach Europe both on their territory and in the Mediterranean. One must ask what kind of a life this is for the people warehoused in Libya, or in Europe? If they make it to Europe, they are at risk of being deported. Migrants and refugees become footnotes in a European world that seems to celebrate Africans post-mortem, not in life.

The European political establishment is well aware of the problems faced by migrants and asylum seekers in Libya, yet security goals take clear precedence over human rights. The border and security focused agreements between Italy and Libya as well as other agreements between Italy and Tunisia, Italy and Egypt, all violate international human rights norms. Yet this security oriented approach is presented as beyond public debate. National law enforcement is countenanced to advance ad hoc initiatives in the arena of migration policy.[23] This approach was only further reinforced after the tragic shipwreck of April 2015 when some 800 African migrants perished after departing from Tripoli on their way to Italy. In the aftermath of the tragedy, the EU held a summit meeting in Brussels where they agreed to admit 5,000 refugees and repatriate the rest. Some 150,000 who had reportedly made it to Italy alone in 2014 were to be sent back as irregular migrants in accordance with to the rapid-return program coordinated by the EU border agency, Frontex. In a now normalized highly racialized image, the *Guardian* news while reporting on the summit meeting included a photograph of Black Africans on the side of a ship with all but their hanging legs covered by a netted fence. The caption read: "Migrants wait to disembark for an Italian navy ship in Salerno…" Another man standing on the shore beside the ship is entirely covered in a protective white uniform except for his forehead and the blue hospital gloves he is wearing.[24] Such images have become iconic. Against these distancing representations, many artists such as the Senegalese photographer Omar Diop and Italian Ghanaian filmmaker Fred Kudjo Kuwornu produce photographs and films that re-present people of African ancestry in a manner that suggests their profound participation in the ongoing making of Europe.[25]

The Italian-Libyan agreements permit Italy to deport African refugees to Libya without first screening their asylum claims, bypassing the Geneva Convention. Libya does not have a viable refugee program in place to process asylum requests and has not ratified the UN Convention on Refugees. Before Civil War broke out in 2011, Libya had reduced the movement of immigrants out of its country by some 90%. In just the first week after the formal operationalization of the agreement, Italy returned some 500 boats to Libya (Blake 2010). Refugees have confirmed their exposure in Libya to inhumane conditions, and indefinite detention.

Asylum seekers are not interviewed upon arrival. They're given a form to complete in English.

A news story reported by a journalist from the Italian paper, *Il Manifesto,* that was covered little if at all by the popular Italian daily press met with international criticism in the summer of 2010. Some 250 Eritrean asylum seekers and migrants were reportedly turned away from Italian shores in 2009 and sent to Libya. The story broke at the end of June when the Eritreans were reportedly being transferred from a migrant center to a criminal prison in the Libyan dessert via an eleven-hour journey on foot without rest break or water after which many were severely beaten. Although Libya does not have a system in place for refugees, as a signatory of the Geneva Convention, Italy is in violation by sending asylum seekers to a country that doesn't recognize refugees. In a press release, the UNHCR, IOM (International Organization of Migration), and Save the Children on April 20, 2013 denounced the widespread practice deployed by Italian authorities of preventing hundreds of asylum requests by North, Sub-Saharan Africans, and Egyptians from lodging asylum requests and summarily returning them to their presumed and often fallacious countries of origin.

In 2014 Human Rights Watch (HRW) documented abuses in Libya's nineteen official camps that hold between 1,000 and 6,000 people. Refugees were crammed into miniscule cells with stopped and overflowing toilets. Their researchers had observed some sixty boys and men shoved into rooms as small as 30 square meters (322.92 feet). Hundreds of detainees were warehoused in tiny spaces and hallways flooded with sewage. HRW witnessed people detained in shipping containers, vacant government offices, and private abandoned buildings. As in slavery in the Americas and Caribbean, people were hung upside down from trees, and whipped with cables. Migrant girls and women were strip-searched and raped. Refugees from Sub-Saharan Africa were especially targeted. Many tried to escape and locate boats to take them across the Mediterranean. A 27-year old Somali man in Libya told Human Rights Watch,

> Since I came here (earlier this year) the guards attacked me twice. They whipped me with metal wire and beat and punched me all over my body. I also saw them hang four or five people upside-down from the tree outside the entrance door and beat them and whipped their feet and stomach.[26]

Libyan authorities claimed some of the violence deployed on detainees was a "form of punishment" for attempting to flee. But for the most part there was "no apparent reason" for it. After visiting nine of the nineteen facilities and speaking with 136 detainees, most who had reported some form of torture, HRW called on Italy to suspend its financing of the Libyan detention camps with millions of euros annually until the UN could determine that the torture had ceased.

At the end of 2015, Europe began to enhance its intra-governmental surveillance technology by focusing resources on the formation of preemptive frontiers or 'hot spots' on the southern borders, the majority in Italy and Greece. As Glenda Garelli and Martina Tazzioli write in *Open Democracy*, the hot spot in Lampedusa, Italy is intended to operate as a migration-management model. Hot spots function as official "states of exception," where Schengen regulations are suspended in the effort to keep refugees and migrants out of Europe. European agencies establish strengthened infrastructures where Frontex (the European border agency), the Europol (the European police), Eurojust (the EU Juridical cooperation agency), and EASO (the European Asylum Support Office) are deployed to help bolster the frontiers between Europe, Africa, and the Middle East. As Garelli and Tozzioli suggest, these organizations use biotechnologies to racially patrol, classify, and exclude or include asylum seekers and migrants; fingerprinting, identifying, and assigning migratory profiles as either "economic migrants" or "refugees" filtered by nationality and other biographical information (cf. Browne 2015). In principle, refugees are to be resettled, but this is a highly exclusionary practice where only the co-nationals of asylum seekers with at least 75% EU wide recognition are eligible for resettlement (Garelli and Tozzioli 2016).

Italian NGOs and activists have denounced the "nationalist" approach of the arrangement that separates "economic migrants" from "persons in real need of protection," based principally on their national origin. "On the spot" people coming from West African countries, for instance, are excluded from protective mechanisms, both through relocation programs and the possibility of claiming asylum in the country of the hotspot (Garelli and Tozzioli 2016). Eritreans, Syrians, and Iraqis are authorized to begin asylum procedures, and the rest are to be handed expulsion orders and told to leave the country within seven days. However, as they are expected to pay for their own return, they remain in Italy as undocumented migrants, and a highly exploitable workforce (Garelli and Tozzioli 2016; see also Mezzadro and Neilson 2003). Garelli and Tozzioli describe protests, for instance among Somali women who have refused to be fingerprinted because they do not wish to remain in Italy, rejecting the Dublin Convention requirement that asylum seekers must be fingerprinted and file claims in the European country where they first set foot, and prohibiting them from making any such requests in other European countries. However, authorities in these hot spots have responded to such refusals to be fingerprinted by holding asylum seekers in overcrowded detention centers on Lampedusa Island.

Detention and Mobilization

In 2014, I spoke with another group of Somali refugee women at the Alma Mater intercultural women's center in Turin. They spoke in Somali; their words were translated into Italian by a Somali woman and member of Alma Mater. They had gathered there to speak with a member of parliament about their ongoing crisis and neglect by the Italian government as refugee women in Italy.

They urged the Italian government to institute policies that would allow refugees to live in Italy with dignity. Just as in 2010, most were homeless, moving in and out of shelters from one day to the next and or sleeping on park benches. The oldest woman in the group who appeared to be in her 50s stated,

> We have to be clear that we want a place to live, and jobs. You can put two or three of us together like we've always done in our country. But we need to have work – the dignity of this is fundamental for us. We are not here to ask for charity.[27]

Several of the women pleaded with the parliamentarian to urge the Italian government to change the Dublin agreement that stipulates application for asylum in the country of first entry, as this precludes them from applying for asylum in other European countries with better refugee policies. One pleaded for her fingerprints, "Just change the Dublin treaty and give me my fingerprints and I'll go somewhere else." Some described having had positive experiences in other countries, for instance one woman went to Norway where she found work and was given a place to sleep. Another had spent some time in Germany where she was given an apartment, 300 Euros monthly, and had just begun school when she was sent back to Rome! The police took her to the airport and upon her arrival in Rome they instructed her to "Stay here. Go." She and other women expressed the experience of having departed from one inferno, only to enter another. The youngest woman in the group declared,

> If I knew it would be like this, I would have gone elsewhere. I need to have a life of dignity. I am young. I can learn. So if Italy isn't going to do anything for me they should give me back my fingerprints. They should not have taken them.

For these Somali refugees and the thousands of others who arrive on Italian territory the policy is to take their fingerprints and place them in some form of detention for a period of time, officially not to exceed three months, but in practice for up to eighteen months. Many are sent from Lampedusa or Sicily to a detention center on the mainland, where they wait. Italian policies are not uniform, for every city processes asylum applications in different ways, some more rapidly than others. One Somali woman described having been held in a CARA or Center for Reception and Asylum in Crotone, Calabria for five months. In 2013 this CARA held 1700 people, double the legal capacity.[28] She described terrible conditions, "very ugly" where they ate little or nothing, or were given "pig food." The military police were a prominent presence that "treated people very roughly." This woman was then issued a three-year status as refugee. Another who arrived in Lampedusa was sent to Sicily, held for eight months, and prohibited from leaving the center. After the eight months, she was given a ticket, "It was cold. It was winter. I didn't know where to go." The refugee women spoke about their experiences with reluctance, stating that talking never leads to any changes. One stated, "We are in prison without people knowing that we are in prison. We are treated like animals. You end up losing your mind."

Before reaching Turin, many asylum seekers and refugees had been placed in one of Italy's Detention Centers, or CIEs, Centri di Identificazione ed Espulsione, CDIs Centri di Accoglienza, CARA, Centri Accoglienza Richiedenti Asilo for people without documents who are requesting political refugee status. These are holding centers, frequently managed by the Red Cross or other voluntary organizations, and guarded by Italian military police. Italian detention centers have blocked most inspectors from accessing the facilities, but some have managed to enter and have reported deplorable living conditions. The international human rights observers, FIDH (International Federation for Human Rights) reported that new arrivals often sleep on the floor and are not provided with blankets; conditions are unsanitary with overflowing toilets; and people sleep in excrement (FIDH 2005).

The organization LASCIATECIENTRARE (Let us in), founded by journalist Gabriella Guido in 2011, has worked doggedly to contest the Ministry of the Interior's circular prohibiting journalists from accessing the CIE and CARA facilities. Their protests have resulted in government recognition of the right of entry, yet journalists and other monitors face considerable difficulties when seeking access as permissions are considered at the discretion of local administrators. LASCIATECIENTRARE now campaigns for the abolition of detention centers in Italy and revision of immigration policies in a campaign named "Mai Piu CIE" (Never again CIE).

The organization has gathered numerous testimonies from people detained in the centers and who have been exposed to physically and psychologically repressive and abusive conditions. Testimony from a man held in the Ponte Galeria detention center in Rome described the facility as "like a Lager." He added, "Psychologically, we're destroyed." He described how he'd suddenly found himself in a detention prison after opening his apartment door one day to carabinieri announcing that he was to be deported to "his country." Holding a wad of documents he spoke of his family in Italy, his Italian children ages 8 and 13, and how he had been forced to leave Algeria in 1990 when civil war had erupted, "This is hurting my children, not just me. They're killing not one person, but three." Many, who like this man are held in detention centers as if criminals, had built their lives in Italy over the course of decades.

For every person arrested and sent to a CIE for expulsion, the contracted organization managing the facility is given approximately 41 Euros by the Italian state (2014 figures). In Gabriella Guido's interview with the Mayor of Modena, Giorgio Pighi, regarding the now former CIE there, he described a popular fear of an "invasion" that fueled the "business of immigration," costing the Italian state some 500,000 euros annually.[29] However, local residents seemed to be indifferent, partly because, as Pighi explained to Guido, there was no normal interchange between the community members and the detention centers. Therefore, community members ignore or are unaware that it exists. The place, and people, are outside their field of vision and community.

Algerian Italian author and social critic, Tahar Lamri has said that for him and other former migrants, the detention centers are difficult to think about. They are as he put it,

> indefensible from every point of view … Putting people into places where they have no rights and where they are in effect "non-persons" and under police or military surveillance is even hard to talk about. Guantanamo and the CIE are the same things.[30]

The CIE embody a state of exception where the people held are deprived of basic human rights to move. Like the deaths along the Mediterranean crossing, the very fact that people especially of African and Arab descent are at all times vulnerable to being seized by police and forced into expulsion centers emotionally impacts Black and Arab Europeans in ways that remain imperceptible to people who do not share in any way in this traumatic and ongoing past (cf Sharpe 2016). Lamri describes how challenging it is for him to even talk about the CIE, because the very knowledge that his brother, who has the same roots as he does, could be placed in a center and deported simply because he has traveled, is unbearable, "I can't even express how that feels to me. I'm at a loss for words." He adds, "A wealthy Arab can go where he wishes. It's only a poor Arab who cannot go where he wants to go – so that he doesn't have even the minimum possibility to improve his situation…." What is needed to change this, Lamri argues, is beyond the laws. It is only at the "human level," in human contacts on a daily basis, where these practices will really change. His words resonate with those of the American legal scholar, Michelle Alexander, who having written a popular and influential book on the New Jim Crow as the system of mass incarceration in the United States recently decided to teach at a divinity school because transforming taken-for-granted practices requires more than the transformation of legislation. These black spaces are fueled by a profound anti-black animus, pleasure from the infliction or spectacle of black suffering, or at best a twisted knowledge and indifference.

Scholars whose work is principally focused on the United States employ a language of the *neoliberal carceral state* to describe the practice of warehousing and sentencing to oblivion large numbers of people (De Genova and Peutz 2010; Morin 2013; Morin and Moran 2015; Golash-Boza 2015). Some of their recent studies have highlighted race. The penal system has become a major engine of social stratification and cultural division characterized by legalized violence in concentration camp-like spaces exempt from outside scrutiny, where treatment of detainees is exterior to the scope of law (Morin 2013; Gregory 2006). The security state has replaced the welfare state, with a racialized punitiveness and intensified militarization and authoritarian culture. Upon scrutiny, government claims to national security, emergency, or states of exception on the basis of a War on Terror are really in the business of producing fear and violence in order to nourish the larger agenda of the neoliberal security state. This security state is also a racial state that asserts and reproduces a taken-for-granted anti-blackness.

Detention centers have become symbolic representations of the government's ability to control the external borders and protect the 'insiders' whose right to protection is believed to be an entitlement. Detention is an immigration policing and social control tactic that provides nation states with performative value as punitive spectacle. These centers contain, document, scatter, and redirect migrants, performing the state's right to violence. Detention sites that in Italy encompass asylum and reception centers serve disciplinary and social functions.

Immigration was criminalized in Italy for well over a decade, until parliament voted to change this in 2014.[31] Yet many of the punitive and fortress-like provisions remain. In April 2014, United Nations Special Rapporteur Crepeau criticized Italy's detention system for its substandard conditions and inadequate access to justice. He cited insufficient safeguards. A European Committee for the Prevention of Torture in November 2014 condemned overcrowding in prisons and ill treatment especially of foreigners by Italian police and carabinieri. There are many informal reception centers close to the shore serving as both reception and detention facilities that are only nominally part of the Italian territory, so European and Italian laws are not applied there. These are classified as off-shore sites where the rights guaranteed in Italian and European legislation need not be applied. The Pozzallo site in Sicily, for example, is a hangar in the industrial part of the harbor. There are many similar structures where people are detained for long periods of time.

Detainees, refugees, and migrants launch countless spontaneous and organized protests against immigration and refugee policies, living conditions, lengthy waiting periods on asylum applications, and acts of local violence fueled by racial hatred.[32] Their opposition has taken the form of setting fire to detention centers, waging hunger strikes, marching in streets, holding public rallies, occupying buildings, and waging and sit-ins. These protests intersect with broader struggles for democracy, human and social rights, and have been supported by many autonomous Italian groups. A culture of protest is emerging among immigrants, refugees, and Italian activists engaged in struggles for rights and recognition. Political and social subjectivities are being produced around these spatial-racial configurations, and the systems of social relations they generate.

Notes

1 Again, I write this as an externally defined White woman with intimate knowledge and empathy, but without having grown up Black in a racially hierarchical society.

2 I have substituted a pseudonym.

3 I did not record this informal interview. My quotations are approximations, from field notes I took directly after our conversation.

4 Asylum seekers are legally entitled to food and medical care, psychological support, and 2,50 E per day – nowhere near the amount needed to live.

5 Several Italian organizations support refugees in the Ex-MOI, such as the *Comitato di solidarietà per rifugiati e migranti,* which created a collective to organize demonstrations about residence as a right for everyone, and school. As Giorgio de Cesare, their Media and Communications liason told me, Italy doesn't recognize residence among refugees. This means they don't have the right to receive social services: "There are some 40,000 without residence." The Comitato di Solidarieta helped refugees mobilize sit-ins at city hall that pressured the municipal government to supply an address for the 'homeless' refugees, which is done for Italian homeless. Tired of the demonstrations, in December 2013 the urban government granted refugees at the Ex-MOI a "Casa Comunale" residence. Much more needs to be done. De Cesare commented, "It's worse than unethical; it's inhuman. But they keep saying they don't have the resources." The Comitato's aim is to forge ties of solidarity with refugees and the urban poor. Their motto is, "You need, I help."

6 Eurostat: http://ec.europa.eu/eurostat/data/database.

7 See *Other Europe/Altra Europa,* 2011.

8 Alice Rossi argues that squatters are not homogenous; there are internal tensions and differences among non-Italian, and between Italian activists and squatters. Even among the homeless there is a continuous process of hierarchization and differentiation, including a growing distance between citizens and noncitizens that is part of a dynamic of racialized dependency performed and produced in social welfare services and institutions (Rossi 2014).

9 Also see Valarie Blake (2010). She argues that Italian police single out persons of African descent, asking for their documents.

10 The term, "ghetto" originates in Venetian dialect, from "geto" from the Italian verb, "gettare," meaning to throw away, so that which is disposed of. It was first used in the 16th century to refer to the segregation of Jews in Venice, site of one of the first 'Jewish Ghettoes' in Europe.

11 The documentary film, *Crips and Bloods: Made in America* (2009) by Stacy Peralta, visually portrays the national and state manufacturing of black imprisonment and the suppression of dissent in contained 'ghettos' in the US.

12 Peter Nyers argues that being an 'authentic refugee' includes being expected to display the qualities associated with 'refugeeness', including speechlessness, placelessness, invisibility, and victim status. The Convention on Refugees classifies them in relation to the human emotion of fear, and as human outcasts who because they lack reasoning capacity are incapable of self-governing subjectivity. They are, Nyers suggests, human beings in the 'raw', not rational, mentally disordered (Nyers, 2006, 45).

13 Lampedusa's local government has built a cemetery, and is trying to establish a museum of the deceased that will display objects recovered by fishermen (see Nicolini and Bellingreri 2013).

14 The war between Ethiopia and Eritrea officially ended in 2000, but border conflicts have continued to erupt.

15 A humanitarian crisis has been unfolding in Somalia for over a decade. The World Bank ranks Somalia with one of the highest infant and maternal mortality rates in the world. Internationally sponsored regime change has led to the ramping up of unbridled warfare, including crimes that *Amnesty International* and *Human Rights Watch* have documented. In 2006, the Ethiopian army pushed ousted the Islamic courts Union (ICU) that had established various degrees of relative stability in the country, including Mogadishu. In the name of counter-terrorism, the US, along with the UN, EU, AU

(African Union), and League of Arab States supported this move. On the coattails of Ethiopia's routing of ICU militias, the Somalia Transitional Federal Government (TFG) was installed in Mogadishu. Almost immediately, the insurrection lead by former supporters of the ICU began to intensify, followed by counter insurgency by the TGF and Ethiopian forces, leading to the further destruction of Mogadishu. Thousands of people were killed or injured and hundreds of thousands forcibly displaced. Over 7 million Somalis have been displaced. In 2008 there were US airstrikes against Al Shababb. This has helped create and intensify torture, rape, and summary killings, but the UN Security Council has refused to investigate. This is a situation where there is no regard for civilians, where women and children under 14 account for 50% of the war related trauma cases, and where health care and education have been almost inexistent for over a generation. The internationally sponsored regime change and support for ongoing unbridled warfare in Somalia have made it extremely difficult even for humanitarian aid organizations to help a beleaguered Somali population.

16 Sergio Carrera, a research fellow at the Brussels-based Centre for European Policy Studies, BBC March 7, 2009.

17 In an unusual, and for Italy unprecedented mass welcoming act toward migrants on November 1, 2016, approximately 1,000 Italians in Milan threw a block party to welcome a group of some 80 migrants being moved to a re-purposed former military barracks, Caserma Montello. In the preceding days, the barracks were the site of anti-immigrant protests by members of the Lega Nord party, *Casa Pound*, and residents of the quarter, holding up signs: "Italians first." Associations organized the welcoming party. *Washington Post*, Nov. 1, 2016, "Italians throw part to welcome migrants in Milan," Colleen Barry of the Associated Press. Zaccaria, a 22 year old from Ethiopia emerged from the barracks and said, "We are human beings, like everyone else. And human beings will be respected." *La Repubblica* on line, R.it by Elena Peracchi.

18 This agreement was rescinded in the aftermath of an attempted coup in Turkey, followed by the blackout of news and massive political repression.

19 On November 3, 2016, the eurobserver (https://euobserver.com/migration/135750) posted an article by Nikolaj Nielsen, "Amnesty: Italian Police tortured migrants to meet EU target" responding to a 56-page *Amnesty International* report documenting human rights abuses by Italian authorities. In the photo accompanying this online article, six African men held bags and luggage, with the caption, "Italy recently signed a repatriation agreement with Sudan." Nielsen reports that Italian police have used electric shocks and beaten refugees in Italy's "hot spots" in an effort to force them to be fingerprinted and their information entered into 'Eurodac,' an EU database employed to identify asylum seekers and determine which country is responsible for them, in accordance with the Dublin regulations. Amnesty International collected 24 testimonies of 16 beatings, including that of a 16-year-old Sudanese boy who reported that police had shocked him with stun batons. A 25-year-old woman from Eritrea said she was repeatedly slapped until she agreed to be fingerprinted. Others reported being sexually humiliated and tortured. The EU commission ruled in 2014 that "proportionate use of coercion" was permitted to ensure fingerprinting.

20 Women of Somali origin who are Italian citizens have worked tirelessly to represent and translated for refugee women from Somalia. They have told me that few could have make it across the deserts without being raped. Some were pregnant from the rapes when they arrived in Italy, and others had young or infant children from sexual assaults.

21 A May, 2016 *European Commission* report cautioned that children had become the favored targets of criminal gangs taking advantage of Europe's "migration crisis" to force more into sex work and other forms of slavery. Police and government officials are complicit in this underground capture and sale of human beings. The EU report

suggests that at least 10,000 unaccompanied children who arrived in Europe have simply dropped off the radar. Criminal networks capture children from between the ages of 6 months to 10 years and sell them for 4,000–8,000 Euros. The report notes a sharp increase in Nigerian women and girls arriving in Italy from Libya and Italian authorities reporting a 300% increase in the Nigerian victims of trafficking. EU law expects countries to provide trafficking victims with at least one-month of accommodation, medical care, and legal advice. (Jennifer Rankin, May 19, 2016, *The Guardian* online). Human trafficking is the fastest growing crime in the world, and it has reached epidemic proportions. Eighty percent of victims are women and children. The International Labor Organization (ILO) has estimated profits from this business in slavery as generating some $150 billion annually (EndSlaveryNow, April 21, 2015, Philip Hyldgaard). In October 2015, the International Organization for Migration (IOM) called on governments to monitor victims of sex trafficking more carefully. They warned of a surge in the sexual assault of women smuggled from West Africa across the Mediterranean Sea (Lisa De Bode, "EU refugee crisis heightens sex trafficking concerns, officials warn," *Al Jazeera America*).

22 The use of DNA testing to identify migrants is troubling, a form of eugenic classification that harkens back to Nazi exterminations. DNA testing is also quite problematic because not nearly enough reference groups have been tested, and there is a high risk of sending people back to countries where they have no history.

23 Emmanuela Paoletti, "Migration Agreements between Italy and North Africa: Domestic Imperatives versus International Norms" Dec. 19, 2012. Middle East Institute (accessed online July 21, 2015).

24 Guardian on line. "EU summit to Offer Resettlement to only 5,000 refugees." Alan Travis. 23 April 2015. Accessed July 21, 2015.

25 Against this epistemic discourse and field of vision, many artists like the Senegalese photographer Omar Victor Diop and Italian Ghanaian filmmaker Fred Kudjo Kuwornu, produce photographs and films that re-present people of African ancestry in a manner that suggests their profound participation in the making of Europe. In his "Project Diaspora," a series of photographs of himself portraying paintings of Africans in Europe from the 15th through the 19th centuries and the contemporary world of soccer, Diop replaces the representation of Africans as external to Europe with figures who defy the normalized expectations of Africans in the diaspora. Examples include Albert Badin, a Swedish court servant and diarist in the 18th century (See Allan Pred (2004), *The Past is Not Dead*), and St. Benedict of Palermo, a 16th century Franciscan friar in Sicily known for his charity and patience and venerated as a saint by Pope Benedict XIV in 1743. Filmmaker Fred Kuwornu also re-presents the presence of people with African ancestry in Italy as war heroes, citizens, and actors (see "Inside Buffalo" (2010)).

26 Human Rights Watch, June 22, 2014. "Libya: Whipped, Beaten, and Hung from Trees." www.hrw.org/news/2014/06/22/libya-whipped-beaten-and-hung-trees.

27 The women spoke Somali, translated by a Somali-Italian woman who works as a cultural mediator and advocate.

28 See Struggles in Italy, https://strugglesinitaly.wordpress.com/.

29 As greater numbers of asylum seekers and migrants have arrived in Italy under the ageis of a "national emergency." The Italian state has outsourced their care to charities, cooperative associations, and businesses across the country. The state has implemented a policy of paying shelter operators approximately 35 Euros per day for every adult they lodge (some reports indicate 41). This is a lucrative business. A landlord who runs a shelter may receive over a million Euros annually if they house 100 people. People not housed in reception centers may be sent to smaller properties operated by hotel managers or restauranteurs. Social activists argue that this system is ripe for corruption, easily exploited by organized criminal groups able to take advantage of the national

emergency. Housing asylum seekers is reportedly more profitable than illegal drug sales.

30 Taken from a series of interviews from the Lasciatecientrare website, from 2014: www. lasciatecientrare.it/j25/

31 The Italian government passed Law No. 177, the "Bossi-Fini" law by decree in July 2002, introducing criminal sanctions for people found to enter the country illegally. Under this law a person found without a residence permit should be accompanied to the border and immediately deported or arrested and later deported. This law firmly links the residence permit to the work contract. The law extended the time limit for containment in detention centers while awaiting deportation, and for asylum seekers placed in detention while awaiting asylum review. This law contravenes Article 5 of the *European Convention on Human Rights*, which states, "Everyone has the right to liberty and security of person." Gianfranco Fini of the National Alliance, Umberto Bossi of the Lega Nord, and with members of Italy's governing coalition proposed the law. The new law passed despite protest by members of Italy's Roma community, other immigrant groups, and allies.

32 For more on immigrant protests in Italy and beyond, see Wendy Pojman (2008), and Vittorio Longhi (2013).

CONCLUSION

Re-Imagining Future Geographies

The eventual achievement of an end to black subordination will require, among other things, a redrawing of the conceptual political maps on which this subordination does not even appear.

Charles W. Mills, Blackness Visible

I came to Italy to find help, but have found myself in the same situation I was in when in Somalia and being bombed (by US backed Ethiopian aircraft). Look at my scars from shrapnel and bullets. Two of my children were killed and another seriously wounded ... But I came here to find myself in the same situation ... The police chase us from one place to another. I'd go back to my country if not for the war, because at least in my country you don't go hungry. We are here without husbands, without children, without homes. We're animals. We don't exist. Italians have destroyed our minds. They have mentally colonized us. All we think about are our problems. The police tell us to leave, and they're supposed to be the ones to help us. The world doesn't care. Nobody does anything.

A Somali refugee in Turin

Anti-blackness has played a crucial role in European, American, and global social imaginaries for centuries. Blackness has been maintained and periodically reinvigorated as a symbol of potentially harmful alterity in relation to Whiteness, in spite of diverse contradictions. Black people are the only people on this earth whose skin color was transformed into a form of merchandise. No other group was so widely inhibited from developing independently of Europe, while struggling to be seen and heard by it. Nevertheless, there is an implicit knowledge that Africans-Europeans are intertwined; contacts are made that affect people and contribute to the continual making of the West. We urgently need to revisit, excavate, and reinterpret histories from the perspective of an ever shifting present so that the past can reveal itself as other than what it has earlier appeared to be. A future present is waiting to be re-made.

Critical social theory advances our ability to make sense of a complex social world, including the operation of power relations over time and in particular places. Social theory builds tools to analyze how and why our racialized ideologies and practices emerge and persist. Critical theory can be deployed as a guide to identify and understand the meanings and patterns that constitute the present world behind the veil of racial structures. Racial capitalist power demarcates fixed oppositions of blackness and whiteness that preclude collective politics. Deeply binary cultural ideologies prevent us from understanding our common humanity and interests, and from embracing our mutually constituted realities.

Black spaces is a concept and an argument that Black people occupy space and place in the modern Western world. They do not merely vie for a place in it. For hundreds of years, Africans and African diasporic people have *inhabited and been present* in the West, have been intrinsic to the West in manifold ways. Power has registered and demarcated black spaces as sites of acceptable violence, and de-humanity. Black spaces also refuse and radically diverge from social norms; they survive, seek social justice and transformation. My idea of Black spaces names a foundational modern epistemology and ontology – a way of knowing and being in the world. Black spaces are part of Western discourse and practice, where Black people are produced as racialized subjects persistently disqualified from the 'family of man.' Black spaces are also symbolic and material sites where Black people, and those who identify with them, create social lives and relationships that are quite divergent from the prevailing narratives of social control that elicit fear and anger.

A great deal has shifted over the past half of a century, legally and to an extent in social representations and access to resources. But, not nearly enough. As Angela Davis and Michelle Alexander argue, legislative and policy changes are necessary but insufficient remedies to anti-black racism (Davis 2016; Alexander 2016). More will be required in order to transform the patterns of racial hierarchy and oppression with which the West was seeded and codified over a period of five centuries. The West is comprised of many diverse cultural variants, yet the strains of its foundational religions, political and social philosophies, cultural notions of self, place, and belonging, are consistent. As afro-pessimist thinkers point out, a profoundly anti-black ontology and set of material practices orients the Euro-American world. I do not support the idea that the ontology and materiality of anti-blackness is as *fixed* as afro-pessimists seem to suggest. However, if our aim is to transform the profound racial structures that have been inherited "like a nightmare on the brains of the living," it is crucial for us to understand how racialized forms of culture and power have worked historically and continue to operate institutionally and in the everyday.

In focusing attention on the lived experiences of people of African origins or ancestry in Italy, on their perspectives and material realities, I aim to generate a geographically informed scholarship and activism. Blackness is not the exclusive domain of Black people, nor is Whiteness the unique domain of White people. It is important to remember this when we consider how to build a viable, ethical, politics in the present moment of danger (Merrill and Hoffman 2015). A necessary precondition for active anti-racism is to develop knowledge of social-racial systems of classification and how they have colonized our minds in ways not necessarily of our own choosing. How can we learn to educate ourselves to become racially literate? (See Twine 2011). To pay attention to everyday lived experiences? How can we use our knowledge to effect substantive social structural changes? Who benefits from anti-black racism? Which social practices and beliefs do racialized divisions and animosities sustain? Who and what do we lose as a society by allowing these divisions to be reproduced? And what can we do to undermine these taken-for-granted systems of domination without falling prey to them?

The study of anti-black racism and blackness is a challenging undertaking. Interrogating how white supremacy operates through culture, politics, and economy as a modality of social power, and how one lives in such conditions, is a scholarly undertaking all its own. Even though racial ideologies were produced in part as a strategy to separate working classes, racism is not merely an epiphenomenon of social class dynamics. And fascism was rooted not just in capitalist political economy, but also in racist ideologies built on nationalism, transatlantic slavery, and colonization. Nor is anti-black racism one of many intersecting forms of power equivalent with gender, sexuality, age, ethnicity, religion, or disability. The belief in a superior race intersects these social classifications and relations of power, but as a crucial and highly persuasive foundation of modern Western systems of knowledge and power, it should first be studied and understood in its own terms.

My study of Italy has aimed to bring attention to the humanity of people who build solidarity and sustain communities in the face of racialized social erasure, everyday expressions of symbolic and material violence. Their lives involve complex, transcultural ways of thinking, being, and acting. If acknowledged and bolstered, this transculturalism can offer routes to building more just ways of knowing and being, beacons for the present-future. For we are living in a context in which, sadly, many have come to accept the normalcy of racialized violence that is at once denied and routinely sanctioned by states and local populations. By studying and truly understanding race and racism we can, as James states in the excellent documentary film, "James Baldwin: The Price of the Ticket," "(I truly do believe that) people can change the way they are, but the price is enormous. And I'm not sure people are really willing to pay it" (Thorsen 1989). This requires nothing less than sustained investments in collectively refocusing and redesigning our system of social values, knowledge, and the social, political policies that represent them.

The dearth of compassion for African immigrants and refugees in Europe and Africa is demonstrated in countless everyday expressions of inaction and neglect, and affected by popular and enduring representations. When civil war erupted in Syria in 2011 and millions of civilians were displaced, the international press began to circulate countless photographs of sorrowful Syrian children and families. Many newspapers captured mournful images of destroyed innocence that elicited empathy even from the self-absorbed US president, Donald Trump. There is an undeniable humanitarian crisis in Syria. There have also been ongoing humanitarian crises in Africa, yet the world has only been informed and expected to be concerned about the lives of Syrian refugees. What is happening in Syria is an indisputable human tragedy where an estimated 6 million people have been internally displaced and 4.8 million have crossed national borders as refugees. But what most people do not know, because neither political figures nor the international media have represented refugees in the same manner, is that one-third of the world's 20 million people displaced by war and conflict are on the African continent. At least 12.4 million Africans have been displaced, and another 5.4 million are refugees who have crossed national borders. When I did a simple Google search for photographs and stories of displaced Africans and refugees I generally found abstract and detached representations of people as so deeply scarred that they lack the innocence and vulnerability portrayed in the emotionally moving photos of desperate Syrian refugees. The representations of Africans illustrate a shortage of empathy for their suffering. They are presented walking or looking away, with hands over their faces, staring blankly at photojournalists, as if in a world apart. Africans are frequently depicted in groups featuring body parts, with their legs hanging over the sides of ships, listlessly laying on mats, and children already emotionally old and resigned to their inhuman living conditions. They appear to be children who do not, or cannot, feel pain. Many photographs seem to be designed to elicit pity, horror, and or indifference, instead of compassion. We learn little if anything about Africans as human beings, and the message conveyed is that their lives don't matter; they are presumed to be outside the social order. Africans are *invisible* as part of the global refugee crisis, represented if at all as economic migrants with illegitimate claims to humanitarian protection (Carter 2010). We need social theory in order to make sense of what accounts for this seemingly naturalized, prevailing racial hierarchy of refugees and immigrants and images.

It is taken-for-granted that the "European," who is presumed White, represents the human norm, while the 'native' is foreclosed as external to the human fold. The European colonial notion of a native other with nothing to give and who must therefore be permanently expelled from modern Western consciousness has allowed the Western subject to emerge and narrate itself as the universal "human," to erase Black and other lives from the social terrain. It may appear contradictory that Syrians, who lived under a French colonial mandate in the early 20th century and are widely assumed to be Arab are being presented in a more or less empathetic manner. But while they are certainly not widely embraced in Europe or the United States, in relative terms Syrians are presented as White or almost white (especially if they are assumed to be non-Muslim), which renders them as at the very "least" human, not animal. Africans are depicted as fundamentally different strangers instead of as human beings with full weight and complexity, from places with which Europe has had an ongoing relationship (Cesaire 2000; Fanon 2008; Baldwin 1998). In common representations, Black *people* with real lives disappear under the weight of an abstraction. Their bodies, symbols of suffering and pain, are used as instruments for lessons about what it means to be culturally White (King 2008). Having been disciplined to distinguish oneself racially, it becomes easy, even 'natural' for many people to deny compassion to people of African descent. In stark contrast to this, Senegalese photographer Omar Victor Diop represents Mbororo refugees in Cameroon with the color blue to demonstrate the hope, resilience, and calmness of these pastoralists and merchants who fled unrest in the Central African Republic. Diop describes his sadness in hearing people refer to Africa as a place of wild animal life, starvation, war, and misery while the world forgets that there are a billion people on the continent with very different fates, yet who share a common culture of resilience when faced with excessive hardship.

The epigraph above from a Somali refugee in Italy conveys the lived experience of many women and men abandoned beyond the usual neglect of the country's poor and Southern Italians who have been compared with colonized peoples (Lombardi-Diop and Romeo 2013). My friends and research participants in Turin have described third and first generations of Southern Italians, including grandchildren and their grandparents who emigrated to the north in the post-war period for work in the burgeoning factories, as retaining the most anti-black among generally racist attitudes toward immigrants and refugees. They describe a worsening situation for Africans in Italy where people who in the 1990s and at the turn of the century were ashamed to openly show anti-black racism recently feel free to openly express their views. My interlocutors blame the Italian government for condoning and encouraging racist attitudes and behavior, especially the political left that has never confronted the Italian history of fascism and colonialism. As one told me in a group discussion, "They will do all sorts of things for Palestine and Afghanistan and Iraq, but nothing for Somalia or Eritrea."

Over the past fifty or so years, conditions have improved for some Africans after struggling for independence from Europe, and for African Americans who through political activism acquired better access to resources and active citizenship. Yet we are not close to reaching a post-racial social order. The racialization of immigrants and refugees is not limited to Italy or even Europe. They are global problems, rooted in modern European culture, economy, and politics, and are central for understanding how systems of social value operate and what they mean. There is still a basic, foundational social psychology of racial caste that W.E.B. Du Bois wrote of in the early 20th century supported by public policy that defends "race" separation and white supremacy to defend against domination of blacks by whites (Du Bois 1999; 2007). This concerns those of us who, as Fannie Lou Hamer and Ella Baker argued and exemplified, believe in social justice, inclusion, respect, reason, and society.

While Prime Minister of Great Britain, Margaret Thatcher said that there was "no such thing as society," meaning that individuals must look to themselves for help instead of to a government that would represent and guarantee their ability to live. Her statement characterized a turning point in global history, when the neoliberal ethos of private gain for the few, basic survival for others, and destitution or a virtual death sentence for many, would become policy among the leading political and economic powers (Harvey 2007). Instead of seeking to provide opportunities and safeguards, they would begin to openly institute systems of "law and order," ramp up policing, and build prisons where primarily nonwhite people would be warehoused and their labor exploited. As happened in the late 19th century United States after the Civil War, the instruments of collective control in the government encompassing the police, courts, schools, and health services were in the hands of whites, while blacks would have little or no power in the face of white aggressors. Racial distinctions including the demonization of non-whites and symbolic and material separation, are useful technologies with which to unite white wealthy classes with poor whites, dividing white and black workers and neighbors through fear, jealousy, and hatred. Common interests between people are obscured by the habit of white social superiority and privilege taking root more deeply in Italy, even among many Southern Italians who until recently did not really see themselves as White or even as fully "European" (Pugliese 2008; Merrill 2013).

We can learn a great deal from the Black Radical tradition that emerged during the slave trade in Africa, the middle passage and enslavement in the Americas, and colonialism in Africa, for it speaks to the struggle for freedom among all people. People everywhere regardless of race, religion, or ethnicity can claim this tradition, which may involve fugitivity. What is needed, as Angela Davis argues, is a broad idea of politics that includes transnational ties between people who share a collective relationship to a history that is not even the past, that haunts and damages us all (Davis 2016). We must unlearn the assumption that racial thinking is about individual attitudes that we can train people to change, because it is the structures of racism that must be dismantled.

People of African descent in Italy, including first and second generations, citizens, immigrants, and recently arrived refugees, live in Black spaces of social life where complex techniques are employed and expressed in unspoken shared experiences, the creation of life sustaining rituals and daily practices. Diverse, frequently improvisational, and traditional cultural practices are important as ways of being that integrally intersect with and inflect the worlds they are represented as distinct from, and also as ways of being that Clyde Woods described in the ethical epistemology of the Mississippi blues tradition in the United States. Local intellectual traditions may hold some of the keys to how we may together build geographical knowledges, philosophies, and social realities that involve more sustainable development, democratically just and ethical, local and global forms of governance (Woods 2007). Change is often perceived as the principal reserve of governments, media, and corporate bodies that effect social discourses and policies, but it can and has frequently been generated collectively, from the ground up. Black southern working class communities and First Nations in the United States maintained not only a sense that life, love, and movement must daily be affirmed, but also a counter-mobilization against resource monopolies, racial, ethnic, class, and gender polarization, and the surveillance of thought, work, language, family, community, and national borders.

Relational places are everywhere, but we have been trained to focus on discrete locations that demarcate a people with essential qualities and characteristics. The so-called 'cultural turn' of deconstruction, social critique of essentialized gender, racial, and other social categories at the end of the 20th century put forward notions of socially constructed worlds, and methods of making sense of them. In spite of this, Africa continues to be a site of anachronistic time and place, of people perceived if not always explicitly, as irreversibly different from 'Europeans.' One is told "a single story," as writer Chimamanda Ngozi Adiche has suggested.[1]

Representations of Africa and Europe as materially and culturally separate have consequences. They constitute social relations, and social borders. As I have argued, however, there is considerable evidence that Africa and Europe are relationally intertwined. Africans have been part of the Western world for centuries, even though our dominant system of knowledge keep us from seeing and understanding these interconnections. Scholars have begun to invoke the concept of a "Black Mediterranean" in order to bring attention to the profound relationality of place and people in the Mediterranean, and to promote a decentered politics (Di Maio 2012; Raeymaekers 2017; 2015). In order to overcome the conditions that have led to the systematic obscuring of the social and economic underpinnings of uneven development, our representations of cultural difference must be subjected to rigorous and prolonged collective (re)thinking and (re)envisioning. Dominant representations of otherness are underwritten by implicit constructions of selfhood and subjectivity.

Benhabib has argued that with the rise of the global free movement of capital, territorial jurisdiction by states is anachronistic and we need compassionate practice of "just membership." The international system of peoples and states is enormously interdependent, with an historical criss-crossing of fates and fortunes (Benhabib 2004). Post-national solidarity is for Benhabib a moral project that requires a new politics of membership and solidarity in a global community. However, the trouble with discussions of refugee and human rights is that anti-blackness is foreclosed. Hannah Arendt argued that imperialist encounters with Africa permitted European nations to transgress the moral limits that would normally control the exercise of power at home, to call for a state of exception (Arendt 1973). The state of the exception has now become the rule in the 'black sites' that I have compared with Black spaces, especially regarding Africans in Europe or offshore locations where anything can be done with impunity, where all is classified and by definition unknowable.

As Lewis R. Gordon has argued, anti-black racism exposes a world that believes it would ultimately be better off without blacks. Blacks from this point of view have to continually justify their very being, "What could blacks offer when it is their legitimacy that is called into question?" (Gordon, 2000, 15). Blackness is invisible by virtue of being too visible, and therefore there is nothing more to be known about it. All that is required is the identification of the social role for a plethora of other judgments.

States and the capital that fuels them are invested in securitization of internal and external borders, and the suppression of neglect and discontent through unseen violence is part of this equation. Violence against Black people has a very particular and ongoing history, but even the drone warfare today is aimed over-whelmingly at nonwhite populations (Gregory 2006; 2015). Increasingly, the racialized are extremely vulnerable to being warehoused, and abandoned. The use of the language, "black" for the CIA's "black sites" is quite telling. Black in the West signifies a lack of something, of spaces vacant for the playground of power. Blackness represents, as Heidi Nast and Mike McIntyre have suggested, a 'necropolis,' where biopolitics are not needed where people don't count as internal to a social order (McIntyre and Nast 2011; also see Mbembe 2017).

The occupation of urban spaces in Italian neighborhoods like the Ex-MOI in Turin represents an alternative to the legal and social norms that dole out racia-lized class privileges. Under circumstances in which they are treated as though, "we do not exist," they take collective measures to sustain their lives and the lives of their families. These are Black spaces that interrogate the positioning of humanness in relation to Whiteness. As Harney and Moten (2013) suggest, blackness is by definition insurgency in the flesh, meaning that one operates in alternative and disruptive ways against being socially erased and or rendered abstractions. Refugees and immigrants in Italy are asserting their right to be in Europe.

My aim in this book is to activate thinking and scholarship across academic disciplines, followed by dialogue, debate, and critique, with an ensuing collective organizing, further analysis, and political activism. When we are led to recognize and have compassion for only the suffering of the White 'transparent I' or presumed universal human, we become partial humans who mechanically follow the whims of others with power and whose interests in division and control we serve instead of our own or those of our community. As for the powerful, there are deeply damaging costs on a human scale (see Cesaire 2000). For to live a full and rich human life is to question, reflect, and feel. As Robin Kelley argues, to love, study, and struggle (Kelley 2016). Even when it is very difficult, hurts us, and makes us feel ashamed.

The lives of people of African descent are no less or more important than other lives around the globe, yet they have been the most denigrated. For centuries, Africa has been represented as a source of empty darkness, holding nothing of value aside from forced labor and natural resources. Place and people have been conflated, while the ongoing participation of African people and her descendants in the making and remaking of the West has been effaced. This is a global system with diverse iterations produced daily in place and time, from which Italians are not exempt. The racial system of social classification that we tend to take-for-granted as natural to human beings is, upon transdisciplinary examination and attention to lived experiences, entirely arbitrary except insofar as it serves to reproduce existing social hierarchies. This limited understanding of who we are and fear of letting go of what we believe to be fixed social differences can only nourish the growing concentration of wealth, expansion of immiseration, and hatred in the world today. By reflecting on our values and gathering collectively to determine priorities and strategies for organizing, we can learn to see, value, and experience things differently in our own lives and in the lives of others. We can stop this train from crashing.

Note

1 TED Talk, 2016.

BIBLIOGRAPHY

Abbay, Alemseged (1998). *Identity Jilted or Re-Imagining Identity? The Divergent Paths of Eritrean and Tigray Nationalist Struggles*. Trenton, NJ: The Red Sea Press, Inc.

Agamben, Giorgio (1995). "We refugees." Trans. Michael Rocke. *Symposium* 49(2), 114–119.

Agamben, Giorgio (2005). *State of Exception*. Chicago, IL: University of Chicago Press.

Agamben, Giorgio (2008). "Beyond human rights." *Social Engineering* 15, 90–95.

Ahmed, Sara (2012). *On Being Included: Racism and Diversity in Institutional Life*. Durham, NC: Duke University Press.

Ahmida, Ali Abdullatif (2006). "When the subaltern speak: memory of genocide in colonial Libya 1929 to 1933." *Italian Studies* 61(6), 175–190.

Albahari, Maurizio (2015). *Crimes of Peace: Mediterranean Migrations a the World's Deadliest Border*. Philadelphia: University of Pennsylvania.

Alderman, Derek and Owen Dwyer (2008). *Civil Rights Memorials and the Geography of Memory*. Atlanta: University of Georgia Press.

Alexander, Elizabeth (1994). "'Can you be BLACK and look at this?': Reading the Rodney King video(s)." *Public Culture* 7, 77–94.

Alexander, Michelle (2016) "Women of Spirit: Michelle Alexander Livestream/Union Theological Seminary." September 15.

Andall, Jacqueline and Derek Duncan eds. (2005). *Italian Colonialism: Legacy and Memory*. Oxford: Peter Lang AG.

Andall, Jacqueline (2000). *Gender, Migration, and Domestic Service: The Politics of Black Women in Italy*. Burlington, VT: Ashgate Press.

Andall, Jacqueline ed. (2003). *Gender and Ethnicity in Contemporary Europe*. London: Bloomsbury Academic.

Anderson, Benedict (2016). *Imagined Communities: Reflections on the Origin and Spread of Nationalism*. Verso.

Andrijasevic, Rutvica (2009). "Deported: The right to asylum at EU's external border of Italy and Libya." *International Migration* 48(1), 148–174.

Andersson, Ruben (2014). *Illegality, Inc.: Clandestine Migration and the Business of Bordering Europe*. Berkeley: University of California Press.

Antonsich, Marco (2015). "The 'everyday' of banal nationalism – Ordinary people's views on Italy and Italian." *Political Geography* 54: 32–42.

Antonsich, Marco (2016). "International migration and the rise of the 'civil' nation." *Journal of Ethnic and Migration Studies* 42 (11): 1790–1807.

Arendt, Hannah (1973). *The Origins of Totalitarianism*. New York: Harcourt, Brace, Jovanovich.

Atkinson, David (2000). "Nomadic strategies and colonial governments." In Ronan Paddison, Chris Philo, Paul Routledge and Joanne P. Sharp eds. *Entanglements of Power: Geographies of Domination/Resistance*. New York: Routledge, 93–121.

Atkinson, David (2003). "Geographical knowledge and scientific survey in the construction of Italian Libya." *Modern Italy* 8(1), 9–29.

Atkinson, David (2012). "Encountering bare life in Italian Libya and colonial amnesia in Agamben." In Marcello Svirsky and Simone Bignall eds. *Agamben and Colonialism*. Edinburgh: University of Edinburgh Press, 155–177.

Baldwin, James (1963) (1992). *The Fire Next Time*. New York: Vintage Press.

Baldwin, James (1965) (1995). "Goin to Meet the Man." In *Going to Meet the Man: Stories*. New York: Vintage.

Baldwin, James (1984). "On Being White and Other Lies." *Essence*, April.

Baldwin, James (1998). "A Stranger in the Village." In James Baldwin and Toni Morrison. *James Baldwin: Collected Essays*. New York: Library of America.

Baldwin, James (2012). "Many Thousands Gone." In *Notes of A Native Son*. Boston, MA: Beacon Press.

Barrera, Giulia (2003a). "The construction of racial hierarchies in colonial Eritrea: The liberal and early Fascist period (1897–1934)." In Patricia Palumbo ed., *A Place in the Sun: Africa in Italian Culture from Post-Unification to the Present*. Berkeley: University of California Press, 81–118.

Barrera, Giulia (2003b). "Mussolini's colonial race laws and state-settler relations in Africa Orientale Italiana (1935–1931)." *Journal of Modern Italian Studies* 8(3), 425–443.

Barrera, Giulia (2005). "Patrilinearity, race, and identity: The upbringing of Italo-Eritreans during Italian colonialism." In Ruth Ben-Ghiat, and Mia Fuller eds. *Italian Colonialism*. London: Palgrave Macmillan, 97–108.

Bartoli, Clelia (2012). *Razzisti per Legge: L'Italia che discrimina*. Bari: Laterza.

Baxter, P.T.W., Jan Hultin and Alessandro Triulzi (1996). *Being and Becoming Oromo: Historical and Anthropological Enquiries*. New Jersey: The Red Sea Press, Inc.

Ben-Ghiat, Ruth (2005). "The Italian colonial cinema: Agendas and audiences." In Ruth Ben-Ghiat and Mia Fuller eds. *Italian Colonialism*. London: Palgrave Macmillan.

Ben-Ghiat, Ruth and Mia Fuller eds. (2005). *Italian Colonialism*. London: Palgrave Macmillan.

Ben Jelloun, Tahar (2005) (2016). *Il razzismo spiegato a mia figlia* (Italian edition). Milan: Bompiani.

Benhabib, Seyla (2004). *The Rights of Others: Aliens, Residents, and Citizens*. Cambridge: Cambridge University Press.

Berger, John (1990). *Ways of Seeing*. New York: Penguin

Berman, Marshall (1998). *All That Is Solid Melts into Air: The Experience of Modernity*. New York: Penguin Books.

Best, Stephen and Saidiya Hartman (2005). "Fugitive justice." *Representations* 92(1), 1–15.

Blake, Valarie (2010). "Mass African migration into Europe: Human rights and state obligations." *Hamline Journal of Public Law and Policy* 32, 135.

Blakely, Allison (2009). "The emergence of Afro-Europe: A preliminary sketch." In Darlene Clark Hine, Trica Danielle Keaton, and Stephen Small eds. *Black Europe and the African Diaspora*. Urbana: University of Illinois Press, 3–28.

Blunt, Alison (1994). *Travel, Gender, and Imperialism: Mary Kingsley and West Africa*. New York: Guilford Press.

Bourdieu, Pierre (1977). *Outline of a Theory of Practice*. Cambridge: Cambridge University Press.

Bourdieu, Pierre (1989). *Distinction. A Social Critique of the Judge of Taste*. Cambridge, MA: Harvard University Press.

Bressey, Caroline and Hakim Adi eds. (2013). *Belonging in Europe – The African Diaspora and Work*. London: Routledge.

Bressey, Caroline and Claire Dwyer eds. (2008). *New Geographies of Race and Racism*. London: Routledge.

Brown, Jacqueline Nassy (2005) *Dropping Anchor, Setting Sail: Geographies of Race in Black Liverpool*. Berkeley: University of California Press.

Browne, Simone (2015). *Dark Matters: On the Surveillance of Blackness*. Durham: Duke University Press.

Bugul, Ken. (2008). *The Abandoned Baobab: The Autobiography of a Senegalese Woman*. Charlottesville: The University of Virginia Press.

Campbell, Ian (2010). *The Plot to Kill Graziani: The Attempted Assassination of Mussolini's Viceroy*. Addis Ababa: Addis Ababa University Press.

Campbell, Ian (2014). *The Massacre of Debre Libanos Ethiopia 1937: The Story of one of Fascism's Most Shocking Atrocities*. Addis Ababa: Addis Abbaba University Press.

Campbell, Ian and Degife Gabre-Tsadik (1997). "La repressione fascista in Etiopia: La riconstruzione del massacro di Debra Libanos." *Studi piacentini* 11(21), 79–128.

Campt, Tina M. (2012). *Image Matters: Archive, Photography, and the African Diaspora in Europe*. Durham, NC: Duke University Press.

Campt, Tina M. (2017). *Listening to Images*. Durham, NC: Duke University Press.

Carter, Donald (1997). *States of Grace: Senegalese in Italy and the New European Immigration*. Minneapolis: University of Minnesota Press.

Carter, Donald M. (2010). *Navigating the African Diaspora: The Anthropology of Invisibility*. Minneapolis: University of Minnesota Press.

Carter, Donald M. (2013). "Blackness over Europe: Meditations on culture and belonging." In Eve Rosenhaft and Robbie Aitken eds. *Africa in Europe: Studies in Transnational Practice in the Long Twentieth Century*. Liverpool: Liverpool University Press, 201–216.

Carter, Donald M. and Heather Merrill (2007). "Bordering Humanism: life and death on the margins of Europe." *GeoPolitics* 12(2), 248–264.

Cerreti, Claudio ed. (1994). *Colonie africane e cultura italiana fra Ottocento e Novecento: Le esplorazioni e la geografia*. Roma: Istituto italo-africano.

Cesaire, Aime (1972) (2000). *Discourse on Colonialism*. Trans. Joan Pinkham. New York: Monthly Review Press.

Cesaire, Aime (2010). "Culture and colonization." *Social Text* 28(2), 127–144.

Chambers, Iain (2008). *Mediterranean Crossings: The Politics of an Interrupted Modernity*. Durham: Duke University Press.

Chen, Kuan-Hsing and David Morley (1996). *Stuart Hall "What is this Black in Black Popular Culture?": Critical Dialogues in Cultural Studies*. London: Routledge Press.

Ciafaloni, Francesco (2011). *Destino della classe operaia*. Roma: Edizioni dell'asino.

Clark Hine, Darlene and Kathleen Thompson (1998). *A Shining Threat of Hope: The History of Black Women in America*. New York: Broadway Books.

Coates, Ta-Nehisi (2015). *Between the World and Me.* New York: Spiegel and Grau.

Cole, Jeffrey (2005). *The New Racism in Europe: A Sicilian Ethnography.* Cambridge: Cambridge University Press.

Colombo, Asher and Giuseppe Sciortino (1990). *Stranieri in Italia: Assimilati ed Esclusi.* Bologna: Il Mulino.

Cooper, Anna Julia (1998). *The Voice of Anna Julia Cooper: Including A Voice From the South and other Important Essays, Papers.* New York: Rowman & Littlefield.

Coronil, Fernando (1996). "Beyond Occidentalism: Toward nonimperial geohistorical categories." *Cultural Anthropology* 11(1), 51–87.

Crehan, Kate (2002). *Gramsci, Culture, and Anthropology.* Berkeley: University of California Press.

Crehan, Kate (2016). *Gramsci's Common Sense: Inequality and Its Narratives.* Durham: Duke University Press.

Dal Lago, Alessandro (1999). *NON-PERSONE: L'Esclusione dei migranti in una società globale.* Milan: Feltrinelli.

Darden, Joseph T. and Sameh M. Kamel (2000). "Black residential segregation in the city and suburbs of Detroit: Does socioeconomic status matter?" *Journal of Urban Affairs* 22(1), 1–13.

Davidson, Joyce, Liz Bondi and Michael Smith (2007). *Emotional Geographies.* Burlington, VT: Ashgate.

Davis, Angela (2016). *Freedom in a Constant Struggle: Ferguson, Palestine, and the Foundations of a Movement.* Chicago, IL: Haymarket Books.

Da Silva, Denise Ferreira (2007). *Toward a Global Idea of Race.* Minneapolis: University of Minnesota Press.

De Marco, Roland R. (1943). *The Italianization of African Natives: Government Native Education in the Italian Colonies 1890–1937.* Teachers College, Columbia University New York: Bureau of Publications.

Decimo, Francesco and G. Sciortino (2006). *Stranieri in Italia. Reti Migranti.* Bologna: Il Mulino.

Del Boca, Angelo (1986). *Gli Italiani in Libia: Tripoli Bel Suol D'Amore 1860–1922.* Roma-Bari: Laterza.

Del Boca, Angelo (1987). "Un lager del fascismo: Danane." *Studi Piacentini* 1, 59–70.

Del Boca, Angelo (1996) (2007). *I gas di Mussolini. Il fascismo e la guerra d'Etiopia.* Roma: Editori Riuniti.

Del Boca, Angelo (2002). *L'Africa nella coscienza degli Italiani: Miti, memorie, errori, sconfitte.* Milano: Mondadori.

Del Boca, Angelo (2003). "The myths, suppressions, denials, and defaults of Italian colonialism." In Patrizia Palumbo ed. *A Place in the Sun: Africa in Italian Colonial Culture From Post-Unification To The Present.* Berkeley: University of California Press, 17–36.

Del Boca, Angelo (2005). *Italiani, brava gente?* Vicenza: Nera Pozza Editore.

Del Boca, Angelo and Nicola Labanca (2002). *L'impero africano del fascismo nelle fotografie dell'Istituto Luce.* Rome: Editori riuniti.

De Genova, Nicholas and Nathalie Peutz eds. (2010). *The Deportation Regime: Sovereignty, Space, and the Freedom of Movement.* Durham: Duke University Press.

Desjarlais, Robert and C. Jason Throop. (2011). "Phenomenological approaches in anthropology." *Annual Review of Anthropology* 40, 87–102.

Deschamps, Benedicte (2011). "The Italian press in a global perspective." In Graziella Parati and Anthony Julian Tamburri eds. *The Cultures of the Italian Migration: Diverse Trajectories and Discrete Perspectives.* Maryland: Farleigh Dickinson Press.

De Vries, Leonie Anselms, Glenda Garelli, and Martina Tazzioli (2016). "Mediterranean migration crisis: Transit points, enduring struggles." *openDemocracy*, Februrary. www.op endemocracy.net/

Di Carmine, Roberta (2011). *Italy Meets Africa: Colonial Discourses in Italian Cinema*. New York: Peter Lang Publishing.

Dickie, John (1999). *Darkest Italy: The Nation and Stereotypes of the Mezziogiorno, 1860–1900*. New York: St. Martin's Press.

Di Maio, Alessandra (2009). "Black Italia: Contemporary migrant writers from Africa." In Darlene Clark Hine, Danielle Keaton, and Stephen Small eds. *Black Europe and the African Diaspora*. Bloomington: University of Indiana, 119–144.

Di Maio, Alessandra (2012). "Mediterraneo Nero. Le rotte dei migranti nel millennnio globale." In *La citta cosmopolita*. *Palermo*. In Manuela Line ed., *Nord, Sud, Est e naturalmente Ovest: Pratiche di attraversamento*, 143–163.

Douglass, Frederick (2013). *Narrative of the Life of Frederick Douglass, a Slave*. Cincinnati Ohio: Simon & Brown.

Douglas, Mary (1966) (2002). *Purity and Danger: An Analysis of Concepts of Pollution and Taboo*. New York: Routledge.

Du Bois, W.E.B. (1994). *The Souls of Black Folk*. Mineola, New York: Dover Publications.

Du Bois, W.E.B. (1999). *Black Reconstruction in America, 1860–1880*. New York: Free Press.

Du Bois, W.E.B. (2007) *The World and Africa. Color and Democracy*. Ed. HenryLouis Gates, Jr. London: Oxford University Press.

Ehrkamp, Patricia (2005). "Placing identities: Transnational practices and local attachments of Turkish immigrants in Germany." *Journal of Ethnic and Migration Studies* 31(2), 345–364.

Fanon, Frantz (1961) (2005). *The Wretched of the Earth*. Trans. Richard PhilcoxNew York: Grove Press.

Fanon, Frantz. (1967) (2008). *Black Skin, White Masks*. New York: Grove Press.

FIDH (International Federation for Human Rights) (2005) *Right to Asylum in Italy: Access to Procedures and Treatment of Asylum Seekers*. FIDR report.

Frankenberg, Ruth (1993). *White Women, Race Matters: The Social Construction of Whiteness*. Minneapolis: University of Minnesota Press.

Franklin, Todd (2018). "Baldwin Bears Witness" in James Haille II ed., *Thinking Through Baldwin*. Lexington Books. Forthcoming.

Frederickson, George M. (1982). *White Supremacy: A Comparative Study in American and South African History*. Oxford: Oxford University Press.

Frisina, Annalisa and Camilla Hawthorne (2017). "Italians with veils and Afros: gender, beauty, and the everyday racism of the daughters of immigrants in Italy." *Journal of Ethnic and Migration Studies*, online, August 2, 1469–9451.

Fuller, Mia (1996). "Wherever you go, there you are: Fascist plans for the colonial city of Addis Ababa and the colonizing suburb of EUR '42." *Journal of Contemporary History* 3 (2), 397–418.

Fuller, Mia (2000). "Preservation and self-absorption: Italian colonization and the walled city of Tripoli, Libya." *The Journal of North African Studies* 5(4), 121–154.

Gabaccia, Donna R. (2000). *Italy's Many Diasporas*. Seattle: University of Washington Press.

Garelli, Glenda and Martina Tazzioli (2016). "The EU hotspot approach at Lampedusa." *openDemocracy*, February 26. www.opendemocracy.net

Garb, Tamar (2013). *African Photography from the Walther Collection. Distance and Desire: Encounters with the African Archive*. Critique d'art. Göttingen; Steidl; New York: The Walther Collection.

Gatti, Fabrizio (2007). *Viaggiare, Lavorare, Morire Da Clandestini*. Milano: Rizzoli.

Ghermandi, Gabriella (2007). *Regina di Fiori e di Perle*. Roma: Donzelli.

Ghirelli, Massimo and Patrizio Valenti (2005). *Bell'Abissina: L'Italia coloniale nelle foto private*. Turin: Agenda Nonsolonero.

Giglioli, Ilaria (2016). "Producing Sicily as Europe: Migration, colonialism and the making of the Mediterranean border between Italy and Sicily." *Geopolitics* 22(2), 407–428.

Gilman, Sandor (1985). *Difference and Pathology: Stereotypes of Sexuality, Race, and Madness*. Ithaca: Cornell University Press.

Gilmartin, Mary (2008). "Migration, identity and belonging." *Geographical Compass* 2(6), 1837–1852.

Giuliani, Gaia and Cristina Lombardi-Diop (2013). *Bianco e Nero: Storia dell'identità razziale degli italiani*. Milano: Mondadori.

Goffman, Erving (1986). *Stigma: Notes on the Management of Spoiled Identity*. New York: Touchstone.

Goglia, Luigi (1985). "Una diversa politica razziale coloniale in un documento inedito di Alberto Pollero del 1937." *Storia Contemporanea*.

Goglia, Luigi (1988). "Note sul razzismo coloniale fascista." *Storia contemporanea* 19(6). 1223–1266.

Goglia, Luigi ed. (1989). *Colonialismo e Fotografia: il caso italiano*. Messina, Sicily: Sicania.

Golash-Boza, Tanya (2015). *Deported: Immigrant Policing, Disposable Labor and Global Capitalism*. New York: New York University Press.

Goldberg, David Theo (1993a). "'Polluting the body politic': Racist discourse and urban locations." In Malcolm Cross and Michael Keith eds. *Racism, the City and the State*. London: Routledge, 45–60.

Goldberg, David Theo (1993b). *Racist Culture: Philosophy and the Politics of Meaning*. Wiley-Blackwell.

Grillo, Ralph and Jeff Pratt eds. (2002). *The Politics of Recognizing Difference: Multiculturalism Italian-style*. Burlington, VT: Ashgate.

Grillo, Ralph, Valentina Mazzucato, Bruno Riccio, and Rubah Salih (2015). *Living with Difference: Essays on Transnationalism and Multiculturalism*. B and RG Books of Lewes.

Gordon, Lewis R. (1995). *Black Faith and Antiblack Racism*. New Jersey: Humanities Press.

Gordon, Lewis R. (2000) *Existentia: Understanding African Existential Thought*. New York: Routledge Press.

Gray, Kevin Alexander, Joann Wypijewski, and Jeffrey St. Clair eds. (2014). *Killing Trayvons: An Anthology of American Violence*. CounterPunch Books. Gregory, Derek (2004). *The Colonial Present*. Malden, MA: Blackwell Publishing.

Gregory, Derek (2006). "The black flag: Guantanamo Bay and the space of exception." *Geografiska Annaler. Series B, Human Geography*. 88(4), 405–427.

Gregory, Derek (2015) "Moving targets and violent geographies." In Heather Merrill and Lisa Hoffman, *Spaces of Danger: Culture and Power in the Everyday*. Atlanta: University of Georgia Press, 256–298.

Gregory, Steven (1999). *Black Corona: Race and the Politics of Place in an Urban Community*. Princeton, NJ: Princeton University Press.

Gress, Melissa and Gregory T. Seigworth eds. (2010). *The Affect Theory Reader*. Durham: Duke University Press.

Grillo, R.D. (2003). "Cultural essentialism and cultural anxiety." *Anthropological Theory* 3(2), 157–173.

Guillamin, Colette (1995). *Racism, Sexism, Power and Ideology*. London: Routledge.

Hall, Stuart (1991). "Old and new identities, old and new ethnicities." In Anthony D. King ed. *Culture, Globalization and the World System*. London: Macmillan, 41–68.

Hall, Stuart (1993). "What is the 'Black' in Black popular culture?" *Social Justice* 2(1/2), 104–114.

Hall, Stuart (1997). *Race, The Floating Signifier*. Dir. Sut Jally. Northhampton MA: Media and Education Foundation.

Hall, Stuart (2003). "Cultural identity and diaspora." In P. Williams and L. Chrisman eds. *Theorizing Diaspora*. London: Blackwell, 233–246.

Hall, Stuart (2015). "Creolite and the process of creolization." In Encarnacion Gutierrez Rodriguez and Shirley Anne Tate eds. *Creolization in Europe. Legacies and Transformations*. Liverpool: Liverpool University Press, 12–25.

Hanchard, Michael (2006). *Party/Politics: Horizons in Black Political Thought*. Oxford: Oxford University Press.

Harney, Stefano and Fred Moten (2013) *The Undercommons: Fugitive Planning and Black Struggle*. Brooklyn, NY: Autonomedia.

Hartman, Saidya V. (1997). *Scenes of Subjection: Terror, Slavery, and Self-Making in Nineteenth-Century America*. Oxford University Press.

Hartman, Saidya V. (2007). *Lose Your Mother: A Journey along the Atlantic Slave Route*. New York: Farar, Straus and Giroux.

Hartman, Saidya V. and Frank B. Wilderson, III (2003) "The position of the unthought." *Qui Parle* 13(2), 183–201.

Harvey, David (1991). *The Condition of Postmodernity: An Enquiry into the Origins of Cultural Change*. London: Blackwell.

Harvey, David (2007). *A Brief History of Neoliberalism*. London: Oxford University Press.

Hawthorne, Camilla (2015). "Italian writer Igiaba Scego rewrites the Black Mediterranean." October 14. http://africasacountry.com/2015/10/italian-writer-igiaba-scego-re writes-the-black-mediterranean/

Hawthorne, Camilla (2017). "In search of black Italia: Notes on race, belonging, and activism in the black Mediterranean." *Transition* 123, 152–174.

Hawthorne, Camilla (forthcoming) *There Are No Black Italians? Race and Citizenship in the Black Mediterranean*. Forthcoming dissertation UC Berkeley.

Hawthorne, Camilla and Pina Piccolo (2016). "Antirazzismo senza razza." In *La machina sognante: Contenitore di scritture dal mondo*. October 1. www.lamacchinasognante.com/a ntirazzismo-senza-razza-camilla-hawthorne-e-pina-piccolo/.

Hess, Robert L. (1966). *Italian Colonialism in Somalia*. Chicago: The University of Chicago Press.

Hesse, Barnor (2014) "Escaping liberty: Western hegemony, black fugitivity." *Political Theory* 42(3), 288–313.

Holston, James (2009) *Insurgent Citizenship: Disjunctions of Democracy and Modernity in Brazil*. Princeton University Press.

hooks, bell (1992). *Black Looks: Race and Representation*. First Edition. Boston: South End Press.

hooks, bell (1999). *Yearning: Race: Gender and Cultural Politics*. Boston: South End Press.

Hyndman, Jennifer (2000). *Managing Displacement: Refugees and the Politics of Humanitarianism*. Minneapolis: University of Minnesota Press.

Ifekwunigwe, Jayne (1999). *Scattered Belongings: Cultural Paradoxes of Race, Nation and Gender*. New York: Routledge.

Inwood, Joshua F. J. and Deborah G. Martin (2008). "Whitewash: White privilege and the racialized landscapes of the University of Georgia." *Social and Cultural Geography* 9(4), 373–395.

Inwood, J. (2016). "Critical pedagogy and the fierce urgency of now: Opening up space for critical reflections on the U.S. Civil Rights Movement." *Journal of Social and Cultural Geography*. www.aag.org/galleries/about-aag-files/Critical_Pedagogy_Inwood.pdf.

Iyob, Ruth (1997). *The Eritrean Struggle for Independence: Domination, Resistance, Nationalism 1941–1993*. Cambridge: Cambridge University Press.

Iyob, Ruth (2003). "From Mal d'Africa to Mal d'Ethiopia? The ties that bind." In Duncan and Andall eds. *Italian Colonialism: Legacy and Memory*. Peter Lang, 255–282.

Iyob, Ruth (2005). "*Madamismo* and Beyond: The Construction of Eritrean Women." In Ruth Ben-Ghiat, and Mia Fuller eds. *Italian Colonialism: Legacy and Memory*. Peter Lang AG.

Jackson, Michael (2002). *The Politics of Storytelling: Violence, Transgression and Intersubjectivity*. Museum Tuscalanum Press.

Jackson, Michael (2005). *Existential Anthropology: Events, Exigencies, and Effects*. Berghahn Books.

Jackson, Michael (2012). *Lifeworlds: Essays in Existential Anthropology*. Chicago, IL: University of Chicago Press.

Jacobs, Harriet (1861) (2001). *Incidents in the Life of a Slave Girl*. Unabridged. New York: Dover Publications, Inc.

Jayne, Mark, Gill Valentine, Sarah L. Holloway (2010) "Emotional, embodied and affective geographies of alcohol, drinking and drunkenness." *Transactions of the Institute of British Geographers* 35(4), 540–554.

Jonas, Anthony (2011). *The Battle of Adwa: African Victory in the Age of Empire*. Cambridge, MA: Harvard University Press.

Jordan, Winthrop D. (2012). *White Over Black: American Attitudes toward the Negro, 1550–1812*. Chapel Hill: The University of North Carolina Press.

Keaton, Danielle Trica (2006). *Muslim Girls and the Other France*. Indianapolis: Indiana University Press.

Keaton, Danielle Trica (2013). "Racial profiling and the 'French exception'." *French Cultural Studies* 24(2), 231–242.

Kelley, Robin D.G. (1996). *Race Rebels: Culture, Politics, and the Black Working Class*. Florence, MA: Free Press.

Kelley, Robin D.G. (2000) "Introduction" to Aime Cesaire, *Discourse on Colonialism*. Trans. Joan Pinkham. New York: Monthly Review Press.

Kelley, Robin D.G. (2003). *Freedom Dreams: The Black Radical Imagination*. Boston: Beacon Press.

Kelley, Robin D.G. (2016). "Black study, black struggle." *Boston Review: A Political and Literary Forum*, March 7.

King, Debra Walker (2008). *African Americans and the Culture of Pain*. Charlottesville: University of Virginia Press.

Kleinman, Arthur. (2000). "The Violence of Everyday Life: The Multiple Forms and Dynamics of Social Violence." In Veena Das, Arthur Kleinman, Mamphela Ramphele, and Pamela Reynolds eds. *Violence and Subjectivity*. University of California Press, 226–241.

Kobayashi, Audre and Linda Peake (2000). "Racism out of place: Thoughts on Whiteness and an antiracist geography in the New Millennium." *Annals of the Association of American Geographers* 90(2), 392–403.

Kuwornu, Fred (2014) "18 IUS Soli" A film.

Kyenge, Cecile (2014). *Ho sognato una strada. I diritti di tutti*. Milano: Edizione Piemme.

Labanca, Nicola ed. (1992). *L'Africa in Vetrina: Storie di musei e di esposizioni coloniali in Italia. Pese*. Treviso, Italy: PAGVS Editions.

Labanca, Nicola (1999). "Il razzismo coloniale Italiano." In Alberto Burgio ed. *Nel nome della razza: il razzismo nella storia d'Italia 1870–1945.* Bologno: Il Mulino, 145–161.

Labanca, Nicola (2002). *Oltremare: Storia dell'espansione coloniale in Italia.* Bologna: Il Mulino.

Labanca, Nicola (2005). "Italian colonial internment." In Ruth Ben-Ghiat and Mia Fuller eds. *Italian Colonialisms.* London: Palgrave Macmillan, 27–36.

Lamont Hill, Marc (2016). *Nobody: Casualties of America's War on the Vulnerable: From Ferguson to Flint and Beyond.* New York: Atria Books.

Larebo, Haile (2005). "Empire building and its limitations: Ethiopia (1935–1941)." In Ruth Ben-Ghiat and Mia Fuller eds. *Italian Colonialisms.* London: Palgrave Macmillan, 83–94.

Leitner, Helga (1997) "Reconfiguring the spatiality of power: The construction of a supranational migration framework for the EU." *Political Geography* 16(2), 123–143.

Levi, Primo (1958) (2015) *Se questo é un uomo.* Turin: Einaudi.

Lewis, I.M. (1965) (1980). *A Modern History of SOMALIA: Nation and State in the Horn of Africa.* New York: Longman.

Lipsitz, George (2006). *The Possessive Investment in Whiteness: How White People Profit from Identity Politics.* Philadelphia, PA: Temple University Press.

Lipsitz, George (2011). *How Racism Takes Place.* Philadelphia, PA: Temple University Press.

Lombardi-Diop, Cristina and Caterina Romeo eds. (2013). *Postcolonial Italy: Challenging National Homogeneity.* New York: Palgrave Macmillan.

Lombardi-Diop, Cristina and Caterina Romeo (2015). "Italy's postcolonial 'question': Views from the southern frontier of Europe." *Postcolonial Studies* 18(4), 367–383.

Longhi, Vittorio (2013). *The Immigrant War: A Global Movement against Discrimination and Exploitation.* Bologna: SEOPS.

Lowery, Wesley (2016). *They Can't Kill Us All: Ferguson, Baltimore, and a New Era in America's Racial Justice Movement.* New York: Little, Brown and Company.

Lucht, Hans (2011). *Darkness before Daybreak: African Migrants Living on the Margins in Southern Italy Today.* Berkeley: University of California Press.

Macedo, Donald and Panayota Gounari, eds. (2005). *The Globalization of Racism.* New York: Routledge.

Malkki, Liisa (1992). "National Geographic: The rooting of peoples and the territorialization of national identity among scholars and refugees." *Cultural Anthropology* 7(1), 22–44.

Mamdani, Mahmood (1996*). Citizen and Subject: Contemporary Africa and the Legacy of Late Colonialism.* Princeton, NJ: Princeton University Press.

Mangano, Antonello (2010). *Gli Africani Salveranno l'Italia.* Milan: BUR, Futuropassato.

Marable, Manning ed. (2008). *Transnational Blackness: Navigating the Global Color Line.* New York: Palgrave Macmillan.

Massey, Doreen. (1994). *Space, Place, and Gender.* University of Minnesota.

Maxwell, Joseph A. (2013). *Qualitative Research Design: An Interactive Approach.* Los Angelos: Sage Publications.

Mbembe, Achille (2001) *On the Postcolony.* California: University of California Press.

Mbembe, Achile (2003). "Necropolitics." *Public Culture* 15(1), 11–40.

Mbembe, Achille (2009). "Figures of multiplicity: Can France reinvent its identity?" In C. Tshimanga, C.D. Goldola, and P.J. Bloom eds. *Frenchness and the African Diaspora: Identity and Uprising in Contemporary France.* Indiana University Press, 55–69.

Mbembe, Achille (2017). *Critique of Black Reason.* Trans. Laurent Dubois. Durham: Duke University Press.

McCormack, Derek P. (2003). "An event of geographical ethics: Spaces of affect." *Transactions of the Institute of British Geographers* 28(4), 488–507.

McIntyre, Michael and Heidi Nast (2011). "Bio (necro) polis: Marx, surplus populations, and the spatial dialectics of reproduction and 'race.'" *Antipode* 43(5), 1465–1488.

Mckittrick, Katherine (2006). *Demonic Grounds: Black Women And The Cartographies of Struggle*. Minneapolis: University of Minnesota Press.

Mckittrick, Katherine (2011). "On plantations, prisons, and a black sense of place." *Social & Cultural Geography* 12 (8), 947–963.

Mckittrick, Katherine ed. (2015). *Sylvia Wynter: On Being Human As Praxis*. Durham: Duke University Press.

Mckittrick, Katherine and Clyde Woods eds. (2007). *Black Geographies and the Politics of Place*. Boston: South End Press.

Mcklintock, Anne (1995). *Imperial Leather: Race, Gender, and Sexuality in the Colonial Context*. London: Routledge.

Memmi, Albert (1957) (1991). *The Colonizer and the Colonized*. Boston: Beacon Press.

Meret, Susi, Elisabetta Della Corte, and Maria Sangiuliano (2013) "The racist attacks against Cecile Kyenge and the enduring myth of the 'nice' Italian." *Open Democracy*, August. Online.

Merrill, Heather (2001). "Making space for anti-racist feminism in a northern Italian industrial city." In France Winddance Twine and Kathleen Blee eds. *Feminism and Anti-Racism: International Struggles*. New York: University Press.

Merrill, Heather (2004). "Space agents: Anti-racist feminism and the politics of scale." *Gender, Place, and Culture: A Journal of Feminist Geography* 11(2).

Merrill, Heather (2006). *An Alliance of Women: Immigration and the Politics of Race*. Minneapolis: University of Minnesota Press.

Merrill, Heather (2011). "Immigration and surplus populations: Race and deindustrialization in Northern Italy," *Antipode: A Radical Journal of Geography* for special issue, "Bio (necro)polis: Marx, Surplus Populations, and the Spatial Dialectics of Reproduction and 'Race'," 43(5), 1542–1572.

Merrill, Heather (2013). "Who gets to be Italian? Black life worlds and white spatial imaginaries in Turin." Chapter 6 in France Winddance Twine and Bradley Gardener eds. *Geographies of Privilege*. New York: Routledge, 135–161.

Merrill, Heather (2014). "Postcolonial borderlands: Black life worlds and relational place in Turin, Italy." *Acme: An International E-Journal for Critical Geographies* 13(2), 263–294.

Merrill, Heather (2015). "In other wor(l)ds: Situated intersectionality in Italy." In Heather Merrill and Lisa Hoffman eds. *Spaces of Danger: Culture and Power in the Everyday*. Athens, Georgia: University of Georgia Press.

Merrill, Heather and Lisa Hoffman eds. (2015). *Spaces of Danger: Culture and Power in the Everyday*. Athens, Georgia: University of Georgia Press.

Mezzadra, Sandro and Brett Neilson (2003) "Nè qui nè altrove: Migration, detention, desertion: a dialogue." *Bologna: Borderlands Journal* 2(1).

Mezzadra, Sandro and Brett Neilson (2016). *Border as Method, or, The Multiplication of Labor*. Durham: Duke University Press.

Mills, Charles W. (1998). *Blackness Visible: Essays on Philosophy and Race*. Ithaca: Cornell University Press.

Mills, Charles W. (1999). *The Racial Contract*. Ithaca, NY: Cornell University Press.

Mitchell, Katharyne and Key MacFarlane (2016). *Crime and the Global City: Migration, Borders, and the Pre-Criminal*. Oxford Handbooks Online.

Moraga, Cherrie and Gloria Anzaldua, eds. (2015). *This Bridge Called My Back, Fourth Edition: Writings by Radical Women of Color*. State University of New York Press.

Morin, Karen M. (2013). "Carceral space and the usable past." *Historical Geography* 41. E-journal. https://ejournals.unm.edu/index.php/historicalgeography/article/view/3045/html_3.

Morin, Karen M. and Dominique Moran eds. (2015). *Historical Geographies of Prisons: Unlocking the Usable Carceral Past.* New York: Routledge.

Morley, David and Kuan-Hsing Chen eds. (1996). *Stuart Hall: Critical Dialogues in Cultural Studies.* London: Routledge.

Morrison, Toni (2007). *Beloved.* New York: Vintage; reprint edition.

Morrison, Toni (1993). *Playing in the Dark: Whiteness and the Literary Imagination.* New York: Vintage Press.

Mosse, George (1997). *Toward the Final Solution: A History of European Racism.* New York: Howard Fertig.

Moten, Fred (2003). *In the Break: The Aesthetic of the Black Radical Tradition.* Minneapolis: University of Minnesota.

Moten, Fred (2008). "The case of blackness." *Criticism* 50(2), 177–218.

Moten, Fred (2013). "Blackness and nothingness (mysticism in the flesh)." *The South Atlantic Quarterly* 112(4), 737–780.

Mountz, Alison (2010). *Seeking Asylum: Human Smuggling and Bureaucracy at the Border.* Minneapolis: University of Minnesota Press.

Muhammad, Khalill Gibran (2010). *The Condemnation of Blackness: Race, Crime, and the Making of Modern Urban America.* New York: Harvard University Press.

Muhlhahn, Klaus (2010). "The concentration camp in global historical perspective.." *History Compass* 8/6, 543–561.

Negash, Tekeste (1987). *Italian Colonialism in Eritrea, 1882–1941: Policies, Praxis and Impact.* Stockholm: Uppsala University Press.

Negash, Tekeste (2005). "The ideology of colonialism: Educational policy and praxis in Eritrea." In Ruth Ben-Ghiat and Mia Fuller eds. *Italian Colonialism.* London: Palgrave Macmillan.

Nicolini, Giusi and Marta Bellingreri (2013). *Lampedusa: Conversazioni su isole, politica, migranti.* Torino: GruppoAbeli.

Novati, G.C. (2005) "National identities as a by-product of Italian Colonialism: A comparison of Eritrea and Somalia." In Jacqueline Andall and Derek Duncan eds. *Italian Colonialism: Legacy and Memory.* Peter Lang AG, 47–74.

Nyers, Peter (2006). *Rethinking Refugees Beyond States of Emergency.* London: Routledge.

Oakley, Judith (1996). *Own or Other Culture.* London: Routledge.

Ong, Aiwa (1996). "Cultural citizenship as subject-making. Immigrants negotiate racial and cultural boundaries in the U.S." *Current Anthropology* 37(5), 737–762.

Pagliai, Valentina (2009). "Conversational agreement and racial formation processes." *Language and Society* 38(5), 549–579.

Palumbo, Patricia ed. (2003). *A Place in the Sun: Africa in Italian Colonial Culture from Post-Unification to the Present.* Berkeley: University of California Press.

Pandey, Gyanendra (2013) *Unarchived Histories: The "Mad" and the "Trifling" in the colonial and postcolonial world.* New York: Routledge.

Pankhurst, Richard. (1969a) "Fascist racial policies in Ethiopia: 1922–1941." *Ethiopia Observer* 12(4), 22–41.

Pankhurst, Richard (1969b). "Ethiopian patriots." *Ethiopia Observer* 12(2), 92–127.

Pankhurst, Richard (1972). "Education in Ethiopia during the Italian Fascist Occupation (1936–1941)." *The International Journal of Historical Studies* 5(3), 361–396.

Pankhurst, Richard (1998). "History of education, printing, and literature in Ethiopia." *Addis Tribune*, 6 November.

Pastore, Ferruccio and Luca Trinchieri (2008). "La Libia nel sistema migratorio mediterraneo. Dinamiche di mobilita e riposte politiche." *Mondo Migranti*. 21–53.

Pastore, Ferruccio, Paolo Monzini and Giuseppe Sciortino (2006). "Schengen's soft underbelly? Irregular migration and human smuggling across land and sea borders to Italy." *International Migration* 44(4).

Patterson, Orlando (1985). *Slavery and Social Death: A Comparative Study*. Cambridge, MA: Harvard University of Press.

Pennacini, Cecilia ed. (1999). *L'Africa in Piemonte tra '800 e '900: Imagini e colonie*. Turin: Archivio di Stato.

Pickering-Iazzi, Robin (2003). "Mass-mediated fantasies of feminine conquest, 1930–1940" in Patrizia Palumbo ed. *A Place in the Sun: Africa in Italian Colonial Culture from Post-Unification to the Present*. Berkeley: University of California Press, 197–223.

Pierre, Jemima (2012). *The Predicament of Blackness: Postcolonial Ghana and the Politics of Race*. Chicago, IL: University of Chicago Press.

Pieterse, Jan Nederveen 1995. *White on Black: Images of Africans and Blacks in Western Popular Culture*. New Haven: Yale University Press.

Pile, Steve (2010) "Emotion and affect in recent human geography." *Transactions of the Institute of British Geographers*, 35(1), 5–10.

Pinelli, Barbara (2011). *Attraversando Il Mediterraneo. Il Sistema Campo in Italia: Violenza e Soggettività Nelle Esperienze delle Donne*. Firenze: Leo S. Olschki.

Pojmann, Wendy ed. (2008). *Migration and activism in Europe since 1945*. London: Palgrave MacMillan.

Ponzanesi, Sandra (2012). "The color of love: Madamismo and interracial relationships in the Italian colonies." *Research in African Literatures* 43(2), 155–172.

Ponzanesi, Sandra (2016). "Does Italy need postcolonial theory? Intersections in Italian postcolonial studies." *English Literature* 3, 145–161.

Pratt, Geraldine (2005). "Abandoned women and spaces of the exception." *Antipode* 3(5), 1052–1078.

Pred, Allan (1995). *Re-Cognizing European Modernities: A Montage of the Present*. London: Routledge.

Pred, Allan (2000). *Even in Sweden: Racisms, Racialized Spaces, and the Popular Geographical Imagination*. Berkeley: University of California Press.

Pred, Allan (2004). *The Past is Not Dead*. Minneapolis: University of Minnesota Press.

Pugliese, Enrico (2002). *L'Italia tra migrazione internazionali e migrazioni interne*. Bologna: Il Mulino.

Pugliese, Joseph (2008) "Whiteness and the Blackening of Italy: La Guerra cafona, extracommunitari and provincial street justice." *Journal of Multidisciplinary Studies* 5.

Puwar, Nirmal (2004). *Space Invaders: Race, Gender and Bodies out of Place*. London: Bloomsbury.

Quashie, Kevin (2012). *The Sovereignty of Quiet: Beyond Resistance in Black Culture*. New Brunswick, NJ: Rutgers University Press.

Raeymaekers, Timothy (2015). "Working the Black Mediterranean/Liminal geographies." Blog.

Raeymaekers, Timothy (2017). "Black Mediterranean/liminal geographies." Blog.

Rankine, Claudia. 2015. "The condition of Black life is one of mourning." *The New York Times Magazine*, June 22.

Riccio, Bruno and Chiara Brambilla (2012). *Transnational Migration, Cosmopolitanism, and Dis-located Borders*. (Quaderni del CE.R.Co) (Italian Edition). Kindle Edition.

Robinson, Cedric J. (1983) (2000). *Black Marxism: The Making of the Black Radical Tradition*. Charlotte: The University of North Carolina Press.

Rochat, G. (1978). "Colonialismo." In *Il Mondo Contemporaneo: Storia d'Italia*. Firenze: Nuova Italia.

Rochat, George. (2005). "The Italian Air Force in the Ethiopian War (1935–1936)." In Ruth Ben-Ghiat and Mia Fuller eds. *Italian Colonialism*. London: Palgrave Macmillan, 37–46.

Roedigger, David R. (1991). *The Wages of Whiteness: Race and the Making of the American Working Class*. New York: Verso.

Rossi, Alice (2014). "Evictions, urban displacement and migrant re-appropriation in Turin (Northern Italy)." *Planum. The Journal of Urbanism* 29(2), 1–11 (online).

Said, Edward (1994). *Culture and Imperialism*. New York: Vintage Press.

Salih, Ruba (2003). *Gender in Transnationalism: Home, Longing and Belonging Among Moroccan Migrant Women*. London: Routledge Press.

Samers, Michael (2003). "Invisible capitalism: Political economy and the regulation undocumented immigrants in France." *Economy and Society* 32(4), 555–583.

Saraceno, Chiara, Nicola Sartor and Giuseppe Sciortino eds. (2013). *Stranieri e disuguali: Le disuguaglianze nei diritti e nelle condizioni di vita degli immigrati*. Bologna: Il Mulino.

Sbacci, Alberto (1977). "Italy and the treatment of the Ethiopian aristocracy, 1937–1940." *The International Journal of African Historical Studies* 10(2), 209–241.

Scego, Igiaba (2015). *Adua* (Italian Edition). Bologna: Giunti.

Schneider, Jane (1998). *Italy's "Southern Question": Orientalism in One Country*. New York: Bloomsbury.

Scott, James C. (1987). *Weapons of the Weak: Everyday Forms of Peasant Resistance*. New Haven, CT: Yale University Press.

Segre, C. (1996). "Italy and classical theories of the 'New Imperialism': The missing case." In *Fonti e Problemi della Politica Coloniale Italiana, atti del convegno Taormina-Messina*, 23–39 Ottobre 1989, pp. 536–546.

Sexton, Jared (2010) "People-of-color-blindness: Notes on the afterlife of slavery." *Social Text 103* 28(2).

Sexton, Jared (2011) "The social life of social death: On Afro-pessimism and Black optimism." *InTensions* Issue 5.

Sexton, Jared (2016). "Afro-pessimism: The unclear word." *Rhizomes* Issue 29.

Sharpe, Cristina (2016). *In the Wake: On Blackness and Being*. Durham, NC: Duke University Press.

Smith, Andrea (2013) "Unsettling the privilege of self-reflexivity." In France Winddance Twine and Bradley Gardener eds. *Geographies of Privilege*. New York: Routledge, 263–280.

Smith, Iain R. and Andreas Stucki (2011). "The colonial development of concentration camps (1868–1902)." *Journal of Imperial and Commonwealth History* 39(3). 417–437.

Smith, Maya (2015). "Multilingual practices of Senegalese immigrants in Rome: Construction of identities and negotiation of boundaries." *Italian Culture* 33(2), 126–146.

Sniderman, Paul M., Pierangelo Peri, Rai J.P. de Figueiredo Jr., and Thomas Piazza eds. (2002). *The Outsider: Prejudice and Politics in Italy*. Princeton University Press.

Sorgoni, Barbara (2003). "Italian anthropology and the Africans: The early colonial period." In Patricia Palumbo ed. *A Place in the Sun: Africa in Italian Colonial Culture from Post-Unification to the Present*. Berkeley: University of California Press, pp. 62–80.

Spillers, Hortense J. (2003). "Mama's baby, Papa's maybe: An American grammar book." In Hortense J. Spillers, *Black, White, and in Color: Essays on American Literature and Culture*. Chicago, IL: University of Chicago Press, 203–209.

Spivak, Gayatri Chakravorty (1987). *In Other Worlds: Essays in Cultural Politics*. New York: Methuen.

Stolcke, Verena (1995). "Talking culture: New boundaries, new rhetorics of exclusion in Europe." *Current Anthropology* 3(1), 1–24.

Tabet, Paola (1997). *La pelle giusta*. Torino: Einaudi.

Taddia, Irma (1996). *Autobiography Africane: Il Colonialismo nelle memorie orali*. Milan: FrancoAngeli.

Taddia, Irma (2005). "Italian memories/African memories of colonialism." In Ruth Ben-Ghiat and Mia Fuller eds. *Italian Colonialism*. London: Palgrave Macmillan, 209–220.

Taylor, Keeanga-Yamhtta (2016). *#BlacklivesMatter to Black Liberation*. Chicago, IL: Haymarket Books.

Thorsen, Karen (1989). "James Baldwin: The Price of the Ticket." A documentary Film.

Thrift, Nigel (2005). "Intensities of feeling: Towards a spatial politics of affect." *Geografiska Annaler*, Series B: Human Geography, 86(1), 57–78.

Tolia-Kelly, Divya P. (2006) "Affect – an ethnocentric encounter? Exploring the 'universalist' imperative of emotional/affective geographies." *Area* 38(2), 213–217.

Tripodi, Paolo (1999). *The Colonial Legacy in Somalia: Rome and Mogadishu: From Colonial Administration to Operation Restore Hope*. New York: St. Martin's Press, Inc.

Trouillot, Michel-Rolf (1997). *Silencing the Past: Power and the Production of History*. First Edition. Boston: Beacon Press.

Trouillot, Michel-Rolf (2003). *Global Transformations: Anthropology and the Modern World*. New York: Palgrave Macmillan.

Triulzi, Alessandro ed. (1995). *Fotografia e storia dell'Africa: Atti del Convegno Internazionale Napoli-Roma 9–11 settembre 1992*. Napoli: Istituto Universitario Orienale.

Twine, France Winddance (2011). *A White Side of Britain: Interracial Intimacy and Racial Literacy*. Durham, NC: Duke University Press.

Twine, France Winddance and Bradley Gadener eds. (2013). *Geographies of Privilege*. New York: Routledge.

Tyner, James (2005). *The Geography of Malcolm X: Black Radicalism and the Remaking of American Space*. New York: Routledge.

Van Houtum, Henk (2013). "Human blacklisting: The global apartheid of the EU's external border regime." In France Winddance Twine and Bradley Gardener eds. *Geographies of Privilege*. New York: Routledge.

Vargas, Joao H.Costa (2008) (2010). *Never Meant to Survive: Genocide and Utopias in Black Diaspora Communities*. Lanham, MD: Rowman and Littlefield.

Walston, James (1997). "History and memory of the Italian concentration camps." *The Historical Journal* 40(1), 169–183.

Weheliye, Alexander G. (2014). *Racializing Assemblages, Biopolitics and Black Feminist Theories of the Human*. Durham, NC: Duke University Press.

White, Deborah Gray (1999). *Ar'n't I a Woman? Female Slaves in the Plantation South*. New York: W.W. Norton & Company.

Wilder, Gary (2015). *Freedom Time: Negritude, Decolonization, and the Future of the World*. Durham, NC: Duke University Press.

Wilderson, Frank B.III (2009) "Grammar & ghosts: The performative limits of African freedom." *Theatre Survey* 50(1), 119–125.

Wilderson, Frank B.III (2015) *Incognero: A Memoir of Exile and Apartheid*. Durham, NC: Duke University Press.

Williams, Raymond (1995) (1973). *The Country and the City*. London: Chatto and Windus.

Willis, Deborah and Carla Williams (2002). *The Black Female Body: A Photographic History*. Philadelphia, PA: Temple University Press.

Wilson, Bobby (2002). "Critically understanding race-connected practices: A reading of W.E.B. Du Bois and Richard Wright." *The Professional Geographer* 54(1), 31–41.

Wilson Gilmore, Ruth (2002) "Fatal couplings of power and difference. Notes on racism and geography." *The Professional Geographer* 54(1), 15–24.

Wilson Gilmore, Ruth (2007) *Golden Gulag: Prisons, Surplus, Crisis, and Opposition in Globalizing California*. Berkeley: University of California Press.

Winant, Howard (2004). *New Politics of Race: Globalization, Difference, Justice*. Minneapolis: University of Minnesota Press.

Woods, Clyde (2007). "Sittin' on top of the world." In Katherine McKittrick and Clyde Woods eds. *Black Geographies and the Politics of Place*. Boston, MA: South End Press, 46–81.

Wright, Melissa (2006). *Disposable Women and Other Myths of Global Capitalism*. New York: Routledge.

Wright, Richard and Mark Ellis (2000). "Race, region and the territorial politics of immigration in the US." *International Journal of Population Geography* 6, 197–211.

Wynter, Sylvia (2003). "Unsettling the coloniality of being/power/truth/freedom: Towards the human, after man, its overrepresentation – an argument." *The New Centennial Review* 3(3).

INDEX